Power and Stability in the Middle East

edited by

Berch Berberoglu

Zed Books Ltd
London and New Jersey

Power and Stability in the Middle East was first published by
Zed Books Ltd, 57 Caledonian Road, London N1 9BU, UK, and
171 First Avenue, Atlantic Highlands, New Jersey 07716, USA,
in 1989.

Cover design by Andrew Corbett
Typeset by EMS Photosetters, Rochford, Essex
Printed and bound in the UK by Biddles Ltd,
Guildford and King's Lynn

British Library Cataloguing in Publication Data

Class, power and stability in the Middle East.
1. Middle East. Politics.
I. Berberoglu, Berch.
320.956.

ISBN 0-86232-808-X
ISBN 0-86232-809-8 pbk

Library of Congress Cataloging-in-Publication Data

Power and stability in the Middle East/edited by
    Berch Berberoglu.
        p.   cm.
    Bibliography p.
    Includes index.
    ISBN 0-86232-808-X. – ISBN 0-86232-809-8 (pbk.)
    1. Middle East – Politics and government – 1979–.
I. Berberoglu, Berch.
DS63.1.P69   1989
320.956–dc 20

Contents

Tables

Acknowledgements

A book of this sort requires the cooperative effort of a large number of people over an extended period. I began working on this project in the early to mid-1980s, when it became apparent to me and other colleagues in the field that comprehensive, comparative/historical treatments of states and issues in the Middle East were few and far between. This, at a time of increasing conflict and crisis in a strategically important region of the world. It was the recognition of this fact by Robert Molteno at Zed Books that made the launching of this project possible in the mid-eighties.

I would like to thank, first and foremost, all the contributors to this volume, who, in addition to producing excellent pieces of research and writing commissioned especially for this volume, have endured the long and arduous process of publication with great patience. I would especially like to thank David Seddon, Fred Lawson, Farideh Farhi and Julie Peteet for their prompt response at various stages of this project, as my thanks go to Fikret Ceyhun, Ghassan Salamé, Paul Saba, and Ahmad Azim for their cooperation and help in making the completion of this volume possible. Additionally, my thanks go to the editors of the *Journal of Palestine Studies* and *MERIP Middle East Report* for permitting the publication of the articles by Pamela Ann Smith and Joe Stork, as well as allowing the publication of a revised version of articles by Seddon and Salamé which have previously appeared in the *Report*.

I would also like to thank David Dickens, Cyrus Bina, Sohrab Behdad, Ertugrul Tonak, Hamid Hosseini, and Behzad Yaghmaian for their input through discussion on various topics involving the Middle East.

My thanks also go to Peggy Hart, who typed and retyped numerous versions of most of the articles in this book, with countless hours spent in front of the computer; her work is much appreciated.

Finally, I would like to thank Robert Molteno and Michael Pallis of Zed Books for their commitment and dedication to the project in seeing to it that a solid piece of important scholarly work on the subject is produced and made available to a broad audience in Middle East studies in a timely fashion.

Needless to say, any errors in fact or interpretation remain those of the authors of individual articles, while I, as editor, assume responsibility for selection and inclusion of the essays that make up this book, as I do for my introductory comments and observations that constitute the opening pages.

B.B.

About the Contributors

Ahmed N. Azim is an Egyptian economist, now an associate professor of organizational theory and policy analysis at the University of Calgary, Canada. He is currently engaged in research on the political economy of Egypt and the Middle East.

Fikret Ceyhun is a graduate of the Faculty of Political Science at the University of Ankara, Turkey, and is currently a professor of economics at the University of North Dakota, USA. His articles have appeared in *Economic Forum* and the *Review of Radical Political Economics*. He is currently engaged in research on the political economy of Turkey.

Farideh Farhi is an Iranian social scientist, now an assistant professor of political science at the University of Hawaii at Manoa. She is presently engaged in research on a comparative analysis of the revolutions in Iran and Nicaragua.

Fred H. Lawson is assistant professor of government at Mills College in Oakland, California, where he teaches international relations and Middle East politics. He is the author of *Bahrain: The Modernization of Autocracy* (Boulder, Co: Westview Press, 1987).

Julie Peteet received her Ph.D. in Anthropology from Wayne State University in Detroit. She has taught at the American University of Beirut and Georgetown University in Washington, and conducted fieldwork on Palestinian women in Lebanon in 1980–82. She was more recently a senior research fellow at Yarmouk University in Jordan. Her publications include articles on Palestinian women in Lebanon in the *Journal of Palestine Studies* and *MERIP Reports*.

Paul Saba is a practising attorney in Tucson, Arizona. He is presently doing work on the Jewish National Question, the history of the Bund and leftwing Zionism and implications of Gramsci's work for socialist strategy in the developed capitalist countries.

Ghassan Salamé is a Lebanese social scientist. He teaches political studies at the American University of Beirut, and Saint-Joseph University in Beirut. He is the author of *Saudi Foreign Policy Since 1945* (Beirut, 1980).

David Seddon is reader at the School of Development Studies, University of East Anglia, where he teaches North African and Middle Eastern development. He is the author of *Moroccan Peasants*, and is currently editing a collection on *The Political Economy of Agrarian Change in Turkey* (with Caglar Keyder).

Pamela Ann Smith is a journalist specializing in Middle East studies, and is the author of *Palestine and the Palestinians, 1873–1983* (New York: St. Martin's Press, 1984).

Joe Stork is editor of *Middle East Report* in Washington, DC and co-founder of the Middle East Research and Information Project (MERIP). He writes and lectures on contemporary development in the Middle East and United States policy there.

About the Editor

Dr Berch Berberoglu is associate professor at the Department of Sociology, University of Nevada, Reno, USA. He is an internationally recognized scholar specializing in the Middle East and in political economy, class analysis, and comparative/historical studies on a world scale. His writings have appeared in the *Journal of Contemporary Asia, Development and Change, International Studies* and *Research in Political Economy,* among others. His recent book *Turkey in Crisis: From State Capitalism to Neo-Colonialism* (London: Zed Press, 1982) is the first comprehensive radical history of the 20th Century Turkish political economy to appear in English. His most recent book, *The Internationalization of Capital* (New York: Praeger Publishers, 1987) examines the nature and contradictions of imperialism and capitalist development on a world scale. He is also the editor of a two-volume collection of classical and contemporary Marxist writings on India: Vol. I: *India: National Liberation and Class Struggles*; Vol. II: *Mode of Production, Class Struggles and Revolution in India* (both published by Sarup & Sons, Publishers, Meerut, India in 1986 and 1987, respectively).

Introduction

The most recent crises in the Middle East centring around the civil war in Lebanon, the Iran–Iraq war, and the Palestinian uprising in the West Bank and Gaza, are part and parcel of the larger crisis engulfing the region for the past 40 years. Clearly, the period from the establishment of the state of Israel in 1948 to the present is replete with critical events unfolding in a continuous drama of social and political struggles, war and revolution. The origins of these crises in the Middle East, however, go much further back in history – to the disintegration and collapse of the Ottoman Empire and the invasion of its territories by the European powers at the beginning of this century. By the end of World War I, Ottoman Turkey had lost most of its territories to Britain, France, Italy, Greece, and other Western powers who divided these lands amongst themselves, turning them into colonial possessions. Thus, Britain came to possess the Persian Gulf region and today's Iraq, Kuwait, Jordan, Israel, Egypt, and parts of North Africa; France established a mandate over Syria and Lebanon, while continuing its colonization of Tunisia, Algeria, and Morocco; while the United States, Germany, Italy, Greece, and other lesser powers divided Turkey and its adjacent territories between themselves. Western penetration of the Ottoman Empire, which had begun a century earlier, was now complete with its final partition through brute military force.

Thus began a prolonged period of colonial rule in the Middle East, which lasted several decades and led to the development of nationalist sentiment and struggles that resulted in wars of national liberation and revolution by the 1940s and, especially, in the 1950s. It is during this period that an increasing number of countries in the Middle East – including Syria, Lebanon, Iraq, Jordan, Egypt, Tunisia, and Algeria – gained their independence and emerged as 'autonomous' nation states. In Lebanon, nationhood was achieved through a 'peaceful' transition of power to neo-colonial elements who remained within the Western imperial orbit; in Egypt, Syria, and Iraq, nationalist regimes came to power through military coups led by junior officers in the army; and in Algeria a protracted war of national liberation finally forced the French out. These struggles took place in response to Western intervention in and control of the Middle East. The partition of the region into colonial possessions also deprived long-established national/ethnic groups of their homelands and dispersed them across several national/political boundaries, as in the case of the Armenians, the Palestinians, and the Kurds – the peoples at the heart of the three major national questions still unresolved to date.

National and class conflicts in the Middle East have developed with increasing speed since the turn of the century. Class formations and class conflicts have developed and matured during three distinct periods – pre-colonial, colonial, and post-colonial – during which changes in the structure of the economy, society and the state have had a varied effect on different states in the region, bringing about major transformations in some of them, while reinforcing traditional social structures and maintaining stability in others.

Throughout the pre-colonial period, under Ottoman rule, the strong central state dominated most of the Middle East. The despotic central state held sway over the entire region – from the Arabian peninsula to Asia Minor down to Palestine and Egypt and across North Africa. Over the centuries, the state's land allocation and management system allowed warriors and local bureaucrats to extend their own control over the local production process, leading to the development of feudal relations in the countryside. At the same time, a small class of merchants began to develop and prosper in the coastal towns. With the expansion of the European powers into the region and the growing subordination of the Empire to the dictates of European capital, Ottoman landlords and merchants came to play an intermediary role in Europe's complete economic domination of the region by the early 20th century. Thus, these two classes, which posed a threat to the survival of the central state, became instrumental in Europe's subsequent military conquest of the Empire during World War I.

With the colonization of Ottoman territories at the conclusion of the war, Britain, France, and other European powers began to prop up the emergent social formations in which European industrial capital played an important role, as many of these states came to function as colonial outposts of Europe to protect Western business interests. This relationship continued until World War II, when, weakened by the Nazi onslaught in Europe, Britain and France began to lose control over their colonies, and nationalist movements sprang up throughout the Middle East.

In the transition from colonial rule to independence, two distinct alliances set into motion the class dynamic of developments in the post independence period. In some countries, such as Lebanon, landlords and merchants tied to French capital were installed in power to assure incorporation into the Western imperial orbit. In this way, Lebanon came to serve the interests of Western capital in a manner complementary to that of the newly established state of Israel. Together, these two countries consolidated their ties with Europe and the United States, and took up special tasks to secure the region for Western financial and strategic interests. Jordan, Kuwait, Saudi Arabia, and the Gulf states played a similar role in the region under British rule. In this context, control of oil, other raw materials, and shipping lanes became paramount in the struggle over control of the entire Middle East region.

Elsewhere in the Middle East – in Egypt, Syria, Iraq, Iran, and Algeria, among others – nationalist forces tied to local small- and medium-scale capital captured power in the 1950s and launched an anti-imperialist programme to bolster the national economy through state intervention, while keeping tight control over labour and radical social movements within their national territories. However, in other countries of the region such as Turkey, Lebanon, and Iran in the latter half of the decade, a closer alliance with foreign capital moved these countries along a different path dependent on the West, while the stability of the Saudi state and the Gulf sheikhdoms were maintained through tight control over the population by the traditional forces in power throughout this period.

Since the 1950s, many countries in the Middle East have been undergoing important social transformations, thus giving rise to a multitude of power centres that are today diverse in both form and content. Ranging from a military-backed regime in Turkey to the Royal Saudi state to Islamic fundamentalism in Iran to the chaos in Lebanon and beyond, the Middle East has come to embrace both stability and change under the weight of rival political forces. These forces have come to express contradictory class interests in a sea of turmoil which lies beneath the surface manifestations of cultural uniformity that appears to characterize the region and its people.

This volume attempts to provide a background for an understanding of the contemporary situation in the Middle East. The various essays examine the political–economic underpinnings of a number of states in the Middle East, providing us with a wide range of explanations from different, yet complementary, perspectives. They examine the process of development in Egypt, Syria, Turkey, Iran, Iraq, Saudi Arabia, Morocco, Tunisia, and Sudan, as well as the role of women in national liberation struggles in Algeria, South Yemen, and Lebanon, and the Palestinian and Armenian national questions. The authors attempt to provide answers to important questions regarding the sources of stability and change, and locate the role of class, power and the state in this process.

The volume begins with Ahmad Azim's analysis of the role of the state in the Egyptian political economy. Arguing that Egypt has gone through two distinct phases in its economic development since the early 1950s, Azim examines the transformation of a state-directed economy and society into a dependent satellite state, ushered in by Sadat and his *infitah* ('open door') policy. According to Azim, a number of internal and external contradictions set the stage for the transformation of the state-capitalist order into a neo-colonial one and this development is leading the country towards conflict and crises, which, far from bringing order and stability to the country, will increasingly cultivate oppositional politics and struggles for power in the coming period.

In the Syria described in Fred Lawson's article, we find a different and complicated situation, where the Ba'thi state bureaucracy has the upper hand. Here, Lawson examines a process of transformation to an as yet undetermined class structure replete with capitalist and bureaucratic overtones. The dominant theme in Syrian political development since the early 1960s, detailed at length by Lawson, is one of power struggles between different factions within the state bureaucracy which is characterized by coups or threats of coups to maintain power in the hands of the bureaucratic state apparatus, albeit fractionalized along different policy lines. Lawson observes that, while for the moment the position of the current Ba'th regime in Syria appears to be secure, the potential for serious political conflict within Syrian society exists, and overt opposition to the ruling coalition by workers and other adversely affected social forces remains a real possibility. Nevertheless, the strong arm of the state bureaucracy over Syrian society, he argues, gives it an appearance of stability and makes it look less vulnerable to forces that may potentially threaten its rule.

This theme is picked up by Joe Stork in his analysis of the situation in Iraq, which is even more complicated due to a number of additional factors: the presence of a large Kurdish minority, represented by the Kurdish Democratic Party (KDP); the political strength of the Iraqi Communist Party (ICP), the strongest such party in the Arab world; and the war with Iran, which continued unabated throughout the decade of the 1980s. Stork argues that, since its inception to power in the late 1960s, the Ba'th Party, led by Saddam Hussain, has consolidated its rule by purges among its own ranks and physically eliminating the leadership of potential rival forces, such as the KDP and the ICP. Stork also traces the personal rise to power of Saddam Hussain and members of his family, as well as his political monopoly over the Ba'th and the Revolutionary Command Council. He contends that the carefully staged elections in June 1980 and the calculated invasion of Iran and the subsequent war worked to control and stabilize the situation in favour of the regime. Moreover, Stork argues that the regional alliances Iraq has been building with Saudi Arabia and the Gulf states in a front against the rising tide of Shi'i radicalism may give Hussain the leverage he needs to hold on to power for the time being.

Developments in Turkey during the past several decades indicate a quite different situation in that country, as the level of class consciousness, organization and militancy of organized labour has moved the struggle to a higher level, prompting military intervention on a number of occasions. Fikret Ceyhun's analysis of transformations in the Turkish political economy through successive stages of development in the direction of an 'export-oriented industrialization' confirms the changing nature of class relations in Turkey which have given rise to class conflict and class struggles that are common to more advanced capitalist formations. Thus, while the latest military coup in 1980 has stabilized the situation for the time being, the underlying structural contradictions of the Turkish economy, society and polity developing along the capitalist path are likely to result in a renewed cycle of class confrontation and struggles for power, for, as Ceyhun points outs, such struggles are continuing below the surface since 1980 under the powerful force of the repressive state, and will intensify and become more violent as Turkey moves on to the next stage of her transition to popular democracy.

Moving down to the Arabian peninsula, Ghassan Salamé in his article provides an intriguing political analysis of the Saudi state, tracing its historical origins and exposing its present nature. Salame pays special attention to the royal family and its allies and points out that from the beginning the power of the Saudi monarchy has depended on alliances with other social forces inside the kingdom to assure the continuation of its rule. He argues that despite the overarching presence and power of the royal family and its protectors, the institutionalization of power in Saudi Arabia remains very limited and that the regime fears some of its own bases of power, such as the army, as it adamantly intends to keep this force under its thumb as an insurance against a sudden uprising. In assuring the loyalties of a complicated grouping of tribal and clan alliances, the regime has come to rely on two distinct, yet complementary, military corps: the army and the national guard. Salamé shows that with the royal family and its class allies holding absolute political power, the enormous profits generated by the oil boom have created immense wealth for the ruling class and the state, while widening the gap between them and the masses who are becoming increasingly restless in this precarious situation. The client role of the Saudi state, dependent for its survival on the United States, makes this unstable situation all the more volatile. As such, what emerges from Salamé's account of the Saudi state is that behind the facade of a stable, closed, self-perpetuating society, Saudi Arabia remains embedded in a host of deep-rooted contradictions that are setting the stage for long-term social transformations. Salamé concludes that, although the opposition to the regime remains fragmented and disorganized – which makes it difficult if not impossible for a viable political alternative to Saudi rule to take root – the future course of socio-political development in Saudi Arabia is still inconclusive and remains an open question at this juncture.

In contrast to the situation in Saudi Arabia, the Iranian experience over the past several decades has been radically different, culminating in the February 1979 revolution. In her essay on Iran, Farideh Farhi argues that the Shah's military-based dictatorship was a specific outcome of prolonged political struggles; it came to power – with US help – after the defeat of the nationalist challenge and the crushing of the working class movement in the early 1950s. The complete dominance of the state over civil society in Iran allowed the state to pursue a policy of capitalist industrialization based on the use of oil-generated revenues to oversee a gradual expansion of Iranian industry. The results of this policy, however, were not as auspicious as expected. Iran became increasingly dependent on oil exports, and the revenues from oil benefited different sectors and classes unevenly. Farhi argues that the 1979 revolution was certainly a reaction to this uneven capitalist development, but its roots cannot merely be located in economic sources. The Shah's mode of governance also antagonized many sectors of society, allowing for the mobilization of a multi-class coalition against an increasingly corrupt, repressive, and seemingly anti-national state. In this mobilization, Shi'i Islam played an indispensable role, as it became an important source of resistance to the dominant ideology. Islam also played an important organizational role: the traditional religious networks were transformed into vehicles for mobilizing the masses. These networks ultimately enabled the fundamentalist clergy, which had become dominant within the religious community, to defeat violently rival forces and attain political control. Farhi points out that success in gaining political control, however, has not yet translated into hegemonic control of Iranian society. This is why the Islamic regime continues to be plagued by internal contradictions and conflict, and faces widespread popular opposition and unrest, which, while now driven underground due to severe repression, may at a later point resurface, thus destabilizing the regime and ultimately challenging its rule.

Focusing on the recent political turmoil in a number of Arab countries in farther corners of the greater Middle East, David Seddon examines the nature and causes of the riots in Tunisia and Morocco and the rebellion in Sudan. In each of these three countries Seddon sees the economic crisis and the state's unpopular actions in response to it as triggering the mass upheavals of the mid-1980s. Removal of food subsidies and the resultant sudden doubling of bread prices, high unemployment and inflation, coupled with generalized poverty of the masses, were behind the demonstrations and riots which led to violent repression of the masses in Tunisia and Morocco and to the overthrow of the Numairi regime in Sudan. Seddon points out that while the uprisings in all three countries started out as 'spontaneous', what determined the different results in Sudan was the level of political organization and the vacuum filled by the opposition forces. Seddon shows that in Sudan, as in Tunisia and Morocco, the logic of the economic 'liberalism' pursued under an 'open door' strategy of economic development during the 1970s and early 1980s has led directly to the growth of inequality, unemployment and social deprivation, which themselves underlay the discontent and social unrest. Seddon points out that neither the repression of popular protest in Tunisia and Morocco nor the military coup which replaced Numairi in Sudan will be able for long to prevent further social and political unrest, unless new economic policies and strategies can be developed which meet both the demands and the needs of the masses. Such policies and strategies, however, are unlikely to be pursued, unless the social and political contradictions created by previous regimes give rise to a significantly new balance of social forces.

The remainder of the volume addresses the role of women in national liberation struggles in the Middle East and examines the Palestinian and Armenian national questions. Julie Peteet's essay focuses on the political activism of Middle Eastern women in the context of militant national liberation movements, incipient state formation, and state consolidation. Peteet looks at the role of women in national politics in a variety of Middle Eastern settings and argues that, by and large, these cases indicate that the participation of women in national struggles can be extensive without involving substantial changes in the sexual division of labour or the access of women to power in post-liberation states. Peteet contends that women's increased integration into the national political process (and the labour force) has not been accompanied by a transformation in the control over women vested in the family and upheld in the legal system of most Middle Eastern states. Focusing on Palestinian women in Lebanon, she argues that exile, national struggle, and incipient state formation had an uneven impact on Palestinian women. At the same time, statelessness and the national movement have formed the axis around which women have organized, and both inform a certain continuity of position and consciousness. Examining the situation of Palestinian women in the refugee camps in Lebanon, Peteet observes that changes in women's role were initiated by a national crisis, and then materialized, institutionalized, and legitimized by the resistance, which lent them a patriotic, national context. She argues that, while women can be found in all sectors of the resistance – military, political, and social – there is, however, a sexual division of labour within the resistance: women tend to be most concentrated in the social field, and least in the military. Thus, the vast majority of women remain distant from the centres of power and decision making. This division of labour is a replica of that of society at large and tends to reproduce the same types of hierarchical gender relations.

Peteet feels that, without losing sight of advances made in the position of women in a national liberation movement, critical questions should be posed in order to assess the consequences of women's activism for transforming gender relations. When the national question is the primary basis of political unity and struggle, there is a general tendency to perceive the national problem in largely political terms, with social issues relegated to secondary positions. This state of affairs is not peculiar to the Palestinian situation. In many national liberation movements, women are pressured to subordinate their own demands and needs in the interest of the broader struggle. Nonetheless, Peteet argues that, although the resistance did not express a firm commitment to transform gender relations and ideologies, it is hardly likely that permanent changes can take place outside a party or state framework. Political activism of women, even in its limited sense, as in the Palestinian context, can signal the beginning of the process of undermining domesticity as the primary social role and source of status for women.

The last two articles of this volume deal with the national question in the Middle East, focusing on the Palestinian and Armenian struggles for self-determination and a national homeland.

The Palestinian national question gained prominence and widespread recognition with the organization in the late 1960s of the Palestine Liberation Organization (PLO) which came to represent the national interests of the Palestinian people. And in the period from the late 1960s to the 1980s the PLO and its supporters engaged in bitter struggles for national liberation inside and outside of Palestine. In the 1980s, argues Smith, the importance of the nationalist struggle assumed a new dimension for all segments of the Palestinian population, however split their leadership appeared to be to the outside world and irrespective of the support various Palestinians felt for one or another of the contending factions within the PLO. Smith contends that, while in private Palestinians from all social backgrounds have expressed criticism of this or that leader, of the way the PLO is organized, or simply of the divisions themselves, the PLO has nevertheless continued to symbolize the determination to achieve their national goals despite the divisions, the various policies of the Arab states, or the PLO's own inability to translate the world's growing sympathy for their cause into the kind of action needed to make possible genuine progress on a peaceful settlement. Thus by the mid-1980s, writes Smith. Palestinian nationalism had become a national cause that transcended divisions of class. place of exile or origin. religion. and gender. In this, she concludes, the PLO. whatever its other failings, has succeeded.

Finally, Paul Saba examines the historical roots of the Armenian national question. focusing on the role of Armenians in the Ottoman Empire. their constant persecution during the 19th century. and their wholesale massacre by the government of Ottoman Turkey earlier in this century. This genocide, which claimed 1.5 million Armenian lives, was the culmination of a whole series of long-term historical processes – both internal and external – which led to the Young Turk revolution of 1908 and the transformation of the Ottoman state into a modern nation–state based on racial/national lines. The Armenian genocide, argues Saba, is the product of both the internal contradictions of the Ottoman formation and the inter-imperialist rivalries of the 19th and early 20th centuries which had as their object the dismemberment of the Ottoman Empire. At the same time, the historically progressive role of the Armenian nation within the Ottoman Empire and the strength and maturity of the Armenian revolutionary movement were important factors in their selection by the Young Turk government for extinction. Drawing the parallels with the struggles of the Palestinians and the Kurds, who find themselves in a similar predicament. Saba points out that the Armenian revolutionary movement today. like its Palestinian and Kurdish counterparts, is divided between those forces who are seeking a political solution to their oppression and those who have opted for a narrowly military approach to the struggle. The future of all three movements, concludes Saba, hinges on the outcome of this battle.

Taken together, the articles in this volume constitute a collection of readings with some common themes, while at the same time providing varied analyses of specific national experiences in a diverse social setting, extending from Turkey in the north to the Persian Gulf and the Arabian Peninsula in the south, to Sudan, Egypt and across North Africa. On the one hand, one observes the centrality of class and class conflicts as the major determinants of social relations and societal transformation in some countries, while the state. nationalism, religion or other superstructural institutions or phenomena emerge as the key factors in determining the nature and direction of stability and change in other countries. Nevertheless, despite the variations in the nature of social processes at work in different countries of the Middle East. the question of stability, or lack thereof, has become the overriding issue affecting the future of the region as a whole. In this regard, the centrality of an analysis of the class nature of the state as well as an analysis of the class content of nationalism and national liberation movements and of their relationship to the state has to be recognized in any effort to understand the process of transformation across national boundaries in the Middle East. It is clear that, given the complexity of the problems in the Middle East. one needs to focus on specific cases and delineate the forces that foster (or impede) change. thus advance or hamper stability, in the region.

One such source of instability in the Middle East is clearly the still-unresolved Palestinian national question and Israel's iron-clad rule in the occupied territories, where the Palestinian uprising (or *intifadah*) has entered its second year. Another source of instability is the current clerical regime in Iran, which, with its aggressive promotion of Islamic fundamentalism throughout the region, as well as its war with Iraq, which lasted nearly a decade, has brought turmoil and chaos in international relations and exacerbated the political crisis in the region. Elsewhere, in Iraq, Syria, Turkey, Egypt, the Sudan, and North Africa, a fragile situation exists, where the current regimes in power keep the population in check under the watchful eyes of the military. The suppression of human rights, the repression of labour and other popular sectors of society, and the authoritarian rule of the political/military bureaucracy over the people lends the situation in these countries an unstable character that is both unpredictable and at the same time promising of change.

Through the contributions of these authors, it is hoped that this book will provide a new impetus in Middle East studies – one that focuses on the relationship between class, power and the state in a new way. A class-oriented approach that incorporates a concrete analysis of the role of the state, and accounts for national and international forces involved in the struggle for power, as part of the political struggles now developing throughout the region, is indispensable for a clear and correct understanding of the crises in the Middle East. It is precisely for this reason that this volume has been compiled, as it promises to make an important contribution to a much-needed, serious analysis of the complex social, economic, and political landscape of the Middle East.

The detailed observations of the authors in the articles included in this volume on particular states in the Middle East provide us the tools and framework of analysis necessary to evaluate the situation in each of the countries examined and draw our attention to the sources of conflict, stability, and change in this important, and in many ways pivotal, region of the world.

Berch Berberoglu
University of Nevada, Reno, USA
March 1989

1.   Egypt: The Origins and Development of a Neo-colonial State

Ahmad N. Azim

Nasser and national capitalism[1]

Free market mechanisms and private ownership in Egypt underwent heavy regulation and structural changes under Nasser between 1952 and 1970. The new regime inherited a mixed feudal–capitalist system with all the known characteristics, including private ownership of all means of production and concentration of wealth, particularly land, in the hands of the landowning aristocracy. Constituting less than 3 percent of all landowners, the landowning aristocracy controlled over 52 percent of the total arable land, and accounted for the bulk of the profits from rent.

The data in Table 1.1 show the disparity in the distribution of landownership and income. Landowners of two or less feddans constitute an overwhelming 73.3 percent of all landowners; they possess only 16.7 percent of the cultivatable land and earn a weighted average income from rent of only E£16.78. This is significantly below the average income of E£103.2. More importantly, over 50 percent of this group, or 38.7 percent of total landowners, own an average of only one-half feddan of arable land and earn E£11.7 in rental income. In contrast to this, two tenths of one percent of all landowners own 30.4 percent of the cultivatable land and earn an average annual income of E£16,691.7 per person in rental income. Moreover, of the cultivatable land, 52.5 percent of the most fertile land is distributed among 2.9 percent of the landowners. This shows marked inequality in both the quantity and quality of land distribution in Egypt.

In industry, most of the businesses in the private sector were family ventures, and quite small in size. Thus, well over 75 percent of the establishments in the manufacturing sector employed less than ten workers.[2] The private sector also experienced some setbacks due to the political instability which prevailed in the period immediately prior to July 1952.[3] Moreover, trade (particularly external) and finance were controlled by the comprador bourgeoisie through administrative decisions designed to benefit foreign interests. Thus, the regime was faced with a number of serious economic problems:[4]

1. Per capita income was very low, and declining.
2. Distribution of income and wealth was extremely skewed in favour of the few rich.

2 Power and Stability in the Middle East

Table 1.1
Distribution of land and average income of owner
(according to size of property)

Size of Property (feddan)	Number of Owners as a %	Areas as a %	Average Profits from Rent Per Owner in Egyptian £s
Less than 1	38.7	4.4	11.7
1	20.7	5.7	28.4
2	13.9	6.6	49.2
3	8.0	5.5	70.8
4	4.3	3.9	93.3
5	7.8	11.2	138.2
10	3.7	10.2	282.4
20	2.0	12.7	653.5
50	0.7	9.4	1,486.5
100 or more	0.2	30.4	16,691.7
Total	*100.0*	*100.0*	*103.2*

Source: S. Ghali. *Egypt: Portrait of a President* (Zed Press. London. 1981), p. 80.

3. The taxation system was inefficient, unjust, and relied heavily on indirect taxes, which put a higher burden on the poor.

4. Public service was of low quality, and carried a high price.

5. A large section of the economy was owned and/or controlled by foreigners.

6. There was no plan or co-ordination for serious development of the national economy.

Government ownership in the economy was restricted to public utilities: irrigation projects, railways, postal and other communication services and hospitals. The role of the government in the economy was confined to the traditional areas of courts, police, and army.

The economic ideology of the Free Officers
During its initial years of power, the regime supported free market mechanisms and private ownership. This support was given to create confidence among the Egyptian capitalists, and to put an end to the detrimental effects of the political instability which prevailed during the years before the revolution. These years witnessed major political events, including the 1948 Palestine war. the burning of Cairo on January 26, 1952, and the Egyptian movement of July 23, 1952, which had a major effect on business expectations in the country.

The regime issued a number of statements to ensure that it did not bind itself to any particular economic system. Thus, the Minister of Finance issued a statement declaring that 'the state will encourage private projects.'[5] Two years later, Nasser issued a statement declaring that the government of the revolution was a government of all classes and professions which stood equally beside workers, peasants, businessmen, employees, students, the rich, and the poor.[6] Businessmen did not, however, respond favourably to the regime's statements until late 1955. Private investment increased noticeably in 1956, and pioneer capitalists began to praise the regime's policy towards capitalism.[7]

The regime and private enterprises

The regime's main policy was in favour of the private sector, but it found it necessary to ensure optimal utilization of economic resources, particularly capital. In 1952, a decree (No. 213) was issued for the establishment of the Permanent Council for the Development of National Production, whose function was to outline economic and social policies for economic development.

Apart from this and the laws of land reform, the regime directed its efforts towards encouraging the performance of the private sector. It offered many concessions and incentive schemes to private (domestic, as well as foreign) investment. These measures included tax exemptions (applied to incomes and profits), protection of infant industries, loans at easy terms, and loan guarantees. The regime also encouraged small savers to direct their savings towards the economic development of the country. In 1954, a decree (No. 26) was issued to regulate investment in public companies in order to encourage small savers. The minimum share price was reduced from E£4.00 to E£2.00. Managers were required to retire at the age of 60, and their remunerations were limited to 10 percent of the final profits, after distributing 5 percent of the profits to the shareholders. Also, no member of the board of directors was to receive more than E£25,000 per year, and no person could serve as a member on the boards of more than six companies, or as managing director of more than two public enterprises.[8]

The regime's encouragement to private capital was also clear from the following actions:

1. The state appointed big businessmen as members of the Board of National Development.

2. The state stayed away from light industry, which was left entirely to the private sector.

3. The state consulted the Federation of Egyptian Industries on every industrial measure before taking action.

4. The state followed the advice of the Federation of Egyptian Industries in all matters relating to custom duties, taxes, etc.

5. The state required all companies whose capital exceeded E£10,000 to join the Chamber of Industries, which was part of the Federation of Egyptian Industries.

The beginning of conflict between the regime and private capital

The trust which seemed to prevail between the state and private capital in the early years of the regime did not last long. A conflict emerged because of actions on both sides. The regime lost confidence in the private sector because the Egyptian capitalists chose to direct their resources only to projects with guaranteed quick, high profits. The state wanted to build heavy industry, but private capital preferred light industries.[9] This pushed the government into taking certain economic measures to direct investment away from building and construction towards other productive industrial projects. New ventures valued at more than E£500 were subject to official licensing.[10] The government also thought that the Federation of Egyptian Industries went too far when asking for guarantees of a minimum investment figure on all projects. Furthermore, the government did not accept the Federation's objections to the establishment of public projects in areas private capital did not find attractive.

Private capital, on the other hand, began to doubt the regime's intentions for a number of reasons:

1. The land reform laws passed in September 1952 created a climate of fear among Egyptian capitalists, although these laws did not affect them directly. The land reform was designed to liquidate a feudal system, put an end to the misery of millions of peasants, and ensure the economy moved towards further industrialization.

2. The foreign policy followed by the regime and, in particular, the Czechoslovakian arms deal in 1955, resulted in a loss of confidence among many businessmen, particularly pro-Western traditional capitalists.

3. The 1956 constitution was not as supportive of free enterprise as hoped for by Egyptian private capital. Although Article 3 of the constitution made it clear that Egypt respects and protects the free market mechanism and private ownership of the means of production, Article 9 stressed that private capital should be directed towards serving the national economy.

4. The introduction of economic planning as a means of co-ordinating economic decisions was not the type of economic policy favoured by Egyptian private capital. Article 7 of the 1956 constitution, which specified economic planning, was not welcomed by Egyptian investors.

5. The nationalization of the Suez Canal and of British and French firms, and the Egyptianization of foreign banks created a climate of fear among Egyptian capitalists.

6. The industrial priorities of the state differed greatly from those of Egyptian investors. The latter believed that Egypt did not have the resources, experience, or ability to establish successful heavy industries. The regime, on the other hand, considered that light industries could not achieve accelerated economic development, and that Egypt should manufacture its own capital goods. Thus, the iron and steel industry was at the top of the state's list of priorities. This created a real conflict between the government and Egyptian capitalists, particularly since most of the investment projects suggested by the government were risky and required long gestation periods. Profit maximization was not central to such projects.

7. The political decisions taken by Nasser to isolate some politicians and restrict their political rights, or detain them, evoked a hostile reaction from

private capital, since most of these politicians had close ties with Egypt's capitalists and landlords.

The revolution and controlled capitalism
Despite the conflict between the regime and private capital, it can be said that 1952–1956 was a period dominated by the private sector.[11]

The regime, however, felt that free enterprise was not achieving economic development at the necessary pace, and it decided to take a more active role in the development process. Hence, the idea of directed capitalism was born. The Egyptian economy moved more towards a mixed economy. This transformation was achieved through the following major economic measures:

1. The establishment in 1957 of an Economic Agency, whose aim was to mobilize domestic savings and direct them towards investment in independent industrial projects.

2. The declaration by Nasser in late 1957 of the creation of a 'socialist–democratic–cooperative society.' The aim of such a society was to protect the people against excessive exploitation. The state was seeking a more responsible role in taking economic initiatives for accelerated development.[12] The creation of the union between Egypt and Syria, however, delayed the implementation of these initiatives, as it was difficult to promote the idea of a 'socialist–cooperative society,' which would have threatened the capitalist class in Syria. Nasser therefore declared that the state did not intend to control private industrial establishments, but only to ensure that these establishments operate in the public interest.[13]

3. The government decided to share up to 25 percent of its industrial investment in the First Five-Year Economic Plan with the private sector; the private sector was not too responsive, however.[14] This convinced the government that the private sector was neither interested nor capable of achieving the desired economic targets, and that the state must take the largest share of responsibility in the process of industrialization. A process of nationalization took place, starting with the nationalization in February 1960 of Misr Bank, the largest trading bank in Egypt. By its nationalization, the state controlled not only a major source of finance, but also a very large section of the industrial sector.[15] The bank owned over 50 percent of all industrial shares, and its affiliated companies were responsible for over 20 percent of total industrial production, and over 50 percent of textile production in Egypt. The government felt that this bank was a symbol of financial authority, and its nationalization was needed to avoid misuse of this authority.[16] In June 1960, Egypt nationalized internal and external trade in tea and medicine.

4. The state entered the retail trade sector in 1957 through the establishment of a chain of consumer co-operative societies to compete with the private sector.

5. A number of laws were passed to regulate industry. A Ministry of Industry was established in 1956. The 1958 Act (No. 21) made it compulsory for industrial firms to obtain a licence from the Ministry of Industry before

embarking on the establishment of a new factory or the expansion of an existing one, or changing the line or place of production. The state established a Public Agency to support industry. Also, an Agency for Industrial Control was established to ensure the optimal utilization of industrial resources.

The above clearly suggest that private capital in Egypt after 1956 was not as free as it was in the years from 1952 to 1956. As it has become subject to severe controls, direction, and planning in the post-1956 period, it would be appropriate to call this state 'the stage of controlled capitalism.' This stage started with the establishment of a mixed economy, followed by an expansion in the public sector, then a fuller control over the private sector. This was followed in June 1961 by a series of reforms that led to what Nasser called 'national capitalism.'

Capitalism in Egypt after 1961: the rise of a state bourgeoisie
The regime was not satisfied with the country's economic performance during the dominance of the private sector (1952–56) and the period of controlled capitalism (1957–61). The growth in Gross Domestic Product (GDP) during the two periods was slight, and per capita income was almost at a standstill, as indicated in Table 1.2.

It can be seen from the data in Table 1.2 that GDP increased by an average E£45 million per year during the period 1952–56, while it increased by E£47 million per year during the period 1957–61. Per capita income increased by a mere one pound per year during each of the two periods.

This slow performance led the rising state bourgeoisie to believe that Egypt needed a more radical solution than control and planning. Thus, in July 1961, a number of resolutions were passed nationalizing a great number of private projects in all areas of production. The size of the public sector expanded, and the growth in private enterprise slowed down. The value of the nationalized projects exceeded E£453 million. This resulted in a shift in the ownership of most of the means of production from private hands to the state.

The transformation to state capitalism did not mean eradication of private ownership in Egypt. This was made clear in chapter six of the 1962 National Charter. The charter recognized 'private ownership which is free of exploitation and monopoly, and independent of foreign interference.' Such ownership was called 'national capitalism.' Thus, after July 1961, capitalism in Egypt entered a new era: the era of 'national capitalism.'

The controversy over national capitalism
The years of transformation to state capitalism in Egypt witnessed intense discussions and debate among politicians, economists, and others. Some believed that there was inconsistency in having a 'socialist' economy with some means of production still in the hands of the private sector.[17] The supporters of this view did not make a clear distinction between capitalism in its old dress (with all the symbols of exploitation, monopoly, foreign dependence, and pursuit of private profit) and 'national capitalism,' which interacts with the public sector in order to achieve optimal utilization of resources and realize the

Table 1.2
Gross Domestic Product and per capita income in Egypt,
1952–61

	The Stage of Free Enterprise (1952–56)			The Stage of Controlled Capitalism (1957–61)	
Year	GDP (Millions of E£)	Per Capita Income (E£)	Year	GDP (Millions of E£)	Per Capita Income (E£)
1952	941	44	1957	1,224	51
1953	943	43	1958	1,291	52
1954	1,076	45	1959	1,375	54
1955	1,054	46	1960	1,376	53
1956	1,166	49	1961	1,459	55

Source: Calculated from data given by IMF, *International Financial Statistics, 1982 Yearbook,* p. 205.

object of self-sustained economic growth. Also, private ownership within national capitalism differed from traditional capitalism in that wealth was no longer concentrated in the hands of a few persons, but was spread amongst a large section of the community. The 'big' private ventures no longer existed; they were all nationalized. Small business was the mode of national capitalism in Egypt.

The 1962 Charter defined the area in which national capitalism may operate. As for agriculture, the Charter contended with the laws of land reform which limited private ownership of land to 50 acres. A number of laws were passed to regulate the relationship between the landowners and the peasants. Also, the lines of production and the prices were subject to state control.[18]

Small industries and crafts were left to private ownership on the grounds that these industries did not employ much capital and depended largely on industry skills. Moreover, the public sector extended its control over these industries through the provision of capital goods and raw materials.[19]

In the area of trade, the Charter confined the role of national capitalism to 25 percent of export trade, and to 60 percent of internal trade. But later wholesale trade was nationalized, after it was discovered that only 219 persons controlled wholesale trade in Egypt.[20]

Most of the building sector was left to national capitalism on the grounds that this sector would be regulated by progressive taxation, rent controls, and laws which govern the relationships between tenants and landlords. It was later proven, however, that these measures were not enough to eradicate all means of exploitation.[21] Personal services, including entertainment, local taxis, and limited private education, were left to the private sector, since they depended mainly on individual effort.

A number of variables were responsible for determining the above limitations. These can be summed up as follows:[22]

1. The private sector was given the largest role in areas where only a small volume of capital was needed (e.g., the cottage industries and personal services).

2. Private ownership was encouraged where it was needed in order to have scattered projects of small size (e.g., groceries and workshops).

3. National capitalism was allowed to exist as long as there was no risk of concentration of wealth or power, and no risk of monopoly or excessive exploitation.

4. Private enterprise was allowed where it was difficult to administer the projects either because there were too many of them, or because they were more dependent on personal efforts.

5. Private ownership was encouraged in areas where family ties or personal service and contact are needed (e.g., small agricultural holdings).

6. National capitalism was allowed to expand and grow, as long as it remained within certain prescribed limits.

Table 1.3 gives the relative contribution of the public sector and national capitalism in Egypt in 1970. This data clearly indicates that national capitalism continued to play a very important role in Egypt's state capitalism. In particular, private enterprise dominated the areas of agriculture and retail trade, and played an important role in the areas of transport and communications, and even in manufacturing industries. Thus, the private sector employed 49 percent of all employees in Egypt's manufacturing industries in 1970–71. This sector also contributed 25 percent of total manufacturing output, and 31 percent of total manufacturing value added in the same year.

Table 1.3
The relative contribution of the public sector and national capitalism in Egypt, 1970–71

Economic Activity	Share of Public Sector %	Share of National Capitalism %
Agriculture	20	80
Extractive Industries	88	12
Manufacturing Industries	60	40
Internal Trade	14	86
Transport and Communications	52	48

Source: Ministry of Planning, Egypt (1975).

Performance of the Egyptian economy, 1962–71
The transformation to state capitalism was not without some merit. The Egyptian economy performed much better after 1961 than in either of the two previous periods (1952–56 and 1957–61).[23] This can be seen from the data

in Table 1.4.

It is clear that the growth in both Gross Domestic Product (GDP) and per capita income was much more rapid after the transformation into state capitalism than during the previous period, 1952–61. Thus, while GDP increased by only E£45 million per year during the free enterprise period (1952–56), and by only E£47 million per year during the period of controlled capitalism (1957–61), it increased by over E£163 million per year during the ten years which followed the takeover by the state bourgeoisie. In other words, Egypt's GDP more than doubled in the ten years between the transformation and Nasser's death. Also, while per capita income increased by only a mere E£1 per year in the period from 1952 to 1961, it increased by an average E£3.7 per year during the ten years following the transformation. Although the general price level rose at a faster rate after 1961 than in earlier periods, the statistics support the conclusion that the Egyptian economy performed much better after its transformation to state capitalism than during the periods of private capital and controlled capitalism.[24]

Table 1.4
Performance of the Egyptian economy, 1961–71

Year	GDP (Millions of E£)	Income Per Capita (E£)
1962	1,513	55
1963	1,685	60
1964	1,888	66
1965	2,214	75
1966	2,403	80
1967	2,481	80
1968	2,533	80
1969	2,696	83
1970	2,971	89
1971	3,146	92

Source: Calculated from data in IMF, *International Financial Statistics, 1982 Yearbook*, p. 205.

The improvement in the performance of the Egyptian economy can be attributed not only to the performance of the public sector, but also to the achievements of national capitalism, as may be suggested by the following:

1. The private sector increased its exports of manufactures from E£2 million in 1965 to E£13.5 million in 1970.

2. The value of the private sector industrial output increased from E£213 million to 1964–65 to E£376 million in 1970–71.

3. The percentage contribution of the private sector to total industrial output increased in all lines of production, as can be seen from the data in Table 1.5.

4. Egypt's exports of cotton increased from E£84 million in 1961 to E£175 million in 1971.

5. The service sector in the hands of private capital also expanded during 1961–70, particularly in the areas of local transportation, personal services, and international trade.

Thus, the laws in effect during this period did not put a brake on the performance of national capitalism. Both the public sector and the private sector worked together in achieving economic development during 1961–71.

Table 1.5
The share of national capitalism in Egypt's manufacturing industries, 1963–68

| Industry | Percentage of Total Industry Output | | | | |
	1963–64	1964–65	1965–66	1966–67	1967–68
Food	18.5	17.5	20.5	23.6	25.1
Wood and Products	8.5	8.5	8.4	8.6	8.7
Metal Industries	4.2	7.9	14.9	12.6	14.7
Machinery	15.3	22.3	23.8	24.1	25.6

Note: The figures do not total 100 percent, as smaller industries are not included.

Source: The Centre for Statistics, Egypt (1970).

Contradictions of the state capitalist period
The Egyptian economy suffered many problems and constraints during the Nasser regime. Nasser's reformist economic measures were often frustrated by bureaucratic and hidden bourgeois interests. Other external factors added to the persistent economic weaknesses. The government was unable to provide for the rapidly increasing population. This was, in part, due to the increase in military expenditures during the period following the Arab–Israeli war of 1967 (from E£150 million in 1967, to E£ one billion by 1973, representing a 600 percent increase in military spending). The economic situation continued to deteriorate. A number of factors added to the problem. The state of war with Israel was a continuous drain on the economy – the oil refineries were destroyed; the oil wells came under Israeli control; and millions of people moved from the Suez Canal area to Cairo and other cities in the country. The social and economic relocation problems became severe. In addition, revenues (in hard foreign currency) from ships' passage through the Suez Canal stopped.

The concurrent and continuous rapid increase in population, low economic growth, and the sharp increase of population in urban areas added to the socio-political tensions. The cost of the war added to the retardation of economic growth, the decline in industrialization, and failure of the agrarian reforms.

Sadat's Egypt: *infitah* and the transition to a neo-colonial state

The bourgeois elements within the Egyptian leadership exploited the opportunities available after the war. They advocated the necessity of moving towards reliance on the private sector, and glorified the advantage of an 'open door' economic policy, which would encourage foreign investment. This led, in 1968, to protest demonstrations directed against these bourgeois elements, and forced the Nasserists openly to oppose such views and tighten government control over the economy. Despite the temporary retreat of the traditional bourgeois elements following the 1968 demonstrations, they were nevertheless able to influence government policy during this period, especially the government's encouragement of the private sector. Soon after Sadat's accession to power, more drastic shifts towards privatization of the economy began. Political manoeuvring by the traditional and new bourgeoisie resurfaced, and their class dominance began to be felt.[25]

Under Sadat, the new regime began to announce the importance of activating individual initiatives, but within the overall frame of the primacy of the public sector; and a joint effort on the part of the private and public sectors was to be maintained. Variations in the role of each sector would, however, be necessary from industry to industry.

What were some of the real reasons for the economic policy shifts after Nasser's death? First and foremost was the gradual (but continuous) collaboration of the traditional and new (state) bourgeoisie with US imperialism. Second, after Nasser's death in September 1970, two levels of struggle ensued: the power struggle among those who had been close to Nasser, and the class struggle among the competing groups. Third, Sadat, in his struggle for power, allied himself with right-wing elements that were waiting in the wings. Fourth, the active influence – primarily economic in nature – of conservative Arab regimes increased. Fifth, the active influence of Western powers, in particular the United States, became overwhelming. All these contributed to the transition to a new, 'open door' economic policy called *infitah*.[26]

The objectives of *infitah* were threefold: to attract foreign capital; to encourage the Egyptian private sector; and to alter the nature of the Egyptian public sector. The government stressed the advantages and benefits of foreign capital, and the powerful mainstream mass media campaigned vigorously in favour of inviting foreign capital. The real motive behind such pronouncements, however, was the plan to transform the economic structure in the direction of undermining and dismantling the public sector. The mainstream mass media publicized the advantages that would materialize through adopting the new economic policy, especially in freeing Egypt from economic, technological and political dependence on the Soviet Union. They claimed that the advantages of diversifying foreign sources were the best and fastest way towards economic growth. This was, in essence, an indirect criticism of Nasser's policy of close ties with the Eastern bloc.[27]

It was crucial to hide the real intent of the new economic programme for a number of reasons: to obtain socio-political stability during a potentially turbulent transition stage in the post-Nasser period; to institutionalize the political legitimacy of the Sadat regime by maintaining the appearance of continuity with Nasser's economic statist structure; and, finally, the Egyptian bourgeoisie was interested in learning how well foreign capital can operate in Egypt.

Foreign capital and transformation of the Egyptian economy

The first foreign investment law of 1971 included provisions contrary to the Egyptian constitution. This law expanded the areas of operation of foreign capital, which had previously been restricted. In addition, generous financial and tax privileges and exemptions were provided to foreign capital for the first time since the early 1950s.

The introduction of the 1971 foreign investment law had the appearance of being an isolated act. Due to internal and external political and economic constraints at the time, the 1971 law was introduced as an isolated event to avoid exposing the true aim of transforming the Egyptian economy into a neo-colonial appendage of imperialism. The 1971 law was not, however, perceived by foreign capital as providing sufficient guarantees. As a result, it was replaced by a new law passed in 1974.[28]

The 1974 foreign investment law expanded the privileges granted to foreign capital, and introduced Free Trade Zones. The new law gave foreign capital the opportunity to invest in several areas: industry, mining, energy, tourism, transportation, construction, agriculture, and other sectors. The most crucial aspect of the law was the permission given to foreign capital to open banks. While historically the banking and financial sector had been restricted to national capital alone, foreign banks were now permitted to obtain licences to engage in financial and currency transactions both inside and outside Egypt. In addition, numerous other privileges granted to foreign capital during the period drastically changed the structure of the Egyptian economy in a neo-colonial direction. This also meant the incorporation of the Egyptian bourgeoisie into new relations with imperialism, and its transformation into a comprador class dependent on foreign capital. This was the result of the regime's encouragement of private capital in general, which included the local bourgeoisie (though operating in a subordinate position to imperialism). Thus, the circle of the alliance at the top was enlarged, and in this way Egypt became a part of the world economy,[29] fulfilling its role as an emergent neo-colony of transnational capital dominated by the United States.

Conclusion

In tracing the evolution of the Egyptian political economy over the past three decades, it is clear that Egypt went through two distinct phases of development: an initial state capitalist phase, with its various stages, and a subsequent neo-colonial phase. A comparative analysis of these two periods reveals that the state capitalist phase was characterized by nationalist economic policies bolstered by the state. The main emphasis during this period was on the development of a national capitalism under the guidance and direction of the state. Although this was envisioned by the state to be in the long-term interests of the local capitalist class, the nationalistic policies of the state during this period clashed with the short-term profitability of some medium and large businesses. This, in turn, led to antagonism and conflict between the state and these businesses, prompting local private capital in general to view the Nasserist state as an obstacle to its interests. It is in this context that the numerous internal and external pressures discussed earlier led to the relaxation of the state's hold over local private capital, and set the stage for subsequent developments during the post-Nasserist 1970s.

The death of Nasser and the rise to power of Anwar Sadat in the early 1970s opened the way to a qualitative change in the state apparatus onto the second, neo-colonial phase. With the 'open door' policy towards foreign capital during this latter period, Egypt embarked upon a neo-colonial path dependent on imperialism, where local capital took a secondary but profitable comprador position within the Egyptian economy.

It is within this dynamic of capitalist development in Egypt that the country's current relations with imperialism in general, and the United States in particular, must be understood. The future course of the maturing class struggles and oppositional politics in Egypt will no doubt be in reaction to these relations, and against the class forces responsible for the country's present state of affairs.

Notes

1. This section has benefited to a large extent from a paper presented by Dr Mahmoud Metwally at the State of Art of Middle Eastern Studies Conference held at the University of Calgary, Canada, August 1–3, 1986.

2. *Industrial Production Statistics Yearbook* 1952, Table 5.

3. *Federation of Egyptian Industries Yearbook* 1951/52, pp. 6–10.

4. M. Metwally, 'Nasser and National Capitalism.' p. 12.

5. *Al-Ahram* (December 15, 1954).

6. Nasser's address on the second anniversary of the revolution, July 1954.

7. *Misr Bank Report* (December 31, 1956).

8. M. Metwally, *Egyptian Historical Principles and Their Effects on Egypt, 1920–1961*, p. 245.

9. N. Safran, *Egypt in Search of Political Community* (London, 1961), Cambridge University Press. pp. 185–9.

10. *The Industrial Bank: Annual Report*, p. 15.

11. P. O'Brien, *The Revolution in Egypt's Economic System* (Oxford, Oxford University Press, 1966), p. 84.

12. *UAR Temporary Constitution*, March 1958.

13. Nasser's address on the seventh anniversary of the revolution, July 23, 1959.

14. *The Presidential Resolution No. 1327 for the Year 1960*. The First Five-Year Plan was for the period 1960–1965, and its main objective was to double the national income in ten years.

15. M. Hussein, *Class Conflict in Egypt, 1945–1970* (New York, Monthly Review Press, 1973).

16. Lecture by Dr A. Kysouni, the Egyptian Minister of Finance, delivered in the Faculty of Commerce, Ain Shams University, Cairo (March 5, 1960).

17. *National Capitalism Within a Socialist Economy*, a series of articles written and published by the National Bank of Egypt (Cairo, 1967).

18. Metwally, 'Nasser and National Capitalism,' p. 12.

19. *Ibid.*, p. 13.

20. *Ibid.*

21. P. O'Brien, *The Revolution in Egypt's Economic System*.

22. Metwally, *op. cit.*

23. *Ibid.*

24. The consumer price index in Egypt (1980 = 100) did not show any rise in the period 1962–1964, and increased from 35.2 in 1965 to only 42.2 in 1971.

25. Ghali Shoukri, *Egypt: Portrait of a President* (London, Zed Press, 1981), p. 80.

26. *Ibid.*

27. *Ibid.*

28. *Ibid.*: Nazih N. M. Ayubi, 'Implementation Capability and Political Feasibility of the Open Door Policy in Egypt,' in H. Kerr, et al. (eds.) *Rich and Poor States in the Middle East* (Boulder, Colorado, Westview Press, 1982), pp. 344–413.

29. Gouda Abdel-Khalek, 'The Open Door Policy in Egypt,' in H. Kerr, *Rich and Poor States*, p. 278.

2. Class Politics and State Power in Ba'thi Syria

Fred H. Lawson

Two basic trends have characterized Syrian politics over the last 20 years. On the one hand, the composition of the country's successive regimes appears to have become steadily more exclusive since the coup d'état of March 1963, when military officers associated with the Ba'th party first captured dominant positions within the state. In the years following this event, sectarian affiliation has emerged as a primary focus of political loyalty and collective action among the ruling élite. Both the radical leadership that carried out the coup of February 1966 and the more pragmatic group of officers that overthrew this leadership in November 1970 have been increasingly composed of and identified with individuals from minority communities concentrated in Syria's more peripheral provinces.[1] Furthermore, during the years in which Hafiz al-Asad has presided over the country's affairs, the regime has become more personalist and more closely tied to special units of the Syrian armed forces under the direct command of relatives and confidants of the president.[2]

At the same time, the period after 1970 has been one of the most stable in recent Syrian history. There has not been a successful coup d'état since the ousting of Salah Jadid by al-Asad and his comrades at the end of that year, although dissident officers have periodically been arrested and charged with conspiring to overthrow the current regime. The potential for widespread social revolt, which remained quite high throughout the late 1970s and early 1980s, appears to have dropped markedly following the suppression of a major rebellion in the city of Hamah in February 1982. And most striking of all, the succession crisis of 1983-84 that threatened to split the country's rulers into at least three disparate factions ended up being contained, if not actually resolved, rather handily.[3] By the spring of 1985, knowledgeable observers of Syrian politics were in fact reporting that the al-Asad regime was 'more firmly in control than ever before,' in the wake of the regional party congress in Damascus that January.[4]

Conventional explanations for the evident stability of the present Syrian regime are for the most part inadequate. Although there is little doubt that the current leadership relies heavily upon the armed forces to maintain its domestic predominance, it seems implausible to argue that Hafiz al-Asad and his associates rule the country through brute force alone. As the regime's attempts to suppress the sporadic revolts of the late 1970s demonstrate, efforts to break up opposition groups by force have generally been counterproductive, provoking armed resistance on the part of the Islamic movement and other opposition forces, and leading the state to adopt increasingly violent measures to combat the regime's challengers. Similarly, there is no clear relationship between the breadth of societal support for recent Syrian regimes and their respective degrees of stability. The al-Asad regime has certainly attempted to cultivate a broad basis of support by lifting a wide range of restrictions on economic activity and encouraging local commercial interests to establish ties to outside firms. But the liberalizing regime of 1961–63 also enjoyed widespread support from commercial and industrial interests within the country, without an attendant level of stability. Similarly, the Ba'thi regime of 1963–66 involved a substantially broader social coalition than that underpinning the al-Asad regime, but was unable to achieve a comparable degree of stability in internal affairs.

A more promising way of explaining variations in the level of stability associated with recent Syrian regimes is to connect them to changes in the class relationships that have structured the country's domestic affairs over the last two decades. These changes have resulted in the gradual reduction of fundamental contradictions among the various forces that have composed Syria's successive dominant social coalitions, and have thus enhanced the mutual compatibility of their respective interests. State policy has facilitated this process, but has not played a direct role in creating it. In fact, the changes that have taken place in the country's governing élite – which have usually been identified with shifts in the general orientation of Syrian political and economic affairs – have occurred only after the ruling coalition has rearranged itself in response to altered internal and external circumstances. The coups d'état of February 1966 and November 1970 should thus be seen as consolidating shifts in class relationships that antedated the seizure of state institutions, rather than as moves initiating fundamental transformations in the structure of Syrian society.

Consolidating Ba'thi rule, 1963–65

Little unified the diverse collection of military officers who staged the coup d'état of March 1963, except their common opposition to the civilian government that had come to power in Damascus following Syria's secession from the United Arab Republic in September 1961. This coalition included Ba'thi, independent socialist, Nasserist, and other unionist officers; its members came from the larger north central cities of Homs and Aleppo, from the peripheral districts adjacent to Hamah and Latakia, from the more insular communities of as-Suwayda to the south, and from the largely agricultural provinces of Dayr az-Zur and al-Hasakah in the far north-east. In ideology, these officers ranged from scientific socialists heavily influenced by the concepts of orthodox Marxism to more moderate reformers willing to co-operate with the country's urban and rural bourgeoisie. It is, therefore, not surprising that the new regime's economic policies vacillated between the poles of encouraging the creation of a state-centred socialist society on the one hand and maintaining existing private enterprise, particularly in industry and commerce, on the other.

At first, the Ba'th and its allies moved to limit the role of private capital within the Syrian economy. The new government nationalized local banks and insurance companies in May 1963, and announced a new Agrarian Reform Law in mid-June. The latter set severely reduced ceilings on private landholdings, while easing the terms under which peasants could purchase agricultural land for their own use. These measures reflected the programme advocated by the more radical wing of the Ba'th party, whose supporters were concentrated in the trades unions of Homs and Damascus, and in the poorer farming areas of Dir'a, as-Suwayda, Dayr az-Zur, and al-Hasakah. In districts where officials drawn from the more radical branches of the party were appointed to key administrative posts, the private sector was subjected to increasing state control.

At the same time, however, more moderate components of the regime made a concerted effort to reassure private capital that nationalization would not be pursued against 'productive industrial sectors, which sincerely serve the interests of the people.'[5] Thus, the new minister of the economy justified the nationalization of the banks in terms of the inordinate degree of influence they had exerted over bourgeois politicians and their reluctance to invest more than a small proportion of their available capital in local productive projects. As a sign of their relatively undoctrinaire orientation towards nationalization, state officials relaxed controls on foreign exchange, and began to allow the banks to sell foreign currency on the open market in the latter half of 1963. By taking steps to pacify propertied interests, especially Syria's urban merchants and manufacturers, these officials were able to retain the continued acquiescence, if not the active support, of the country's small-scale tradespeople, a force deeply suspicious of Nasserist forces within the ruling coalition.

Contradictions within the regime became more pronounced in subsequent months. Radical delegates to the Ba'th party congress held in Damascus during October 1963 pushed through a resolution committing the state to the establishment of large-scale collective farms on land expropriated under the terms of the Agrarian Reform Law, while their more moderate colleagues managed to postpone the nationalization of Syria's larger industrial establishments until a comprehensive study of the country's manufacturing sector could be undertaken. When serious inflation hit the larger cities at the end of 1963, the party adopted only token measures to ease the hardship on organized labour. At the same time, state officials avoided extending centralized control over the country's expanding private industrial and commercial firms, whose growth was fuelled by the beginning of oil production and a boom in the construction sector of the domestic economy.

In early 1964, growing conflicts of interest among the forces that constituted Syria's ruling coalition provided an opportunity for opponents of the Ba'th's social programme to challenge the regime's policies. Small-scale merchants carried out a series of strikes and demonstrations in the north central cities of Homs, Hamah, and Aleppo from February to April, prompting the government to deploy regular army units to suppress the demonstrators. When unrest spread to Damascus, the regime sanctioned the creation of armed workers' militias, composed of militant trades unionists from the larger cities. These militias were sent out against striking shopkeepers and other opponents of the regime.[6] The actions of the militias were supported by newly formed cadres of the National Guard that forcibly reopened closed shops and businesses.

Moderates within the regime responded to the rebellions of early 1964 by playing down the importance of state control. Salah ad-Din Bitar, the newly appointed prime minister, announced in late May that the private sector would continue to play a major role in the initial stages of the transition to a more egalitarian economic order. In an effort to combine public and private enterprise with a minimum of conflict, the cabinet proposed creating a 'common sector' within the Syrian economy, in which the state would purchase a 25 percent share of particular firms and assist in managing them in partnership with their private owners. In addition, the regime abandoned its plan to establish state-run collective farms on expropriated agricultural land, and instead initiated a programme of government support for more autonomous agrarian co-operatives. Taken together, these moves represented a resurgence of the more accommodationist wing of the Ba'th, at the expense of the trades unionists and other radicals within the party.

Continual jockeying between the accommodationist and radical wings of the Ba'th provided the impetus for Syrian politics throughout the following year. For the most part, this struggle pitted the country's central administration against provincial officials, drawn largely from the party's rank-and-file. Even as the cabinet continued to mollify an increasingly apprehensive urban private sector, the authorities in Aleppo and Latakia undertook a particularly active programme of dispossessing local notables who had sponsored or taken part in the disorders from February to April 1964. This programme involved the nationalization of a number of major industrial enterprises in these districts, including seven of the country's largest textile firms, which accounted for almost three-quarters of domestic cloth production. At a meeting of the party's branch secretaries in July, the Ba'th leadership attempted to impose some measure of control over the more radical provincial cadres by extending the degree of central supervision over the trades union federations and other affiliated 'popular front organizations,' and making these institutions directly subordinate to the state bureaucracy. Radical forces within the party responded by launching a campaign to 'democratize' Syria's internal affairs.[7] The Ba'thi leadership countered by setting up a General Peasants' Union as a way of harnessing the activities of the diverse collection of rural militants, led by Akram Hawrani, who composed Syria's agrarian movement.

As a result of these tensions, by early 1965 the ruling coalition found itself in a virtually untenable political situation. On the one hand, private property owners in both the cities and the countryside had gradually been pushed beyond the point of reconciliation with the regime by the 'piecemeal nationalizations' its more radical members had implemented after early 1963. Increasingly concerned about the ultimate shape of the regime's economic programme, urban manufacturers refrained both from setting up new operations and from modernizing or expanding existing ones. In addition, private interests pulled substantial amounts of capital out of the country throughout 1964, leaving the north central cities and their surrounding agricultural areas precariously short of financial resources.[8] Moreover, large landowners in the districts around Hamah and Aleppo began to form close tactical alliances with various provincially based peasant organizations, demanding less state intervention in rural affairs, while richer merchants and manufacturers in the north central cities gradually became the primary supporters of the country's rising Islamic movement. Consequently, by early 1965 the opponents of the Ba'th regime posed an increasingly serious threat to its predominance.

On the other hand, those occupying important positions within the state administration came into growing competition with those who controlled the higher echelons of the party and the armed forces. This conflict precipitated a split between the president and leading members of the military committee of the Ba'th, which was only patched over when a minority faction of the committee allied itself with President Amin al-Hafiz in an effort to preserve the state apparatus as a means of co-ordinating the activities of the private and public sectors of the Syrian economy and keeping the more militant trades unionists in line. In a last-ditch effort to stabilize the regime, state officials co-operated with representatives of the more radical wing of the party to implement a series of nationalizations that imposed government control over more than 100 of Syria's largest industrial and commercial firms.

Small-scale merchants reacted to the nationalizations of January 1965 by carrying out a wave of strikes in Damascus and Aleppo. These actions were broken up by the police and workers' militias, who arrested striking artisans and shopkeepers and confiscated their businesses. In late January, a special military court even went so far as to sentence to death eleven men associated with the strikes, on charges that they had conspired to return the country to the hands of 'reactionary elements.'[9] Such measures failed to end the resistance to nationalization; sporadic strikes and demonstrations persisted throughout the spring in most of Syria's north central cities. Consequently, the regime curtailed its nationalization programme, offering modest compensation to the country's remaining small-scale private interests and announcing that it intended to leave the construction sector in private hands as a token that wholesale appropriations of property by the state were to be brought to an end.

The 1965–66 period thus represents a crucial turning-point for Syria's Ba'thi rulers. Prior to this time, the regime had been able to carry out a programme designed to improve the position of smaller farmers and industrial workers without infringing upon the interests of the country's small-scale urban tradespeople and manufacturers. But with increasing state intervention, in conjunction with a persistent shortage of capital in all sectors of the local economy, the petty bourgeoisie of the larger cities and towns found their operations increasingly constrained by the central administration in Damascus. The agricultural shortfall that became evident in the first weeks of 1966 prompted growing popular discontent in the country's north central provinces, and generated increasing support for the various organizations that made up Syria's Islamic movement centred in Aleppo, Hamah, and Homs. These developments led more moderate forces within the regime to begin criticizing the 'inordinate' expansion of the public sector and soliciting economic assistance from Western governments. Disagreement among the members of the military committee of the party over how the ruling coalition should handle its economic and political difficulties precipitated renewed jockeying for predominance among several disparate factions within the governing élite. By mid-February 1966, this jockeying led to the coup d'état in which officers loyal to Generals Jadid and al-Asad displaced the government headed by President al-Hafiz.

Restructuring the regime, 1966–68

The coup of February 23, 1966, represented a triumph for the more militant wing of the Ba'th party in its efforts to use Syria's state administration to substitute public ownership for private capital in the most important sectors of the country's economy. By the first week of March, the party newspaper, *al-Ba'th*, was commenting that the 'mission' of the new government in Damascus was to improve the Syrian economy through 'developing and deepening [its] socialist experience.'[10] In pursuit of this goal, the Jadid regime de-emphasized the pan-Arab nature of the Ba'th party and removed the organization's founders from their leadership positions within the Syrian party command. This move highlighted the difference in social backgrounds between the relatively moderate Salah ad-Din Bitar and Michel Aflaq (who came from the established urban milieux of Damascus and Beirut), and the more doctrinaire Salah Jadid and Yusif Zu'ayyin (whose origins lay in the poor minority communities of the western and southern provinces). The latter had established particularly close ties to Syria's state institutions as a way of improving their disadvantaged social and economic position.

From its first months in power, the Jadid regime carried out a programme designed to further the interests of the country's peasants and industrial workers. In early March, the government proclaimed the end of the first stage of Syria's land reform programme, in which excess holdings of agricultural land had been confiscated from larger farmers, and announced the beginning of a second phase in which expropriated land would be distributed to the peasantry. Furthermore, state officials organized the lands that had been sequestered in the reforms of the mid-1960s into a centralized network of agrarian co-operatives. At the same time, the regime set up extensive state-run agricultural projects on reclaimed lands in the far north-eastern provinces, where centrally administered irrigation systems were being built with the assistance of Soviet advisers.

Industrial policy during the first year or so following the February coup involved a concerted effort on the part of state officials to build up large-scale public sector enterprises in several key sectors of Syria's economy. These included a modern fertilizer factory at Homs, as well as a cotton spinning mill and a steel rolling plant at Hamah. These projects accompanied a marked rise in industrial investment within the country. During 1961–65, annual investment in Syrian industry averaged approximately 113 million Syrian pounds; for 1966–67 this figure rose to approximately 181 million, and reached more than 252 million in 1968–69.[11] Part of this investment went into light industry as well, particularly to firms producing metal and cement pipe, wire, and other items used in manufacturing and transportation.

In an attempt to protect these new public sector enterprises, after 1966 state officials gradually restricted the flow of imported goods entering Syrian markets. Increased customs duties on both European and Arab manufactures, and a devaluation of the Syrian pound, effectively reduced the level of imports coming into the country, while the government entered into a variety of barter arrangements with eastern European countries as a way of managing the importation of vital capital goods.

In late 1966 and early 1967, the government came under pressure from labour organizations who demanded a variety of benefits to workers in the public sector. Among these were an enlarged profit-sharing scheme, a programme administered by the newly-established General Federation of Women to set up day-care centres for working women, and training institutes to provide them with improved industrial and clerical skills. Outlays for programmes such as these kept the public sector operating at the edge of insolvency throughout the first two years of the Jadid regime. This trend enhanced the competitiveness of small-scale manufacturers relative to the larger public firms, enabling them to resist state control over their operations in the months prior to the June war.

By the spring of 1967, the regime's efforts to establish a state-centred 'socialist' society within Syria had driven urban merchants in the cities of north central Syria into active opposition to the Jadid regime. This opposition took two different but related forms. In the first place, private capital stopped investing in local manufacturing and trade; this kept Syrian industrial production virtually stagnant between 1965 and 1968. Second, the country's Islamic movement, which drew its primary support from the small-scale traders and artisans of the north central cities, became increasingly active. In May 1967, prominent religious leaders mobilized anti-Ba'th demonstrations in the streets of Damascus, Aleppo, Homs, and Hamah, protesting against the publication of an article on 'the new Arab socialist personality' in the army weekly, *Jaysh ash-Sha'b*.

Government officials took advantage of the strikes in Syria's larger cities to consolidate their hold over the country's urban economy. As police were forcibly reopening a number of locked shops in the Damascus marketplace in early May, the authorities seized the assets of 45 wealthy merchants. These measures were stepped up as tension with Israel mounted in early June. A series of decrees issued in the days preceding the war ordered rationing of a wide range of staple food items; subsequent orders prohibited the movement of flour from one province to another without a permit from the appropriate state agency.[12] These moves culminated in the government Supply Board's taking charge of the wholesale trade, and the most important aspects of the textile and clothing industry in subsequent months. As a result, Syria's state administration emerged from the June war in a substantially stronger position vis-à-vis private industry, a position that was reinforced with the start of large-scale oil production in early 1968.

Over the next two years private enterprises gradually chipped away at the public sector by making more efficient use of the country's scarce resources. State-owned firms were for the most part unable to be as productive as the remaining smaller privately-held companies, due to the persistent inefficiencies of the former. As a result, by 1968–69 private companies began holding their own against the larger public sector enterprises in specialized areas such as knitwear and confectionery, along with the construction sector, which had been left largely in private hands.

This resurrection of the private sector created a serious crisis within Syria's domestic economy. The rapidly expanding small-scale manufacturing and trading sectors demanded greater access to two critical factors controlled by the central administration: markets for their products and investment capital. Whether or not state agencies should loosen their hold on these two economic levers constituted a point of contention between hardline socialists such as Jadid and Zu'ayyin on the one hand, and more pragmatic advocates of a regulated social order led by al-Asad on the other. The former called for continued efforts to achieve a 'socialist transformation' (*tahwil ishtiraki*) through the expansion of the public sector, and greater support for co-operatives in agriculture and commerce. This faction's approach to the growing challenge facing the regime from urban merchants is evident in its recommendation to the tenth national congress of the Ba'th that the state create two new popular front organizations: a Federation of Craftsmen and a Federation of Small Income Earners, under the supervision of the ministries of economy and supply, respectively.[13]

On the other hand, al-Asad's supporters pushed for the adoption of a considerably more liberal set of policies as a way of addressing the regime's growing economic difficulties.[14] When this faction of the party took over key cabinet positions in May 1969, it began implementing measures designed to deregulate first the commercial sector and then the industrial sector of Syria's economy. Over the next few months, free trading zones were set up in Aleppo and the port city of Tartus. Then in October, the state-run Société Import–Export was broken up into five more specialized trading companies for textiles, industrial machinery, pharmaceuticals, metals, and tobacco. These policies were capped with the promulgation of a law reopening the country to direct foreign investment in both trade and manufacturing.

As the Jadid–al-Asad rivalry escalated, those in charge of Syria's public firms began to adopt the profit-oriented management strategies that had proved so successful in the private sector. Increasing concern for productivity and profit within the country's public sector created a clear convergence of interest between the managers of state-run companies and the larger private merchants and manufacturers of Damascus and Aleppo. These business people were the beneficiaries of the regime's conscious programme of concentrating public enterprise in a limited number of districts as a way of creating economies of scale in construction and transportation. By setting up firms that specialized in supplying goods and services to the public sector, well-to-do merchants, particularly in the capital, guaranteed themselves steady incomes as ancillaries to state companies. This mutuality of interest led to greater efforts by the central administration to crack down on 'black market' operations by unlicensed or unsanctioned entrepreneurs, as well as to a gradual deregulation of state-affiliated enterprises.

In January 1970, state-run import–export agencies reduced restrictions on the importation of a wide range of manufactured goods; duties on 191 products imported from neighbouring Arab countries were lifted entirely. At the same time, government officials announced plans to provide low-interest loans and other subsidies to small private workshops having annual incomes of less than 15,000 pounds.[15] Three months later, the state-controlled Commercial Bank began allowing depositors to open foreign currency accounts, on the condition that they be used to finance government-approved commercial transactions.

By mid-1970, Syria's ruling coalition had become seriously split. The Ba'th apparatus, supported by the various popular front organizations, continued to pursue a programme of state-sponsored large-scale industrialization, combined with administrative control over finance and commerce. This programme had achieved success in several different areas during the late 1960s: gross investment increased substantially after 1967, industrial productivity rose by almost 8 percent per year between 1967 and 1972, and the proportion of agricultural land in the hands of independent small landholders jumped from less than 15 to more than 50 percent by 1969.

By the end of the decade, however, state-sponsored development had also created a variety of problems for the regime. Syria's foreign debt increased dramatically between 1967 and 1971, agricultural production fluctuated widely after 1965, and greater imports of capital goods produced rapidly-growing foreign trade deficits beginning in 1966. Consequently, the Jadid government's persistent efforts to support the public sector at the expense of more efficient private enterprises became unproductive and dangerous, as urban discontent spread after 1968. It was this perception within the party that set the stage for al-Asad's virtually uncontested coup of November 1970, carried out in the name of 'relaxation' (*infiraj*), or 'opening up to the people' (*al-infitah 'ala ash-sha'b*).

Reorienting the Ba'th, 1970-83

As its first move after taking control of the party and state, the regime's new leadership appealed to private enterprise to assist in solving Syria's persistent economic difficulties. In early December, President al-Asad announced his intention, before a delegation of wealthy Damascene merchants, of doing all he could to enhance the role of the private sector in the country's commercial and industrial affairs. In addition, he promised to initiate a wholesale reorganization of the public sector, with a view to improving its overall efficiency. In January 1971, the government altered Syria's foreign trade regulations to make them more accommodating to private importers. By early 1972, state officials had eased the restrictions on imported sugar, rice, and flour. At the same time, the state began encouraging private sector industry; between mid-1971 and mid-1972 the Ministry of Industry issued more than 100 licences to individuals or private companies to set up new industrial ventures.

Private enterprise responded quickly to the state's liberalization measures. The private sector accounted for 29 percent of Syria's foreign trade in 1971, with most of the goods consisting of textile equipment, fruits, vegetables, and canned foodstuffs. Figures for 1972 indicate that private firms provided 35 percent of total manufacturing production, and employed 62 percent of the workforce. Elisabeth Longuenesse reports that by 1973 the private sector 'produced 85 percent of the chocolate, 51 percent of the cotton and silk, 94 percent of the knitted goods, 70 percent of the socks, 56 percent of the paint, 45 percent of medical supplies, and 78 percent of the soap, etc.' for the country as a whole.[16] These proportions are all the more remarkable given the priorities of the third Five-Year Plan (1971-76). Under this plan, almost 80 percent of total investment was earmarked for large-scale public industry, particularly in the larger cities.

Liberalization subverted any potential for overt conflict between Syria's newly-reconstituted ruling coalition and the labour movement, but it soon created co-ordination problems among the various sectors of the economy. As early as April 1971, government officials were forced to reintroduce restrictions on the importation of fruits, vegetables, and consumer goods from Lebanon in order to stem the flow of Syrian currency to Beirut. By the first half of 1972, increased levels of state spending led to sharp increases in prices on local markets. This trend forced the government to cut back on actual expenditures for state-sponsored projects during 1972-73, with the exception of large-scale capital goods plants, such as the proposed cement factories at Damascus, Aleppo and Hamah.

These policies provided the conditions in which a new urban bourgeoisie took root and began to flourish during the mid-1970s. This class was concentrated mainly in the capital, but existed to a lesser extent in Aleppo, Homs, and Latakia as well.[17] Its members made their fortunes by colluding with those who controlled the monopoly enterprises in the public sector, either to supply state firms with necessary equipment and spare parts, or to distribute surplus goods on the growing black market. The nouveaux riches buttressed their position through speculative investments in real estate and foreign trade, creating a booming market in unregulated housing and commercial property in the larger cities.

As this class of wealthy merchants established itself in Damascus and Aleppo during the early 1970s, richer small farmers who had been the primary beneficiaries of the regime's land reform programme, along with scattered scions of the old landowning élite, began consolidating their holdings into larger private agrarian enterprises. This trend was particularly evident in the north central provinces of Aleppo, Hamah, and Homs, although extensive holdings also reappeared in the far north-eastern provinces of al-Hasakah and Dayr az-Zur.[18] On the whole, Tabitha Petran's general assertion that large landholders began to regain a predominant position in rural Syria after 1970 may have to be modified for particular regions. Around Hamah, for example, the 'old landowning "aristocracy"' re-emerged as a powerful force in local politics in the aftermath of al-Asad's coup d'état.[19] Around Damascus and Tartus, on the other hand, no such class reconstituted itself during this period.

Differences in economic organization between Syria's north central provinces and those in the southern and western parts of the country came to be associated with marked differences in the scale and frequency of political violence in the years following 1970. Violent disorder has been most prominent in the rural areas around Hamah. Large landholders in these districts provided a focus for rural discontent. At the same time, landless peasants had little chance of obtaining one of the few smallholdings in this part of the country. Moreover, the considerable numbers of artisans and merchants associated with small-scale industry in the province provided rural dissidents with potential allies capable of supporting organized political action. After 1970, joint action on the part of these forces became more threatening to the regime, as it was carried out under the direction of local branches of the Islamic movement. Major riots led by this movement broke out in both Hamah and Homs in the spring of 1973, and soon spread to Aleppo. No sooner had they been suppressed by state security forces than they recurred in Homs on the occasion of the holiday marking the birth of the Prophet.

Early 1976 marked a high point in the development of overt, organized opposition to the Ba'th regime in Syria's north central provinces. During February, rioting occurred in several north central cities following the death of a widely respected leader of the Islamic movement in a government prison. The most serious of these disorders took place in Hamah, where local merchants and students clashed with police and army units. According to sources close to the Muslim Brothers (*Ikhwan al-muslimin*), these actions substantially increased the level of popular support for the movement throughout Syria's northern provinces. In fact, the official publication of the Islamic movement, *an-Nadhir*, gives February 8, 1976, as the date on which its general struggle against the al-Asad regime was launched.[20]

Syria's rulers responded to the growing threat from small merchants in the north central cities by adopting a variety of programmes, none of which was particularly well co-ordinated with the others. Those in charge of the state bureaucracy ordered military and police commanders to break up dissident organizations by force. These operations were largely entrusted to the Defence Squadrons and Special Elite Forces led respectively by the president's brother, Rif'at al-Asad, and his long-time ally, 'Ali Haydar. At the same time, the managers of Syria's heavy industrial enterprises initiated a programme of large-scale industrialization in the north central provinces as a way of putting that region's artisans and craftspeople under some form of centralized administration. But, by the Spring of 1976, the state's use of armed force against the *Ikhwan* had begun seriously to destabilize working conditions in these areas. State officials and public sector managers thus found themselves working at cross purposes in efforts to weaken their mutual opponents.

This contradiction was exacerbated by the activites of the country's major import–export merchants. By the first months of 1976, the operations of the larger private commercial firms began to hurt not only small-scale manufacturers of household and luxury items, but also state-supported light industrial firms. Government trading companies imported a variety of capital goods in addition to lighter consumer items during this period. This shift enabled these companies to improve their own profitability, but it put them into direct competition with public sector enterprises manufacturing the same product. As competition between these trading and manufacturing firms grew, short-term interest rates rose sharply, while prices for locally produced industrial goods dropped. These two dynamics effectively reduced the returns on investment in Syria's larger, capital-intensive companies, compounding the regime's problems in coming up with enough capital to finance new ventures. These internal difficulties did much to set the stage for the military intervention in the Lebanese civil war.

By intervening in Lebanon, Syria's ruling coalition was able to suppress its domestic political opponents and moderate the most crucial conflicts of interest among its own members.[21] The compromise that emerged from this strategic operation enhanced the dynamism of private commerce and industry and undermined the public sector even further. The expansion of the private sector is evident in the changing distribution of the country's labour force during the late 1970s. In 1971, almost 60 percent of workers were employed in agriculture, approximately 5 percent in construction, almost 10 percent in commerce, and 12 percent in services; eight years later, the proportion employed in agriculture had fallen to around 33 percent, while those for construction, commerce, and services had risen to approximately 14, 10, and 20 percent respectively (see Table 2.1).

On the other hand, during the late 1970s, state administrators continued to concentrate public investment in a limited number of large-scale, capital-intensive operations. The high costs associated with these projects made them less and less feasible as time went by, making 1977–78 a disastrous period in public sector manufacturing. The following year there was a partial recovery in such industries as glass- and pottery-making, cement production, and electrical components; but low rates of output and capacity utilization persisted in such critical industries as textiles, food processing, and fertilizer production.[22] The

Table 2.1
Structure of employment in Syria, 1965–79
(in percentages)

Sector	1965	1971	1975	1979
Agriculture	55.6	58.6	51.1	32.8
Mining and Manufacturing	12.0	11.4	12.4	13.9
Construction	4.3	4.6	7.0	13.7
Commerce	10.6	9.2	10.6	10.4
Transportation	3.1	3.0	4.3	4.6
Services	13.3	12.0	13.4	20.0
Total Labour Force (in thousands)	*1,292.1*	*1,522.3*	*1,750.5*	*2,092.0*

Source: Alasdair Drysdale, 'The Asad Regime and its Troubles.' *MERIP Reports*, No. 110 (November–December 1982) p. 11.

discontent generated by the state's economic policies found expression in elections to local union committees in the major public corporations. In the autumn of 1978, a number of leftists and Nasserists opposed to the regime were elected to these bodies from unofficial lists, competing with those prepared by the party hierarchy. These candidates ran on platforms sharply critical of the emphasis being accorded to private enterprise in the country's development programme.[23]

In an attempt to revive the state-run heavy industrial firms, in early 1979 Syria's central administration instituted a set of individual incentives for public sector employees. The programme provided bonuses to both workers and managers whose performance exceeded prescribed levels. It was followed by a general pay rise in public sector firms, as well as a graduated effort to make each plant less subject to centralized authority and more responsive to local-level management.[24] These moves were accompanied by the imposition of higher tax rates on private manufacturing firms and a concerted effort, particularly in the north central provinces, to direct raw materials away from the smaller private companies and into state enterprises. In the spring of 1981, state officials began requiring private importers to obtain the credit they needed from state financial institutions such as the Commercial Bank, and to take out import licences from the Ministry of Trade. Merchants who sidestepped these new regulations were arrested on charges of smuggling and tax evasion.

These moves provided the context in which small-scale traders and manufacturers in Hamah rose in open revolt in February 1982. This rebellion, which appears to have been triggered by a raid on several buildings in the old marketplace suspected of being hideouts for local Islamic militants, pitted small-scale merchants and resurgent private landholders against provincial authorities and the managers of state-run factories, in a last-ditch struggle against the regime's programme of rationalizing the Syrian economy.[25] Its suppression by élite units of the regular armed forces was facilitated by the refusal of small-scale merchants in Aleppo and Damascus, who enjoyed closer ties to the public sector than did their counterparts in Hamah, to participate in the revolt.[26] This development highlights the regime's success in transforming itself in the two decades following 1963 from a heterogeneous collection of poor farmers, trades unionists, and military officers into a coherent coalition of state administrators and large-scale commercial and industrial interests supervising a hierarchically ordered system of 'popular front organizations.'

Conclusion

Political dissent in Syria did not come to an end with the suppression of the February 1982 rebellion in Hamah. Opponents of the al-Asad regime merged the following month to form a joint National Alliance for the Liberation of Syria. This movement was composed of pro-Iraqi Ba'this, supporters of Akram Hawrani's Arab Socialist Party, and representatives of a number of other dissident groups, in addition to the leaders of the more mainstream Islamic organizations. But the Alliance's charter contained little more than vague pronouncements concerning the need to reform Syria's economic and political systems, and its constituents abandoned their attacks against the Ba'thi regime soon after the Alliance was formed. In late January 1985, the leader of the more militant wing of the Islamic movement surrendered to the authorities, bringing to an end what Yahya Sadowski has called 'the civil war of the late 1970s and early 1980s.' Subsequent debates over the future direction of government economic policy have on the whole reflected co-ordination problems, rather than deep-seated challenges to the ruling coalition.[27]

Nevertheless, the potential for serious political conflict within Syrian society remains. The most salient domestic political issue, that of 'official corruption,' involves not simply the legitimacy of high-ranking state and party officials, but also the basis for collaboration among the forces making up the regime. To the extent that the costs of widespread collusion between Syria's commercial and industrial élite and the leadership of the Ba'th become politically or economically unmanageable, the ruling coalition will face fundamental internal difficulties.

At the same time, the apparent quiescence of the country's trades unionists masks a variety of disconcerting trends within the public sector. Longuenesse has noted that state-run firms suffer from chronic labour shortages and absenteeism. In mid-1984, these problems led to plant closures and lay-offs at a number of public companies. They also precluded the awarding of bonuses to employees, thereby reducing workers' expected incomes and forcing them to moonlight at second jobs in the unpredictable private sector.[28] Given these conditions, the possibility that overt opposition to the ruling coalition could germinate among the rank-and-file of the trades union federations cannot be ruled out. For the moment, however, the position of the current Ba'thi regime appears secure indeed.

Notes

1. See Alasdair Drysdale, 'Ethnicity in the Syrian Officer Corps: A Conceptualization,' *Civilizations*, no. 29 (1974); 'The Syrian Political Elite, 1966–1976: A Spatial and Social Analysis,' *Middle Eastern Studies*, no. 17 (January 1981); 'The Syrian Armed Forces in National Politics: The Role of the Geographic and Ethnic Periphery,' in Roman Kolkowicz and Andrzej Korbonski (eds.) *Soldiers, Peasants and Bureaucrats* (London, Allen and Unwin, 1982); Mahmud A. Faksh, 'The Alawi Community in Syria: A New Dominant Political Force.' *Middle Eastern Studies*, no. 20 (April 1984).

2. Hanna Batatu, 'Some Observations on the Social Roots of Syria's Ruling, Military Group and the Causes for its Dominance,' *Middle East Journal*, no. 35 (Summer 1981); Gerard Michaud, 'The Importance of Bodyguards,' *MERIP Reports*, no. 110 (November–December 1982).

3. Drysdale, 'The Succession Question in Syria,' *Middle East Journal*, no. 39 (Spring 1985).

4. Alan George, 'Firmly in the Saddle,' *Middle East International*, (January 24, 1986).

5. Itamar Rabinovich, *Syria Under the Ba'th, 1963–66: The Army–Party Symbiosis* (New York, Halsted Press, 1972), p. 64.

6. Tabitha Petran, *Syria* (New York, Praeger, 1972), p. 176.

7. *Ibid.*, p. 177.

8. Alan W. Horton, *Syrian Stability and the Baath*, American Universities Field Staff Reports, Southwest Asia Series No. 14 (1965), p. 125.

9. Rabinovich, *Syria Under the Ba'th*, p. 140; chronology entry in *Middle East Journal*, no. 19 (Spring 1965).

10. *Arab Report and Record*, (February 15–28, 1966), p. 45; chronology entry in *Middle East Journal*, no. 20 (Summer 1966).

11. E. Kanovsky, *Economic Development of Syria* (Tel Aviv, University Publishing Projects, 1977), p. 47.

12. *Middle East Record* (1967), p. 502.

13. *Middle East Record* (1968), p. 722.

14. My understanding of these developments has benefited greatly from Yahya Sadowski's unpublished manuscript, 'The Knife's Edge: A Study of the Failure of Liberalisation in Syria.'

15. Economist Intelligence Unit, *Quarterly Economic Review of Syria*, first quarter, 1970.

16. Longuenesse, 'The Class Nature of the State in Syria,' *MERIP Reports*, no. 77 (May 1979), p. 7.

17. Eric Rouleau, 'Syria: Clubbing Together to Beat the System', *Guardian Weekly* (July 24, 1983); Batatu, 'Syria's Muslim Brethren,' *MERIP Reports*, no. 110 (November–December 1982), pp. 19–20.

18. Ziad Keilany, 'Land Reform in Syria,' *Middle Eastern Studies*, no. 16 (October 1980), p. 212.

19. Petran, *Syria*, p. 207; P. J. Vatikiotis, 'The Politics of the Fertile Crescent,' in P. Y. Hammond and S. S. Alexander (eds.) *Political Dynamics in the Middle East* (New York, Elsevier, 1972), p. 226.

20. Umar R. Abd-Allah, *The Islamic Struggle in Syria* (Berkeley, CA: Mizan, 1983), p. 109.

21. Fred H. Lawson, 'Syria's Intervention in the Lebanese Civil War, 1976: A Domestic Conflict Explanation,' *International Organization*, No. 38 (Summer 1984).

22. David W. Carr, 'Capital Flows and Development in Syria,' *Middle East Journal*, no. 34 (Autumn 1980), pp. 459–64.

23. Longuenesse, 'The Syrian Working Class Today,' *MERIP Reports*, no. 134 (July–August 1985), p. 24.

24. Carr, 'Capital Flows and Development in Syria,' p. 465.

25. Lawson, 'Social Bases for the Hamah Revolt,' *MERIP Reports*, no. 110 (November–December 1982).

26. Thomas Mayer, 'The Islamic Opposition in Syria, 1961–1982,' *Orient* (Hamburg) no. 24 (1983), pp. 605–6.

27. Lawson, 'Comment le régime du président El Assad s'emploie à remodeler l'économie syrienne,' *Le Monde diplomatique*, no. 358 (January 1984); Sadowski, 'Cadres, Guns and

Money: The Eighth Regional Congress of the Syrian Ba'th.' *MERIP Reports*, no. 134 (July–August 1985).

   28. Longuenesse. 'The Syrian Working Class Today.' pp. 18–21.

3.   Class, State and Politics in Iraq

Joe Stork

There have been two momentous political revolutions in the Gulf during this era: the overthrow of the British-installed monarchy in Baghdad in 1958, and the defeat of the Pahlavis in 1979. Both were the culmination of protracted popular upheavals against regimes sponsored by the leading imperial powers. The current regime in Baghdad has nurtured Iraq's subsequent reputation as a progressive nationalist country, primarily on the basis of its commercial and military ties with the Soviet Union and its vocal militance in Arab and Third World forums.

This carefully cultivated image has until recently inhibited criticism of Iraq from the left. Even prior to the war with Iran, though, many of the regime's actions posed sharp questions about its political character and commitment. Physical attacks against Palestine Liberation Organization representatives in Europe and the Middle East in 1979 are one case in point. Iraq's closest ally in the region is now Jordan's King Hussein, himself once on the CIA payroll and still regarded by Washington as a key US 'asset,' and earlier Anwar Sadat had announced that Egypt would provide Iraq with arms and ammunition for the war. Iraq's attack on Iran aimed clearly at deflecting, if not reversing, the course of the Iranian revolution, and predictably facilitated a greatly increased US military presence in the Gulf. These developments have produced a tendency to identify Iraq as a 'client' of the US, as if their coincidence of interests made any inquiry into the dynamics of Iraqi politics and society superfluous. What are the circumstances and conditions of Iraq's revolution and its aftermath that produced this apparent metamorphosis?

Modern Iraq – its state apparatus, its social and economic character – had its beginnings in the early phase of European penetration in the mid-19th century and its fitful but persistent integration into the world economy. This provoked a distinct shift from prevailing pastoral and subsistence agriculture to production for the external markets of British India and Europe, and transformed, over many decades, the relationship of shaikh and tribesperson into one of landlord and peasant/serf as communally farmed lands became the private estates of large shaikhs, urban merchants, and state officials.

The formation of the state, combining the vilayets of Basra, Baghdad, and Mosul after the Ottoman defeat in World War I, was dictated by European convenience and the imperative of foreign capital in consolidating its rule. Oil –

the reserves of Mosul and proximity to the Persian fields – was the incentive for British control, sanctioned by a League of Nations mandate. The new state, built on the Ottoman apparatus and financed by indirect taxes that hit the poorest classes hardest, secured international recognition of British hegemony.

In the countryside, where the vast majority of the people lived, the colonial regime shored up the large shaikhs, whose traditional authority was eroding with the accelerating shift to tenure relations based on private property. The urban building blocks for the British-installed monarchy included Iraqi officers from the Ottoman army who had sided with the British in the war, large merchants, and former bureaucrats. These elements forged close ties with the shaikh-landlords in the countryside, as political and military offices were parlayed into large estates and import licences.

The Depression and the sharp fall in world prices for Iraq's chief exports, barley and wheat, precipitated an economic and political crisis that led to 'independence' in 1932. The Iraqi state, however, incorporated contradictions not so easily resolved with 'independence.' The local bourgeoisie was overwhelmingly mercantile, closely tied to foreign capital and the landowners. The construction of railways and ports, the growth of trading activity and workshops, and the expansion of the state apparatus brought into being newer, urban-based social forces: a small proletariat, and somewhat more numerous petty bourgeois and intermediate strata.[1] These forces perceived their interest to lie in the growth of the urban economy, including the state, and they came to articulate widespread resentment of British control and the abuses of the local ruling class.

The instability of Iraqi society was reflected at the state level in a series of military interventions and tribal rebellions during 1936–41. With the outbreak of World War II, Britain intervened to freeze the political situation. The wartime environment of protection and high demand benefited merchants and landlords, but hurt drastically the rural and urban masses. Long-time Western residents in Basra compared the circumstances of the lower classes unfavourably with their conditions in the last years of Ottoman rule. Intensifying anti-British sentiment, added to these explosive social conditions, sparked strikes, demonstrations, and harsh repression. The manager of Iraq's largest bank described the situation in 1948 as 'a political crisis of the first magnitude.'[2]

Oil and revolution

The crisis was met by the unstinting repression of all anti-monarchy and anti-British forces, especially the large and well-organized Communist Party. Soon after, the growth of oil exports and revenues permitted the expansion of construction and trading sectors and the state itself, resolving the financial dimension of the crisis.

Until the 1950s, the economic and social impact of the oil industry in Iraq was slight. Reconstruction of the industrialized capitalist countries after World

Table 3.1
Iraqi oil revenues, selected years

Year	Revenue ($ million)
1950	19
1953	144
1958	244
1964	353
1968	488
1972	575
1974	5,700
1977	9,600
1979	12,180

Source: For 1950–77, Richard Nyrop (ed.), *Iraq: A Country Study* (Area Handbook Series: Washington, DC, 1979), p. 265; 1979 provisional figure from Economist Intelligence Unit Special Report No. 88, *Iraq: A New Market in a Region of Turmoil* (London, 1980), p. 31.

War II required the rapid growth of crude exports from the Middle East. The nationalization crisis in Iran, strong Communist trade union activity in Iraq, and political threats in other oil-producing countries threatened the stability of the region when it was most vital. The US companies, in order to 'get more money into the hands of the conservative governments in the Arab world,' offered to 'share' their profits with the producing regimes.[3] A 1952 agreement between the government and the Iraq Petroleum Company[4] raised revenues from $1.75 to $5.50 per ton. This and increased production brought Iraq's oil revenues from $19 million in 1950 to $144 million in 1953, and $244 million in 1958, a jump proportionately as great as that of the mid-1970s (Table 3.1).

The 1950s were a critical period of transition and dislocation. The first phase of Iraq's incorporation into the world economy was marked by agricultural exports and the formation of large private estates, and a vast peasant class. The oil rent, unlike the agricultural surplus monopolized by the landlord class, accrued to the government and was dispersed from Baghdad. It perceptibly accelerated the shift of economic activity to commodity production and services in the urban areas. The continued dominance of foreign and merchant capital, with its strong links to the monarchy and the landlord class, impeded any easy or quick transformation of social relations. With the influx of oil rent, however, this balance was challenged; the oil revenues nourished a revolution they were designed to pre-empt.

A new demographic dynamic defined this second phase. The locus of domestic production was set for dams and irrigation works, but the social structure restricted benefits to the large landowners, who appropriated over 70 percent of the total production in the rural sector. A vast tide of people moved from the impoverished country to the cities. Squalid slums of cardboard, reed, and mud huts swelled the outskirts of Baghdad and Basra. Tens of thousands of peasants found even the miserable part-time unskilled, poorly paid jobs there an improvement over the oppression and misery of the estates. This massive urbanization increased in later decades, but already it defined the new era. Within three decades after World War II, the proportion of the Iraqi population in the urban and rural sectors was exactly reversed (Table 3.2).

Table 3.2
Iraqi population in urban and rural sectors

Year	Total Population	Urban	%	Rural	%
1947	4,816,185	1,733,827	36.0	3,082,358	64.0
1957	6,298,978	2,445,459	48.8	3,853,519	61.2
1965	8,047,415	4,112,291	51.1	3,935,124	48.9
1977	12,171,280	7,728,763	63.5	4,442,517	36.5

Source: For 1947–65, Central Statistical Organization, Ministry of Planning, 1974, cited in Basil Naim Najar, 'Dynamics of Rural–Urban Migration and Assimilation in Iraq,' unpublished PhD dissertation, Wayne State University, 1976; for 1977, *Iraq: A Country Study*, p. 76.

The social impact of the oil industry was indirect. It accounted for over 35 percent of the country's total production of goods and services in the 1950s, but employed only 0.6 percent of the labour force. Total disbursements, including wages, were only $25 million in 1954, but government revenues financed trade and real estate ventures, construction, and manufacturing projects. There was a marked growth and diversification of wealth and property within the existing élite. By the end of the decade, investments and total profits in manufacturing exceeded those in trade, suggesting the formation of a new fraction of the bourgeoisie, linked with the old but with a different agenda.

Its interests were not served by the feudal-like relations in the countryside, where 1 percent of the population owned 55 percent of the land. The political expression of this budding 'national bourgeoisie' was the National Democratic Party, headed by Kamel Chadirchi.

The political weight of Iraq's small proletariat had developed considerably since military coup leader Bakr Sidqi asked derisively in 1937, 'Where are our factories and our workers? Where are our capitalists and the capital with which they could cause oppression?'[5] British military forces directly employed some 60–70,000 workers in 1943.[6] The number employed by the oil companies grew from 3,137 in 1941, to more than 15,000 by the mid-1950s.[7] Industrial and transport workers numbered over 130,000 by 1954, with more than 43 percent in establishments of over 100 workers. In the first year after the revolution, the General Federation of Trades Unions claimed membership of some 275,000 workers and artisans.[8] Among workers, the nationalist cause – independence and unity – had great sentimental appeal, but in terms of immediate wants and needs the Communists enjoyed a near political monopoly. The ICP (Iraqi Communist Party) organized the largest and most strategic concentrations of

Table 3.3
Iraq: economic statistics

Sector	% GDP	% Labour Force	Rent/ Profits*	Wages/ Salaries	% Increase Profits 1953–56	1956–60
Agriculture	21.0	55.0	ID 62.0 m	ID 26.0 m		
Manufacture, Construction, Utilities	13.8	12.5	ID 27.2 m	ID 25.9 m**	59	48.4
Trade, Banking, Insurance, Real Estate	10.7	15.0	ID 32.5 m	ID 4.2 m	41	15
				(banks	96	26)
Services, Transportation, Communications	12.2	8.6	ID 16.6 m	ID 26.6 m		
Public Admin., Defence	6.5	8.0		ID 21.4 m		

* One Iraq Dinar (ID) = $2.80.
** Includes earnings of self-employed shop owners.

Source: Compiled from data of K. Hasseb. *The National Income of Iraq* (London. 1964).

workers: the state railway, Basra port, and the oil fields.

Between the few who were unmistakably bourgeois in their outlook and material condition and the masses of peasants and workers were the petty bourgeoisie and intermediate strata. Here the lines on the class map were especially blurred: thousands of small handicraft shops that were part of the 'manufacturing sector'; even more numerous one-person stores; professionals and semi-professionals employed in services and the public sector, including the army, and thousands of students looking for scarce jobs, whose orientation was unmistakably towards commerce and the bureaucracy.[9] Newer and younger elements of this class and strata were educated, ideologically articulate, and increasing rapidly. Many were early migrants from provincial towns, or first-generation city dwellers, concerned with expanded employment opportunities, markets, and social mobility.

The survival of Iraq's political order assumed some preservation of the existing balance of social forces, including foreign capital. As new forces emerged and old ones were undermined, as tens of thousands of unskilled peasants and their impoverished families fled the countryside to the largest cities, as even the armed forces came to reflect this shifting balance, the immunity of the regime to radical alteration evaporated. The coup of the 'Free Officers,' led by Colonel Abdul-Karim Qasim on July 14, 1958, was triggered by Iraqi participation in Western manoeuvres against Egypt; but at a more fundamental level it was 'the climax of the struggle of a whole generation of the middle, lower-middle and working classes.'[10]

The revolution shakes down

An open struggle for class hegemony in Iraq lasted a full decade. In the years just after the 1958 revolution, Iraqi society was intensely politicized at every level. Over the decade, though, political struggle was removed from the popular level and increasingly restricted to competition among petty bourgeois and intermediate groupings within the state apparatus.

The social origins and political inclinations of the 'Free Officers' placed them squarely among the petty bourgeoisie. All the parties, notably the ICP and the Ba'th, had adherents among the officers, but the dominant influence on Qasim was exercised by the 'men of substance,' the leadership of the National Democratic Party. Their programme called for restructuring the economy under the leadership of the new urban bourgeoisie, including fiscal protection for new industries, a 'welfare state' array of social services, government salary rises, better working conditions, and regional labour exchanges.[11]

The question of national control of oil grew in importance over these years. Success in this arena was seen as a way of restructuring the economy while avoiding a direct confrontation with the urban class structure of Iraqi society. In Qasim's words:

> We are not combating the oil companies to obtain an additional ID 7 million a year. This is not a fundamental point. We are fighting for the industrialization of our republic and the ending of our dependence on the sale of crude oil. The resulting financial gains will benefit all and improve the lot of the poor without jeopardizing a fair standard of living for the rich.[12]

But confrontation with the oil companies came at a time of declining world crude prices. Nationalization was not fully achieved until 1975, and oil production and revenues stagnated through the 1960s, putting economic and political strains on succeeding regimes in Baghdad.

The main political achievement of this early period was the agrarian reform programme, due in no small part to the vigorous efforts of the ICP. The political strength of the landowning class was broken. Political and economic power was restructured in favour of the urban and petty bourgeoisie, while the principle of private ownership was maintained. But successive governments failed to provide alternate structures and social relations in the countryside, contributing to a deterioration of agricultural production and accelerated migration that has continued to this day.[13]

By 1963, when the Communists had been physically eliminated from political contention, Iraqi politics centred on conflicting interpretations of the appropriate role of the state among self-styled 'radical' and 'moderate' factions of petty bourgeois/intermediate strata nationalists. 'Radicals' favoured an expanded public sector role, 'moderates' wanted that role restricted to the provision of physical infrastructure and basic industries and services beyond the capacity of private entrepreneurs. The character of the economy would be private.

A locus of 'moderate' strength was the Oil Ministry and, after it was set up in 1964, the Iraq National Oil Company (INOC). The struggle over control of oil and disposition of revenues was manifest in the frequent reorganizations of INOC. The 'radicals' wanted it under control of the cabinet, where they often held the edge. The 'moderates' favoured an autonomous body that could function like a commercial company, not bound by civil service salary limits, and could develop Iraq's oil industry in partnership with foreign private or state companies. The 'radicals' enjoyed more popular support, but lacked a coherent ideology and political organization. Typical of their mode of operating was the July 1964 nationalization decree, an unsophisticated imitation of Egyptian measures that transferred overnight the largest, most profitable manufacturing, trading, and financial firms to the public sector.[14]

The 'radicals' relied on popular support without mobilizing it, and without developing a programme to resolve the manifold social and economic crises in the country. After 1966 a drop in oil revenues and another futile campaign against Kurdish nationalists forced the regime to increase taxes, hitting especially those on fixed salaries and eroding public support. Communist activity among the peasants in the south and increased migration to the cities testified to the ineptness of the agrarian reform after 1963. Wages in manufacturing, but not prices, had been stagnating. Officers and bureaucrats, backed by one or another faction of the small Iraqi bourgeoisie or foreign capital, squabbled over political terrain and financial spoils, while economic and political conditions in the society deteriorated close to the point of breakdown. In July 1968, just after the tenth anniversary of the Qasim revolution that brought the diffuse petty bourgeois and bourgeois forces to power, the Ba'th party, in alliance with right-wing military officers, seized power in a bloodless coup.

The Ba'thi movement

The consolidation of power after 1968 by Ahmad al-Bakr and Saddam Hussein in the name of the Ba'th party comprises an important chapter in the evolution of the modern Iraqi state. The Ba'th in 1958 was still relatively new to Iraq and did not play a major role in the revolution. In the struggle for class hegemony that ensued after 1958, though, it emerged as the most significant political instrument of the 'radical' petty bourgeois forces inspired by Arab nationalism.

The Ba'th, in its sporadically effective alliances with nationalist officers, provided the shock troops and the conspiratorial organization for the defeat of the Communist Party, culminating in the bloodbath of February 1963. The Ba'th party's nine-month rule displayed an extraordinary inability to govern. They alienated nearly every element of their potential constituency, and were soon ousted by their erstwhile officer allies in November 1963.[15] (The Ba'thists learned this lesson, and in 1968 hustled the non-Ba'thi conspirators out of the country within two weeks of the coup.)

The years of interregnum were critical in the evolution of the party's social composition and political definition. The Ba'th, inspired by European romantic nationalism, originated in Syria in the 1940s as an amalgamation of several nationalist groupings to represent 'Arab spirit against materialistic communism.'[16] It recruited among the lower strata of the petty bourgeoisie and intermediate social categories, including sons of small shopkeepers and petty officials, and graduates of teacher training schools, the law school and the military academies. In Iraq the party's pan-Arab aspirations had their strongest appeal in the Sunni Arab communities, and specifically those from provincial towns of the north and north-west most seriously affected by Europe's colonial division of the Arab east. It was not restricted to these elements, however; important leaders, like Fuad Rikabi and Ali Saleh Sa'di, were of Shi'i origin.

A number of factors led to more exclusive control of the party by persons from a few Sunni towns. Many officers in the armed forces and security services also hailed from and had relatives in these same towns. In the crackdowns against the Ba'th after 1963, they were more lenient towards those Ba'th cadres from their own localities. Other Ba'this, especially those of Shi'i origin, were imprisoned longer and treated more harshly. In addition, internal party struggles led to the explusion of 'left' elements, a category that included many of the Ba'thi of Shi'i origin. These factors were part of a more general deterioration of party and ideological-based ties in the post-revolutionary period, and the reversion to more traditional, kin-based loyalties.

The split with the Syrian branch of the party also dates from this post-1963 period. Political setbacks left the Ba'th weak and divided in both countries. The recruitment of many junior officers into the party had modified a long-standing aversion to military takeovers, and incorporated a strong tendency towards 'regionalism' – in Ba'thi terms, placing the interest of the Syrian or Iraqi 'region' above the overarching interests of the Arab 'nation.' Civilian leadership of the Iraqi branch was nominally maintained in the person of Saddam Hussein, but in Syria in 1965–66 the 'military committee' of the party outmanoeuvred the traditional 'nationalist' civilian leadership of Michel Aflaq and Salah ad-Din Bitar. The old guard fled to Beirut, from where they maintained influence over the other Ba'thi 'regions,' including Iraq. When the Iraqi Ba'th took power in July 1968, many of them took the first plane to Baghdad. Both Syria and Iraq now had their own Regional Command and National Command, each with adherents in other 'regions,' such as Lebanon, Jordan and Yemen. The conflict then took on a life of its own, quite apart from its doctrinal origins.[17]

Politics under the Ba'th

As a broad social force, the petty bourgeoisie and intermediate strata had identified Iraq's 1958 revolution with its own interests. Its substantial size in the towns and cities, the lack of coherent opposition from the less numerous, now dispirited upper bourgeoisie, and the physical decimation of the Communists had all defined and limited the social content of the revolution; but the dominant elements lacked a political structure and a coherent ideology. In a society in upheaval, ridden with ethnic, sectarian and class division, this fostered the political immobilization and economic deterioration that prevailed in 1968.

In form and content the Ba'thi takeover embodied continuity, rather than any sharp break with the recent past. Its significance, rather, was the ensconcement for the first time of a relatively homogeneous faction of the petty bourgeoisie/intermediate strata displaying a modicum of structure and discipline, and with claim to an Arab nationalist tradition larger than Iraq. The consolidation of Ba'thi rule, though, owed nothing to its scant ideological leverage, and everything to the opportune alliances and selective but thorough repression directed by Saddam Hussein. 'The psychological state and the after-effects of the 1963 experience made any large scale purges intolerable,' a party report observed in early 1974. 'A different method with more flexibility was required to achieve the same objectives.' A special security branch ('the Public Relations Bureau') was composed of party militants 'with little formal experience in this field of work . . . but they were quick to learn and prove their high calibre by liquidating external and internal conspiracies and exposing intelligence networks.'[18] The calibre of the leadership was manifest in the public hanging in 1969 of fourteen 'spies,' nine of them Jewish Iraqis, which established the requisite political climate in which the regime could go about its business. Competing political groupings were alternately cajoled and intimidated. Most of the bloodletting was reserved for purges within the upper echelons of the Ba'th; within several years, all but two of the original coup-makers – President Ahmad Hassan al-Bakr and Vice President Saddam Hussein – had been eliminated. Al-Bakr and Hussein dominated the 'supreme organ of the state,' the Revolutionary Command Council (RCC). The membership of the RCC changed frequently in these first years, and until late 1977 generally consisted of only half a dozen persons.

The regime scored great political gains with the successful nationalization of the IPC in June 1972. The next year political negotiations produced a Progressive National Front government that included the Iraqi Communist Party, some insignificant nationalist groupings, and reserved seats for the Kurdish Democratic Party. The Communists received no voice in the RCC, but did get several insignificant cabinet posts, and were now permitted to function and publish above-ground. The Front proved to be only a tactical manoeuvre, however, allowing the Ba'th to concentrate its energies for a major military campaign against the Kurds in 1974. When the Kurdish situation was again under control, following the Algiers Agreement in 1975, Saddam Hussein turned against the ICP. Communists were arrested in 1976 and executed in 1977, allegedly for political organizing among the armed forces, a privilege reserved under pain of death to the Ba'th. By mid-1979 the ICP was again underground, with thousands of its members imprisoned.

The RCC continued to serve as the vehicle for Hussein and al-Bakr's rule by decree. In February 1977, serious disturbances erupted during the Shi'i religious processions in Kerbela and Najaf which were put down by the army with some loss of life. The RCC appointed one of its five members, Izzat Mustafa, to head a three-man special tribunal. The tribunal quickly sentenced eight persons to death and 50 others to life imprisonment. Shortly thereafter Hussein had Mustafa and Hassan Jassem of the party's Regional Command stripped of all party and official posts and sent into internal exile for 'defeatism' and 'negligence,' presumably for their lenience in the tribunal. Mustafa, a physician and long-time party member, had been on the Regional Command in 1966–68, and in the Revolutionary Command Council from 1969.[19]

In September 1977 the Revolutionary Command Council was enlarged to include all 22 members of the party Regional Command, but there is no evidence to suggest that RCC rule has become more collegial. Batatu's judgment, that Saddam Hussein and his fellow Takritis rule through the Ba'th rather than the other way around,[20] seems to have been borne out by the extensive purge of the party and the regime's upper ranks in July 1979.

On July 12, 1979, Muhyi 'Abdul-Hussein, the secretary-general of the RCC, was dismissed from the government and party, and arrested. On July 17, the anniversary of the 1968 coup, President al-Bakr resigned and transferred formal power to Saddam Hussein. On July 28 the RCC announced that the arrested secretary-general had implicated dozens of top officials in a Syrian 'plot' against the regime. On August 7, a special tribunal of seven RCC members issued 22 death sentences, 33 prison terms, and 13 acquittals. The executions, whose victims included five RCC members, were carried out the next day, in the presence of Saddam Hussein.

The former secretary-general was of Shi'i origin, and according to Egyptian reports was arrested initially for contacts with Shi'i agitators rather than for the 'plot' to which he so readily confessed. The uncharacteristically Islamic cast of Saddam Hussein's address to the nation following the executions, with its inventive comparisons of his regime with the Shi'i hero-martyrs of the first century of Islam, suggested a sectarian dimension to these developments. Most of those executed were Sunnis, however, as befitted their standing in the regime. Moreover, Saddam used the occasion to pull out of prison long-time but inactive foes within the Ba'th – including prominent leftist 'Abdul Khaleq al-Samarrai – and have them shot.

Saddam's accusations of Syrian complicity are not persuasive, but suggest that Iraq's regional policy may have been a key issue. The 'plotters,' by this line of analysis, committed the crime of stressing good relations with Syria and opposing Saddam's close ties with the conservative regimes of Saudi Arabia and the Gulf. Whatever the trigger, the purge exposed the increasingly narrow base of the regime, and concentrated power further in the hands of a few men from the region of Takrit. Saddam's brother-in-law, Defence Minister Khairallah, was made deputy commander of the armed forces. Intelligence chief Sadun Shakir, another local boy made good, became minister of the interior, and Saddam's brother Barzan took charge of intelligence services.

The discrepancy between the pan-Arab rhetoric of the Ba'th and its actual base in Iraq is now more striking than ever before. Saddam moved within weeks to diffuse adverse reaction with a general amnesty on 16 August, and salary increases for military, security and public sector personnel (more than one-fifth of the total labour force) on 29 August. On 19 August, Deputy Prime Minister Tariq Aziz announced elections for a 250-member National Assembly, on the regime's public agenda since 1970.

'After the elections,' President Saddam intoned in January 1980, 'Iraq will enter a new democratic phase.' The remark is uncharacteristically candid for what it says about the Ba'th's first twelve years, but in fact the Assembly's powers border on the ceremonial, and in no way modify the executive and legislative prerogatives of the Revolutionary Command Council. The elections, carefully staged, were held on June 20, 1980. According to the government, 840 candidates stood for 250 seats. Nominations were open, but had to be approved by a special elections committee. Non-Ba'thists were reportedly allowed to stand, although all candidates had to be certified 'believers in the principles of the July 17–30 [1968] revolution.' Communists were excluded on the grounds that they 'follow a foreign [i.e., Soviet] line.' The elections served as a counterpoint to the putschist politics in which Saddam Hussein excels. Just as the Regional Congress of the party is ritually invoked as the authority for the decrees of the party/state leadership, the Assembly provides 'national' countenance to the reality of Takriti rule.[21]

Oil and the state

The substantial role of the Iraqi state, encompassing the major economic institutions of the society, derives from its formation in the period when the territory was directly tied to the wheel of imperialism, and subsequently from its rentier function in relation to Western oil interests. Direct state control of the oil industry was achieved at a time (1972–75) when the exchange value of crude oil escalated considerably. Oil revenues at the disposal of the regime increased from $488 million in 1968 to $5.7 billion in 1974 and $12.2 billion in 1979 (Table 3.1). The consolidation of political power under the present regime thus occurred in conjunction with a momentous expansion of the state's economic functions.

Iraq's historically imposed relationship to the world economy has fostered and financed a measurable margin of autonomy of the state and political apparatus in relation to the economic structure of the society. Nevertheless, the capacity of the political leadership to develop a more modern economic structure is distinctly constricted by this historic formation, by the vulnerability inherent in its role as supplier of a single, albeit major, commodity to world markets, and by reliance on those same markets to provide a growing portion of the goods and services required by Iraq for consumption and capital formation (Table 3.4). A review of developments in the major sectors of the Iraqi economy, with particular attention to the implications for class formation, highlights some of the problems facing the ruling strata in the 1980s.

Table 3.4
Structure of Iraq's Gross Domestic Product, 1976

Sector	$ million	% GDP
Agriculture	1,180.7	8.4
Mining and Quarrying	8,381.0	59.6
Manufacturing	1,098.8	7.8
Utilities	76.2	0.5
Construction	1,202.4	8.6
Total Commodities	11,939.1	85.0
Trade	669.8	4.9
Transportation	737.1	5.2
Finance and Real Estate	558.0	3.9
Social Affairs	147.9	1.1
Total Non-Commodities	2,112.8	15.0
Total	*14,051.9*	*100.0*

Source: Economist Intelligence Unit Special Report No. 88. *Iraq: A New Market in a Region of Turmoil* (London. 1980). p. 3.

Agriculture and the Rural Sector. After seizing power, the regime moved quickly to review and implement the badly lagging agrarian reform programme. Law 117 (1970) further limited the maximum that could be held, eliminating compensation to landowners, and abolished payments by beneficiaries (acknowledging the extremity of peasant indebtedness and poverty). According to the official Agricultural Census of 1971, there were 589,387 holdings (up from 253,254 in 1957). Despite improved tenure patterns, the top 1 percent of the landholders held over 22 percent of the total (down from more than 55 percent in 1957), and the lowest 60 percent owned 14 percent.[22] In 1973 reform beneficiaries farmed 22.7 percent of the cultivatable land; peasants renting sequestered and state land from the government farmed 34.5 percent of the total; and private non-beneficiaries held 34.9 percent.[23] It can be inferred from scanty statistics that the number of reform beneficiaries has increased since then, while the number of those leasing land from the government has declined. The number of agricultural co-operatives and collective farms has also grown somewhat.

It is difficult to assess changes in rural social structure. The little information available and the experience of other countries suggest that new stratification patterns are emerging, characterized by the rise of middle peasants who directly and through leadership of the co-operatives control allocations of machinery and other inputs. As in the cities and towns, affiliation with the Ba'th smooths this path.

Within the agricultural sector as a whole, the deterioration that began before the revolution has not been appreciably halted. The total arable and cultivated land has declined, perhaps by as much as 30 percent between 1958 and 1977.[24]

The factors are numerous: soil salinity and lack of drainage investments on the physical side, and low prices and inadequate development of marketing and credit functions of the co-operatives on the political level. The most distinguishing feature is demographic: the mass migration from the countryside to the towns and cities threatens a virtual depopulation of the countryside. By one calculation, the number of persons employed in agriculture declined from over 1.5 million in 1973 to 943,890 in 1977, or from 51 percent to 30 percent of the total labour force[25] (Table 3.5).

Table 3.5
Structure of the Iraqi labour force, 1977

Sector	Female	Male	Total	% Total
Agriculture	352,824	591,066	943,890	30.2
Petroleum/Mining	2,119	34,716	36,835	1.2
Manufacturing	48,618	235,777	284,395	7.9
Electricity/Gas/Water	949	22,241	23,190	0.7
Construction	5,136	316,560	321,696	10.3
Wholesale/Retail Trade	16,155	207,949	224,104	7.2
Transportation/Storage/ Communications	4,985	172,814	177,799	5.7
Finance/Real Estate/ Business Services	5,066	26,023	31,089 }	32.4
Community, Social and Personal Services	86,100	871,879	957,979 }	
Other	11,979	46,258	58,237	2.0
Unemployed	10,447	64,278	74,725	2.4
Total	*544,378*	*2,589,561*	*3,133,939*	*100.0*

Source: Annual Abstract of Statistics 1979, compiled in EIU, p. 40.

There were reports in 1977 that the government tried to restrict peasants from changing their 'profession' on their identity cards.[26] One can assume that the migrants include a disproportionately high number of peasants with skills, precisely those most needed for the agro-industrial projects now planned.

The establishment of schools, clinics, and utilities have altered the traditional isolation of rural villages, but the higher level of prosperity in rural areas is due chiefly to the infusion of income from the central government rather than increases in productivity. Field research carried out in more than 100 villages in Babylon and Nineveh provinces in 1974–75 indicated that continued impoverishment and deteriorating land and living conditions were the main impetus to migration, rather than the 'pull' of urban jobs and amenities.[27] Agriculture's share in the domestic product declined to an estimated 5 percent in 1980. This has put the burden for meeting rising demand for foodstuffs on imports, which have more than doubled since 1977 and stood at $1.4 billion in 1980, more than the total value of Iraqi agricultural production in that year.[28]

Industrialization and the Manufacturing Sector. The contribution of the manufacturing sector to domestic production rose slowly to a high of 10 percent in 1973, fell to 4.7 percent in 1974 after the oil price rise, and reached 7.8 percent in 1976. Tables 3.6 and 3.7 show the growth of large plants (over 10 workers) and the public sector share. Small manufacturing shops also grew in number, especially after the oil price rise; in 1976 they numbered 37,669 and employed 85,460 (including owner-workers).

Table 3.6
Large manufacturing in Iraq

Year	Companies	Workers
1954	727	44,410
1964	1,202	80,066
1976	1,479	142,740

Source: Kathleen Langley, *The Industrialization of Iraq* (Cambridge, MA, 1961): *Annual Abstract of Statistics* (Baghdad: Central Planning Organization, 1965 and 1977).

Table 3.7
Public sector share of large manufacturing

Year	% Total Companies	% Total Workers	% Total Wages	% Total Input	% Total Output
1964	22	52	64	55	65
1974	27	74	76	74	74

Source: Annual Abstract of Statistics (Baghdad: Central Planning Organization, 1965 and 1975).

The greater part of Iraqi manufacturing is light industry based on local raw materials. Food, beverages, and tobacco processing accounted for about one quarter of the larger firms, workers, and wages, half the inputs, and 38 percent of output in 1974. Textiles accounted for about 20 percent of the firms, 28 percent of the workers, 17 percent of inputs, and 19 percent of output. Twelve large public sector textile firms employed an average of 1,666 workers each, and 139 large private textile firms averaged 35 workers each.[29] The value added per worker is higher in the private sector in food processing and textiles, but public sector dominance in chemicals, oil products, and similar capital intensive industries gives the public sector as a whole a higher input, output, and value added per worker. In the large manufacturing sector, between 1974 and 1976 the private sector expanded at a slightly greater rate than the public.[30] The main area of private sector growth was in consumer durables.

The relationship between the public and private sectors in large manufacturing is reflected in their employment structures (Table 3.8).

Average wage scales in 1976 ran from ID 372 per year for unskilled, to ID 1,594 for highly skilled experts.[31] Above average wages are paid by the public

Table 3.8
Employment structure of large manufacturing, 1976

Workers	% Public Sector	% Private Sector
Production Workers		
Unskilled	60	40
Skilled	78	22
Technicians/High-skilled	93	7
Non-Production Workers		
Services	84	16
Administration/Marketing	68	32
High Administration	20	80

Source: Calculated from *Annual Abstract of Statistics* (Baghdad: Central Planning Organization, 1977).

sector for unskilled and non-production workers; the private sector pays a substantial premium for its small number of technicians and skilled workers. There is considerable wage differentiation between different industries, both public and private.[32]

Large capital-intensive hydrocarbon-based industrial projects have been the centrepiece of the regime's planning since 1973. Their viability is based on projected export of substantial portions of production. The urea plant at Khor al-Zubair will export a million tons of fertilizer a year, more than half its planned output. A phosphate-based fertilizer plant plans to export 85 percent of its output. The steel plant at Khor al-Zubair plans to export 1.5 million tons of concentrated ore a year. The $1 billion petrochemical plant there will produce 150,000 tons of polyethylene and poly-vinyl chloride, and 40,000 tons of caustic soda a year, more than the domestic economy is likely to absorb in the forseeable future. The capital costs of these plants run 50 to 75 percent higher than equivalent costs in industrialized countries. If feedstocks and fuels are not factored in at world market prices, the effect will be a subsidization of those industries with revenues foregone from the direct export of hydrocarbons.

These projects strengthen Iraq's links to the world market as a provider of intermediate-stage resources and reinforce the pattern of an economy whose export sector is the dynamic core, producing most of the value added, earning most of the revenues, but employing a small fraction of the labour force and relying on the multinational corporations for capital in the form of technology and skills. Since the oil price rise, Iraq has imported machinery, equipment and capital goods worth over $2 billion a year, more than twice the value of the country's entire manufacturing sector. Consultant and service fees alone each year amount to hundreds of millions of dollars – more than twice the value of all Iraq's non-oil exports, and more than ten times the total expenditure for local research and development activities.[33]

The Oil Sector. The share of this sector in the national product jumped from 35 percent in 1970 to 60 percent in 1974, a level it has since maintained. Its contribution to total government revenues increased from 52 percent in 1971 to 87 percent in 1976, and crude oil accounted for some 98 percent of total exports in 1975. Decisions over markets, prices, and production levels are narrowly reserved to Saddam Hussein and one or two top lieutenants.[34] The Oil Affairs Committee of the RCC became the Follow-Up Committee for Oil Affairs and the Implementation of Agreements in September 1971. Consisting of Saddam Hussein and (until July 1979) Adnan Hamdani, the committee not only directed the oil sector, but functioned as the highest authority in the entire realm of economic planning.[35] Under the rationale of circumventing cumbersome bureaucratic procedure, the committee can short-circuit such planning components as competitive bidding by declaring a project to be 'strategic.' Most large industrial and infrastructure schemes are eligible for such designation.

Despite consistent rhetoric from the regime concerning the need to diversity the economic structure of Iraq from its dependence on oil exports, the most prominent feature of Iraqi development spending is heavy investment in exploration for additional reserves, and extending the productivity of existing fields.[36] Nearly one-quarter of Iraqi contracts in 1979 were in this sector; nearly half of the total Middle East contracts in this sector were Iraqi.[37]

Construction. This sector now ranks above agriculture and manufacturing in its contribution to the domestic product. Once almost entirely private, there is now a large public sector component which employed 76,479 workers in 1977, far more than the total number of unskilled and semi-skilled workers in both public and private large manufacturing. Average wages for ordinary labourers were relatively high at ID 919.

The prominence of this sector is also reflected in loans by the Estate Bank totalling $223.1 million in 1976. Comparable figures for the Agricultural Bank and the Industrial Bank were $44.6 million and $42.3 million, respectively. Over three-quarters of this construction were buildings, rather than infrastructure. More than half the residential buildings and three-quarters of the commercial buildings were in Baghdad.[38] One recent report noted that 'the predilection of leading Iraqis for real estate investment has been acknowledged in the role allotted to the mixed sector in the development of tourism and in meeting Iraq's chronic shortage of hotels.'[39]

Commerce. An Iraqi Chamber of Commerce report in 1973 estimated the number of retail trade firms had risen from 36,000 in 1965 to 100,000 in 1973, and the number of persons engaged to 200,000. Official figures for 1976 claimed 77,766 establishments, and less than 100,000 persons engaged full time. For the few who were not proprietors, salaries averaged ID 349. Retail trade is increasingly dependent on imported goods, 90 percent of which come through the public sector. Private retail agents get commissions averaging 10 percent for serving as a distribution network.[40]

Services. This is now the largest sector in terms of employment, with over one million persons in 1977. Much of the labour displaced from the agricultural sector in recent years has been absorbed into this sector, and most of it by the state itself. The state is by far the largest single employer. In 1977 the number of government personnel was 580,132, almost as many persons as employed by all large public and private manufacturing firms (Table 3.9). This does not include the armed forces, an estimated 230,000 persons, or nearly 200,000 pensioners directly dependent on the state for their livelihood.

Table 3.9
Growth of the state sector

Year	Personnel
1938	9,740
1958	20,031
1968	224,253
1972	385,978
1977	580,132

Source: 1938, 1958 from Hanna Batatu, *The Old Social Classes and the Revolutionary Movements of Iraq* (Princeton, 1978), p. 482; 1968, 1972 from K. Hameed, 'Manpower and Employment Planning in Iraq and the Syrian Arab Republic,' in United Nations, *Studies on Development Problems in Countries of Western Asia, 1975* (New York, 1977), p. 34; 1977 from *Annual Abstract of Statistics* (Baghdad: Central Planning Organization, 1977), p. 248.

Within the government, the largest employee is the Ministry of Interior, with 136,900 in 1977. An additional 40,819 were employed in the Presidential Affairs Department, many of whom, as in the Interior Ministry, are engaged in 'security' assignments.[41] In November 1979, Interior Minister Shakur announced an unspecified expansion of internal security forces, 'in order to carry out transactions with citizens with greatest possible speed.'[42]

The state as boss

The basis for the expanding role of the state lies in its access to some 60 percent of the national product by virtue of its control of the hydrocarbon extraction and export sector. In the spheres of production the largest enterprises are by definition public. The structures of public and private sectors display the strategic character of state control of the most capital-intensive and technologically advanced industries, established by contract with multinational firms. In the sphere of circulation the state is responsible for virtually all external trade. Its control over internal trade is indirect, but, all considered, state ownership leaves in the hands of the regime the major share of the surplus at the levels of production and exchange.

This control, however, also represents a relationship with millions of Iraqis who have a direct interest in the state's economic capacities. Access to the oil rent provides the regime with extraordinary leverage in meeting expectations and needs with regard to distribution. The current 'guns and butter' policy of Saddam Hussein has provided Iraqi consumers with an unprecedented array and quantity of goods (mostly imported) since the war with Iran was launched (Table 3.10).

At the level of production, however, the regime's capacities are more limited. At a structural level, there is the displacement of labour from the rural sector, and its absorption for the most part in the notoriously unproductive services sector. Since 1974, the state has expressly become the employer of last resort for all university graduates. This suggests that the official unemployment figures are, at the least, a gross understatement. Ironically, the surfeit of non-productive labour in the services sector, and the state in particular, is matched by a serious labour shortage in productive sectors, from skilled and expert labour in industry to agricultural workers. According to one analysis, industrial projects in the 1976–80 plan called for nearly half a million additional semi-skilled workers, 375,000 craftspersons, and 150,000 degree holders. The total output of graduates was annually less than 20,000, and the situation in vocational fields even more inadequate.[43] It is impossible to say how much this labour 'bottleneck,' as opposed to other factors, contributed to the shortcomings of the plan. Japanese firms working on Iraqi projects have had to import thousands of Chinese workers from the People's Republic, and Yugoslav construction firms have an edge in bidding on Iraqi projects, owing to their ability to supply the necessary labour. A World Bank study in the early 1980s estimated that by 1985 Iraq would depend on non-Iraqis for between 4.3 and 10 percent of its entire labour force.[44] The outlook may be further complicated if the armed forces draw more heavily on the limited pool of skilled labour.

Table 3.10
Main sources of Iraqi imports 1975–79
(in millions of dollars)

Country	1975	1976	1977	1978	1979
West Germany	750.9	735.1	800.8	767.9	1,038.3
Japan	760.0	482.2	787.6	945.9	1,612.9
UK	230.1	249.7	306.8	411.5	424.7
France	262.3	270.9	251.5	499.1	803.9
Italy	164.6	165.3	228.0	322.3	668.0
US	363.0	183.5	217.1	315.7	440.5
USSR	103.1	74.0	86.0		
	(433.3)	(546.6)	(449.6)	(1,077.9)	

Source: Calculated from Economist Intelligence Unit Special Report No. 88. *Iraq: A New Market in a Region of Turmoil* (London, 1980). p. 12. Figures for 1975–77 are based on Iraqi trade statistics; figures for 1978–79 are based on exporting country accounts. Figures for USSR in parentheses are from EIU report. p. 74. based on Soviet figures. EIU provides no explanation for the discrepancy.

Given the problems in this area, it is quite remarkable that Iraq's development plans consistently ignore the matter of labour supply and demand.[45] The difficulty of controlling the labour market is reflected in decrees forbidding private firms from hiring skilled workers who have resigned from the public sector. It is also reflected in the Ba'th's policies towards the working class. Trade unions are under the direct control of party functionaries. Other labour organizing is forbidden. To resolve acknowledged tensions between management (public and private) and labour, a scheme of worker participation on the boards of directors of firms was instituted; the worker representatives are selected by the party rather than the workers themselves.

In 1976 the regime, seriously worried by low productivity in both manufacturing and services, instituted a series of 'productivity seminars' in plants and government agencies; the first was conducted by Sadam Hussein himself. Responsibility was rhetorically shared between management and labour, but there was little ambiguity in the thrust of the solutions: stress on surveillance and discipline to raise productivity, and tying wage increases (but not bureaucrats' or professionals' salaries) to increases in productivity. The efforts by the regime to secure working class support early in its reign, particularly through guarantees of job security, now hamper its efforts to reallocate capital and labour, and redefine the terms of their relationship.

Serious confrontation with Iraqi workers has been avoided, owing to the extensive security apparatus of the state and the ability of the regime to implement periodic wage and salary rises, and occasionally price and tax reductions. This is a simple though not directly productive means of partially distributing increases in the oil rent, but further complicates the serious disparity between urban and rural living conditions. It serves the immediate purpose of purchasing political support, or at least acquiescence, but exacerbates an already serious obstacle to the long-term reproduction and accumulation of capital.

The war with Iran

In early September 1980, armed forces of Iraq launched forays at several points across the land border with neighbouring Iran, and staked out claims to some disputed territory. On September 17, President Saddam Hussein revoked the March 1975 Algiers Agreement with Iran sharing sovereignty over the Shatt al-Arab. This waterway marked the southern border between the two countries and provided both with access to the Persian Gulf.

Within days, Iraq mounted deep air strikes against Iranian military and economic targets, and Iran replied in kind. By all accounts, Iraq took the initiative in escalating hostilities between the two countries to the point of open warfare, justifying it as 'retaliation' against Iranian 'defiance' of the Shatt al-Arab 'decision.'

Military activities ebbed considerably during the winter rainy season, but mediation efforts by Islamic and non-aligned nations have repeatedly foundered. Iraq claims to have killed some 20,000 Iranians in the first seven months of war, and Western embassies in Baghdad estimate Iraqi fatalities at 6,000–10,000.[46] Tens of thousands more have been wounded and made refugees. The government in Tehran estimated its war-related costs for 1981 at $5 billion, and Iraq projected an increase of 25 percent in its 1981 budget for imports and investments relating to war damages.[47]

Iraq failed to inflict any decisive defeat on Iran's forces or to secure key strategic points on the ground, but does claim to hold 6,000–8,000 square miles of Iran's oil-producing Khuzetan province. Neither Iraqi withdrawal nor Iranian capitulation seems likely in the near future. The mutual destruction has ended a protracted phase, and Iraqi leaders have threatened to be satisfied with nothing less than the 'dismemberment' of Iran.[48] The political damage has already been incalculable; possibilities for constructive efforts to transcend national, ethnic, and sectarian divisions have been set back for decades.

The proximate cause of hostilities, according to Iraq, was the failure of the new Iranian regime to recognize 'usurped Arab rights' regarding their border, including the Shatt al-Arab, and the three small (non-Iraqi) Gulf islands confiscated by the Shah in 1971. The border, drawn under British tutelage, has never been definitively set. A 1937 treaty between 'sovereign' Iraq and Iran gave Iraq full control over the Shatt, a waterway of considerable economic importance to both countries. Content with this status quo, Iraq refused to negotiate any subsequent alteration following the end of British rule in the region. Iran finally declared the 1937 provisions void in 1969, and dispatched naval craft up the waterway to reinforce its claim. In March 1975, in return for an end of Iranian support for Kurdish insurgents in Iraq, Saddam Hussein signed an agreement in Algiers recognizing Iran's position and following conventional practice in placing the international boundary in the middle of the waterway.

Iraqi Defence Minister Adnan Khairallah no doubt spoke for the Iraqi regime when he told the press on September 25 that in 1975, 'We would not have agreed if we'd had the choice.' The agreement was imposed by the Shah, with all his hegemonic pretensions, and with the covert assistance of Israel and the US, but it was in essence a reasonable settlement. The 1937 treaty, dictated by the British (then ensconced in Baghdad), had little to do with international law or common sense. Complaints from Baghdad about the working of the 1975 agreement were exceedingly scant before late summer 1980. While Iraq is indignant over the manner of the accord, there is little reason to think that Saddam Hussein would risk so much over what is, at bottom, a trivial issue. The dispute over the Shatt, and the other minor border rectifications demanded by Iraq, were a pretext rather than a cause of war. Of course, now that much blood and treasure have been spilt in the name of the 'Arabism' of the Shatt, it is unlikely that the present regime in Baghdad can accept a truce that would once again share sovereignty over the waterway.

A more substantive Iraqi complaint against the new regime in Tehran is its support for al-Da'wa, an underground Shi'i organization. Not long after the downfall of the Pahlavi regime, Iranian broadcasts appealed for the 'overthrow of the atheist Ba'th regime' and its replacement by a Shi'i based Islamic republic. Other forms of incitement mounted in frequency and intensity, and there is little reason to doubt Iraqi charges of Iranian material aid to the underground movement. Popular demonstrations reportedly occurred in predominantly Shi'i cities and Shi'i neighbourhoods of Baghdad, and an assassination campaign in the Spring of 1980 against top Iraqi officials understandably provoked the leadership. The regime cracked down sharply on all Shi'i political manifestations, making membership of al-Da'wa punishable by death. A leading Shi'i religious figure, Ayatollah Muhammad al-Bakr al-Sadr, was arrested and presumably executed. The Iranian leadership only grew more outspoken in its desire that the Iraqi regime, in Khomeini's words, 'be dispatched to the refuse bin of history.'

These exchanges accurately reflect the hostility between the two regimes, but Baghdad's propaganda campaign against Khomeini had been equally fierce, specifically targeted on Khuzestan with its oil and its large ethnic Arab population. Assassinations and economic sabotage, supported by Iraq, plagued Iranian authorities over the same period. The Iraqi regime was more vulnerable to this sort of campaign than the Islamic Republic, but there are no signs that it amounted to a serious immediate threat against the regime. Why did the clashes between Iraq and Iran not remain at the level of propaganda barrages, clandestine small-scale attacks, and occasional border shellings?

The immense popularity of the Iranian revolution made it unwelcome next door in Iraq, where mass political activity is a dim memory from its own revolutionary period. For all of their animosity towards the Shah's regime, the Iraqi Ba'th likewise presided over a narrowly based, highly centralized, and thoroughly repressive political order. The Ba'th's vulnerability was compounded by the ethnic and sectarian composition of Iraqi society. The Shi'i character of the Iranian revolution, providing symbols and language of opposition to the political kingdom as well as organizational resources, posed a potentially hazardous challenge to the regime. The difficulty of insulating Iraqis from the contagion of revolution and mass politics persuaded Baghdad to eliminate the threat at its source.

If vulnerability represents one dimension of the Iraqi calculation, opportunity is another. Domestically the regime seemed secure. In June 1980, 'elections' were held for a long-promised National Assembly. Saddam Hussein used them as a backdrop for an intense media campaign establishing his credentials as a 'man of the people' – touring the provinces, kissing babies, sipping tea with peasants – as popular among Iraqis as Khomeini was among Iranians. Financially and politically he could risk war, particularly a brief campaign in which Iraq held the initiative.

The most likely opponents within the Ba'th regime of an attack on Iran had been purged in July 1979 over related questions of Iraqi policy in the region. A fundamental decision had been taken after the Iranian revolution to align Iraq regionally with Saudi Arabia and the conservative Gulf regimes. The aversion of every Gulf regime to the Iranian revolution was no secret, but only Iraq had the military capacity to pose a credible threat. The disarray and, it seemed, effective disarmament of Iran's military forces had been widely advertised in the Western media, and 'confirmed' by informal Iraqi contacts with European and US military intelligence sources.[49] Finally, the pariah status of the Iranian regime as a result of the hostage crisis led Saddam Hussein to expect that an attack on Iran would be benignly countenanced, if not supported, by the Western powers. He could not hope for a more opportune moment to eliminate the political threat represented by Iran's revolution and simultaneously to renew a strong bid for regional hegemony.

Postscript[50]

From its inception in September 1980, the Iran–Iraq war continued unabated for eight long years, resulting in the deaths of tens of thousands of people on both sides, with many more thousands wounded, while costing billions of dollars in revenue to both countries. The prolongation of the war has not only affected negatively the social–economic development of both Iran and Iraq, but has threatened the entire Middle East region and led to the danger of direct US military intervention in the Gulf, thus complicating the situation in the region even further.

Notes

1. For a discussion of the social components of the intermediate strata in a comparable setting, see Elisabeth Longuenesse, 'The Class Nature of the State in Syria,' *MERIP Reports*, no. 77 (May 1979), pp. 3–11.

2. This remark was made to the US Embassy and passed to Washington in dispatch 890G.51/2-749.

3. Testimony of Ambassador George McGhee to the US Senate Foreign Relations Subcommittee on Multinational Corporations, January 28, 1974; see Joe Stork, *Middle East Oil and Energy Crisis* (New York, 1975), pp. 47–9.

4. A consortium of British Petroleum, Shell, Mobil and Jersey Standard.

5. Hanna Batatu, *The Old Social Classes and the Revolutionary Movements of Iraq* (Princeton, 1978), p. 442.

6. Batatu, p. 473.

7. Fahim Qubain, *The Reconstruction of Iraq, 1950–57* (New York, 1958), p. 143. See also E. A. Finch, 'Social Effects of the Oil Industry in Iraq,' *International Labour Review* (March 1957).

8. Statistics on workers from Kathleen Langley, *The Industrialization of Iraq* (Cambridge, MA, 1961); trade union figure from Batatu, p. 897.

9. Primary schools practically doubled between 1950 and 1958 to more than 2,000; primary students went from 180,779 to 430,475. Secondary schools increased from 95 to 158, and students from 22,706 to 51,934. There were 5,338 students in higher education in 1958. See Abdul-Amir al-Rubaiy, 'Nationalism and Education: A Study of Nationalistic Tendencies in Iraqi Education,' unpublished PhD thesis (Kent State, 1972), pp. 92, 123–47.

10. Batatu, p. 806.

11. Uriel Dann, *Iraq Under Qassem* (New York, 1969), pp. 63–4.

12. Dann, p. 54.

13. Doreen Warriner, *Land Reform in Principle and Practice* (London, 1969); Rony Gabbay, *Communism and Agrarian Reform in Iraq* (London, 1978).

14. Majid Khadduri, *Republican Iraq* (London, 1969), pp. 233–6.

15. For a Ba'thi evaluation of this period, see 'Minutes of the Extraordinary Syrian Regional Congress of the Arab Ba'th Socialist Party following the Events of November 18, 1963, in Iraq,' Damascus, February 2, 1964, published in *al-Muharrir*, March 17–23, 1964, and translated in *Arab Documents, 1964* (Beirut, 1965).

16. The phrase of a recruiting flyer from 1943, quoted in John Devlin, *The Ba'th Party: A History from its Origins to 1966* (Stanford, 1976), p. 11.

17. In the 1970s there was an escalation of bombings, assassinations, and material support for opposition elements in the respective countries. These tapered off in the months after Camp David, and in October 1978 a National Charter for Joint Action was signed by Syrian President Hafiz al-Asad in Baghdad. Conciliation was less durable, however, than the conflict it replaced, and was terminated with the extensive purge in the upper ranks of the Iraqi party in July 1979, ostensibly in reaction to a Syrian 'plot' to overthrow Saddam Hussein.

18. *Revolutionary Iraq: Political Report of the Eighth Regional Congress of the Arab Ba'th Socialist Party in Iraq, January 1964* (Baghdad, 1974), pp. 63, 171–2. This report was republished as *The 1968 Revolution in Iraq* (London, Ithaca Press, 1979).

19. For Iraqi broadcasts relating to these events, see *Foreign Broadcast Information Service* (FBIS), March 24, 1977; see also *Le Monde*, February 26, 1977, and David Hirst's dispatch in the *Washington Post*, May 1, 1977.

20. Shakir Issa, 'Rural Income Distribution in Iraq,' (mimeo) Development Seminar Working Paper No. 8, London University School of Oriental and African Studies (March 1977), p. 3.

21. The head of the Assembly, Naim Haddah, most recently had 'served the revolution' as head of the special court which ordered the executions of August 1979.

22. Batatu, p. 1088.

23. Batatu, p. 1117.

24. 30 percent is Issa's calculation for the decline in arable land based on the 1971 Agricultural Census. According to the Iraqi government's *Annual Abstract of Statistics* (AAS) for 1977 (p. 59), total cultivated area in 1977 had dropped to the 1971 level.

25. Economist Intelligence Unit (EIU) Special Report No. 88, *Iraq: A New Market in a Region of Turmoil* (October 1980), p. 5.

26. *Al-Iraq*, June 23, 1977.

27. Atheel al-Jomard, 'Internal Migration in Iraq,' in Abbas Kelidar (ed.), *The Integration of Modern Iraq* (London, 1979).

28. EIU, pp. 4, 13.

29. *AAS*, 1977.

30. If we include shops of less than ten workers, which are wholly private, the public sector in 1976 accounted for only 43.6 percent of workers, 50.8 percent of inputs, and 49.9 percent of output for all manufacturing large and small.

31. One Iraqi Dinar (ID) = $3.38.

32. *AAS*, 1977.

33. United Nations Conference on Trade and Development (UNCTAD) Report, *Transfer and Development of Technology in Iraq* (June 1978), pp. 27, 30.

34. The major buyers of Iraqi oil are the international majors, as well as foreign state oil companies. France, Italy, and Brazil are among the largest importers. Information concerning production, exports, destinations, or purchasers is extremely restricted. From recent editions of the official Annual Abstract of Statistics, one would not know Iraq ever produced or exported a single barrel of oil.

35. Hamdani was the most prominent official executed in August 1979. Like Saddam, he was a graduate of the Baghdad Law Faculty, and was long a close and trusted ally. After a brief stint as director of Oil Company Affairs at the Ministry of Oil, he became Director General of the Presidential Office, a post he held in conjunction with his duties on the Follow-Up Committee. In 1976 he took over the Ministry of Planning. Hamdani once observed that 'The Ba'th party is not just a ruling party; it has an ideology based on rapid deployment of the economy in a limited period of time. For this we need large revenues.' *Middle East Economic Survey*, June 20, 1975.

36. EIU, p. 54.

37. *Middle East Economic Digest* (MEED). January 25. 1980.

38. *AAS*. 1977.

39. FIU. p. 16.

40. Federation of Iraqi Chambers of Commerce. *Summary of Annual Report, 1973* (mimeo). pp. 22-6.

41. *AAS*. 1977. p. 248.

42. *Al-Thawra*. November 18. 1979.

43. EIU. pp. 67-8.

44. World Bank. 'Research Project on International Labor Migration and Manpower in the Middle East and North Africa' (mimeo: Washington. DC. September 1980). p. 36.

45. See Ismail Aubaid Hummadi. 'Economic Growth and Structural Changes in the Iraqi Economy. with an Emphasis on Agriculture. 1953-75.' (unpublished PhD dissertation: University of Colorado. 1978). p. 97.

46. *Washington Post*. April 22. 1981.

47. *Middle East Economic Digest*. March 13-19. 1981: *Middle East Economic Survey*. January 26. 1981.

48. *Washington Post*. April 19. 1981.

49. *Armed Forces Journal International*. November 1980. p. 44.

50. Written by the editor.

4. Development of Capitalism and Class Struggles in Turkey

Fikret Ceyhun

Until 1950, Turkish society had a predominantly feudal structure, where, by virtue of their dominant economic position in agriculture, the landlords had tremendous economic and political influence. However, during World War II a financially powerful, commercial bourgeoisie emerged as a result of enormous profits made from speculative activities. This newly powerful bourgeoisie began, at the end of the war, to compete with the landlords for influence. The Democrat Party, founded in 1945 when Turkey adopted a multi-party political system,[1] and representing, among other elements, the new commercial class, came to power in 1950, and introduced 'laissez-faire' capitalism marking a turning-point for Turkey, politically, economically, and socially.

With an open-door policy, Turkey attracted some foreign investment and was able to import capital goods and industrial raw materials. In order to finance costly infra-structural investments, Turkey resorted to external borrowing. The liberal economic policy which followed in the 1950s thus helped the merchant class and produced an investment climate which made it possible to channel their finance capital into industrial projects. The accumulation of commercial capital was the genesis of capitalist development in Turkey.[2] Capitalism had the environment to flourish in, and flourish it did; the transition to capitalism greatly accelerated during the 1950s.[3]

Laissez-faire capitalism

The 1950s were the antithesis of the 1930s, which were characterized by autarchic and state-led industrialization. Self-reliant development policies, a form of 'Etatism', were embarked on in 1933, influenced by Soviet economic planning. This experiment was terminated by the outbreak of World War II. After the war, American influence over the region led the new government to shift its foreign policy towards the West. Turkey received military and economic assistance from the US, entered the Korean War, and joined US-sponsored military alliances, most notably NATO, moving completely into the US sphere of influence.

The Democrat Party government encouraged private investment and liberalized foreign trade. Agricultural production increased remarkably, due to the importation of agricultural machinery, increased land use, and suitable weather. Turkey was able to import large amounts of industrial products and consumer goods, in addition to agricultural machinery. The increased imports were financed by three sources: (a) increased agricultural exports, (b) foreign aid, and (c) foreign exchange reserves accumulated during World War II. With the increased importation of industrial raw materials, and both agricultural and industrial machinery, the economy was stimulated into a three-year boom such as Turkey had never seen before. But this boom ended abruptly in 1954 when agricultural production was crippled by bad weather, the real per capita GDP declined by 5 percent, and real gross domestic investment dipped by 4 percent.[4]

The rest of the decade was replete with economic difficulties and crises: the economy was crippled by foreign exchange shortages, economic growth and per capita income declined, inflation increased and trade deficits surged. Agricultural production stagnated, first because of prevailing bad weather, and then because of lack of spare machinery parts. Parts were scarce because the foreign exchange needed to purchase them itself became scarce as the continuing drought reduced the agricultural exports which earned foreign exchange. In a cyclical fashion, one problem exacerbated the other, restricting agricultural output and export earnings. Growing trade deficits made external loans scarce, and reduced imports had other adverse economic effects: many industrial projects were halted. The regime resorted to inflationary and, supposedly, stimulatory economic policies, but rising inflation and scarcity of goods only increased political opposition and repressive reaction.

The open-door policy of the Adnan Menderes government was eventually dropped, due to the difficulties in generating enough foreign exchange to pay for the rising imports and to service debts. The IMF blocked foreign loans. In the second half of the 1950s the lira was sharply devalued (in 1958 over 300 percent), raising the dollar exchange rate from 2.80 liras per dollar to 9.09 liras per dollar. Despite devaluation and IMF austerity measures, economic problems and hardship increased. When social unrest became bloody, and chaos threatened, the military intervened by staging a coup d'état on May 27, 1960. Thus ended Turkey's experiment with laissez-faire capitalism, for the time being.

Import-substitution industrialization

The 1960 military coup created a new atmosphere. Under a new, liberal constitution democratic institutions began to flourish. Civilian government was reestablished in 1961. Democratic institutions began to take hold under this constitution and provided broad civil rights to the populace. With the changes in direction effected by the constitution, economic and social planning was instituted through the agency of the newly created State Planning Organization (SPO). The SPO, which was charged with preparing five-year economic and social plans, charted a new course in Turkey's economy. The

First Five-Year Plan was drafted in 1963, initiating a new economic policy, 'import-substitution industrialization' (ISI). The purpose of the ISI development policy was to avoid the difficulties of the 1950s, caused by the disastrous foreign exchange crunch and economic mismanagement, by producing domestically what had been imported previously.

Under the 1961 constitution, many democratic organizations emerged to challenge anti-democratic state institutions left intact from the previous constitution. Among these were student, teacher, and other professional organizations, which became strong opposing forces on the side of labour against capital and the state. Labour unions became militant under the leadership of DISK (Confederation of Revolutionary Workers Unions), a radical labour confederation which emerged as a break-away from the conservative American-style labour confederation, TURK-IS. For the first time in Turkish political history, a left-wing party, TIP (the Workers Party of Turkey), was established by trade unionists, in 1961. TIP reached its zenith in the 1965 general elections, by gaining 15 seats in the parliament. The Communist Party of Turkey (TKP), which was founded in 1919, is not legally recognized and has remained in exile in Eastern Europe, with some important labour following within Turkey. Another development was the formation of DEV-GENC, a revolutionary youth organization whose members were entirely university students. With the rise of a left-wing press, DISK, TIP, and DEV-GENC, socialist movements became a powerful force for capital to reckon with. The struggles waged by students, teachers, progressive unions, the left-wing press, and other organizations reached their peak in 1970 and 1971. The rising political strife and strikes by the labour unions paralysed certain industries, and social life.[5] The confrontation between labour and capital and the ensuing strife and chaos eventually led to a second military coup on March 12, 1971. In 1973, general elections brought the Republican People's Party (RPP) to power, under Bulent Ecevit. Soon afterwards, however, they lost office to Suleyman Demirel and his Justice Party (JP), in coalition with the Islamic fundamentalist National Salvation Party (NSP) and the neo-fascist Nationalist Action Party (NAP).[6]

The economy survived the 1973 oil shock and the ensuing worldwide recession of 1974–75, largely thanks to the enormous inflow of earnings of Turkish workers in Western Europe.[7] In the second half of the 1970s, however, the Turkish economy showed signs of derailment and ISI was in difficulty with rising inflation, unemployment and trade deficits. Turkey's reliance on external loans continued, despite the increasing return of Turkish workers' earnings from Western Europe. Debt burden and IMF pressure increased, and the trade deficit reached an all-time high in 1980, after the second dramatic rise in oil prices in 1979 (see Tables 4.1 and 4.2 below). Total export earnings were insufficient to pay for the imported oil. During 1978–79, Turkey was hard-pressed by debt, and applied to the IMF for the extension of loans and some concessions. The ensuing negotiations resulted in the imposition of the classical IMF austerity measures, such as a wage freeze, balanced budget, social spending cuts, tight money, reduced regulations, devaluation, and a liberalized trade and foreign investment policy. Budget balancing meant the elimination of government subsidies to state economic enterprises and agricultural producers, including peasants. State economic enterprises, whether making steel, textiles or shoes, had been selling their products at prices lower than the cost of production. These subsidies had been financed by printing money for nearly thirty years. The resulting inflation had become a major problem, and the major focus of IMF concern.

Table 4.1
Turkey's merchandise trade by selected years, 1950–85
(in millions of dollars)

Year	Exports	Imports	Trade Deficits
1950	264	311	47
1955	313	498	185
1960	321	468	147
1965	479	505	26
1970	588	830	242
1975	1,401	4,147	2,746
1980	2,910	6,920	4,010
1985 (est.)	7,127	10,251	3,124

Sources: 1950–60 data from: IMF, *International Financial Statistics*, Supplement on Trade Statistics, Supplement series no. 4 (1982); 1965–80 data from: IMF, *International Financial Statistics, Yearbook 1984*, pp. 582–83; 1985 data from: Republic of Turkey, Prime Ministry, State Institute of Statistics, *Monthly Bulletin of Statistics*, June 1985, p. 33.

Table 4.2
Turkey's merchandise trade by decades, 1950–1985
(in millions of dollars)

	Exports	Imports	Trade Deficits	Exports as percent of Imports	Trade Deficit as percent of Exports
1950–59	3,234	4,367	1,280	70.1	39.6
1960–69	4,338	6,359	2,030	68.2	46.8
1970–79	14,662	34,880	20,220	42.0	137.9
1980–85	33,347	55,928	22,581	59.6	67.7

Sources: 1964–79 data from: IMF, *International Financial Statistics, Yearbook 1982*, p. 455; 1980–85 data from: Republic of Turkey, Prime Ministry, State Institute of Statistics, *Monthly Bulletin of Statistics*, June, 1985, p. 33; for other years IMF, *International Financial Statistics*, Supplement on Trade Statistics, Supplement series, no. 4 (1982), pp. 42–43, 46–47, 120–21, 132–33, 146–47, 152–53, 158–59.

Export-oriented industrialization

The severe shortage of foreign exchange resulted in underutilization of industrial capacity, below 50 percent in some industries. Rising bankruptcies, unemployment, and inflation at a triple digit level, forced the Demirel government, with IMF pressure, to adopt an export-led growth model, similar to some South East Asian and Latin American countries. Not surprisingly, there was considerable resistance to the new economic policies from industrial workers, civil servants, intellectuals, and small businesses threatened with bankruptcies. Unpopular IMF rules were seen as foreign domination and were a source of special resentment. The left, radical unions, including social democratic unions, and many intellectuals condemned the new economic policy. Considerable civil unrest and agitation emerged.[8] There were many acts of violence, an average of 25 killings daily. This prompted the military to intervene in September 1980, the third such intervention in 30 years.

After two years in power the military junta, under external pressure, particularly from European governments and the Council of Europe, began to prepare for civilian rule.[9] A constitution was drawn up by a Constitutional Assembly appointed by the junta and composed of right-wing intellectuals, politicians, and businessmen. The final draft of the constitution, which was submitted to the voters, was similar to a proposed draft by the Employers' Confederation of Turkey (TISK). In a controlled election in November 1982 it was overwhelmingly ratified.[10]

As the *Financial Times* in its special section on Turkey reported:

Since the generals seized power in 1980 the balance between employer and worker has totally changed. The radical union confederation, DISK, has been closed down, its leaders tortured, and a trial accusing them of trying to overthrow the state drags on under conditions which deeply disturb most foreign observers. . . . The generals have just tied Turkey's union movement, hand and foot. Unions are forbidden from giving or receiving support from political parties. Strikes are strictly circumscribed and may not be 'prejudicial to the principle of good will, to the detriment of society or damage national wealth.' The government can impose cooling-off periods of 90 days, followed by compulsory arbitration. Labour go-slows are prohibited, as is picketing.[11]

Since the junta came to power real wages have dropped by 40 percent, based on the official figures on inflation.[12] Overall, real wages have been declining every year (except in 1981) since the late 1970s: the decline was 12.3 percent in 1978, 20.8 percent in 1979, 7 percent in 1980, 44 percent in 1982, and 6.5 percent in 1983. The loss in purchasing power for this period was 46.1 percent.[13] 'In many cases workers have not received any pay since the Spring [of 1983], but cannot change jobs without jeopardizing their social security rights.'[14] In 1984, workers 'were granted a 25 percent pay increase plus 2,000 Turkish lira [about $2] a month, certainly not enough to maintain their purchasing power in a year during which inflation will have reached 50 percent. The Supreme Arbitration Board, which had held sway over all settlements in 1981–83, decides the terms of an agreement and often bans strikes in a particular sector as well; the coal and petroleum industries are good examples.'[15]

The junta, by keeping the labour unions, universities, the press, student organizations, civil organizations and societies under tight control by legislation and by martial law, was ready to move towards civilian rule and 'guided democracy' under the newly created legal system.[16] The new legal system gives broad rights and freedom to capital and constricts labour. Thus legislation has not only provided a framework for civilian rule under the generals' control, but has also prepared the ground for export-oriented industrialization.

Ever since the military coup in 1980, unemployment has remained high (around 20 percent) and price increases have run at twice the level of wage increases. As long as unemployment remains high, there is very little hope for the working class to improve its economic lot. 'Official social security figures suggest that Turkey's workforce has witnessed a decline in income of 40 percent since 1980. . . . What is beyond doubt is that the standard of living of many Turks has declined since 1980 and that unions are still tied . . . in a manner which still allows little room for manoeuvre.'[17] As *Yanki* reports: '1983, from an economic point of view, was the year of the middle class' impoverishment. At the beginning of the year inflation was estimated to be 25 percent, and wages and farm support prices were adjusted accordingly. At the end of the year, the inflation, approaching 50 percent, lowered workers' and peasants' real income by 20 percent.'[18]

The domestic economic difficulties are exacerbated by the changes in external economic factors. The tight money and declining demand in the domestic market, due to foreign exchange shortages, influenced investment decisions in the private and state sectors. The state sector has revised its investment plans every year since 1980. In 1981, the realized investment in the state sector was 94 percent of the planned investment. In 1983 it declined to 85 percent.[19] Total state investment, in constant prices, declined from 963 billion liras in 1981 to 924 billion liras in 1982 and 863 billion liras in 1983.[20] In the private sector, according to Istanbul Chamber of Industry (ISO) research,[21] industrialists are not planning new machinery expansion until they eliminate the present excess capacity. Because of this, the share of private investment in total investment has declined continuously since 1978: private investment, as a percentage of total investment, declined from 53 percent in 1978 to 44.0 percent in 1980 and 39.7 percent in 1983.[22]

In 1983 Turkish industry had an excess capacity in the range of 40–60 percent. In key industries the idle capacity was 50 percent; in others, every six machines out of ten were idle: 'Many factories are working at one-half to two-thirds capacity because of the depressed domestic market. Power cuts are again hitting production, and will worsen if industrial output picks up. Financing costs, running at 35–40 percent in real terms, are driving an increasing number of firms into bankruptcy.'[23]

The minimum real wage has shown continuous decline since 1977 – from 20.32 liras per hour in 1977 to 6.81 liras per hour in January, 1984, as shown in Table 4.3. In 1984, the Minimum Wage Commission agreed to increase the minimum wage by 51.4 percent, from 16,200 liras per month to 24,525 liras per month for a family with two children. However, the wage increases were wiped out before the workers saw the raise in their pay cheques, by a series of price increases following the local elections.

Table 4.3
Minimum wage and price index
(in Turkish liras)

Year	Nominal Minimum Wage (Liras)	CPI (1963=100) in Istanbul	Real Minimum Wage
1972	21.80	213.7	10.20
1974	40.80	301.8	13.25
1976	60.00	429.6	13.96
1977	110.00	541.3	20.32
1979	180.00	1,433.1	12.56
1981	333.00	3,831.2	8.69
1983	540.00	6,548.7	8.24
Jan. 1984	540.00	7,424.6	6.81

Source: Yanki, no. 677 (March 19–25, 1984), p. 21.

Turkey's move to export-oriented industrialization dates back to January 1980. In order to earn more foreign exchange, to pay for the rising imports and the fast-climbing foreign debt, the Demirel government discouraged domestic consumption so that more of the domestic production could be exported. This imposed a great burden on the working class, as many consumer goods were no longer available due to the exports, and what little commodities remained for local consumption were soon priced beyond their reach. Despite the much-emphasized export drive, Turkey's foreign exchange difficulties continued. The country's imports have grown historically twice as fast as her exports. The principal imports are machinery, industrial raw materials, and energy, which are needed for the industries established under the earlier strategy of import-substitution industrialization (ISI). The import-substituting industries required the continuation of imports if these industries were to be operated at the designed capacity. The ISI had done next to nothing to establish the heavy industries to produce fixed capital goods and industrial raw materials; and there was nothing in the government's export promotion policy to establish the capital-goods producing industries that were neglected by the ISI programme, to reduce Turkey's dependency on imported machinery.

The ISI, initially, was designed to take care of local capital's demand for income-elastic luxury goods and some light industries for consumer goods. Many joint ventures with foreign transnational corporations (TNCs) were set up (mostly in assembly line operations where the main components are imported), to satisfy the demands of the upper class, rather than to provide the production of goods which are necessary for internal, self-sustaining, capital accumulation. Many factories in food processing, textiles, pharmaceuticals, chemicals, automobiles, and tyres were established in this manner. Turkey's demand for industrial goods and for energy will thus continue to grow, as will her foreign exchange needs. Fuel imports and debt-service payments, as percentages of total imports, have increased from 31 percent in the 1970s to 64 percent in the 1980s. Current account deficits and debt service payments take 85 percent of export earnings.

As Turkey's industrialization continues, the external debt will grow further and with it so will the debt service. Total exports plus external borrowing are less than total imports plus debt service payments. In other words, for the left and right side of the equation to balance, it is required that new loans (external borrowing) match current account deficits plus debt service payments. Turkey, heavily indebted as a result of a lopsided industrialization strategy, is very vulnerable to a rise in the US interest rate, which would increase Turkey's debt service burden significantly. For instance, a 1 percent rise in the US interest rate would increase Turkey's interest payments by one-quarter billion dollars for a $25 billion debt.[24]

Turkey's economic growth in the first half of the 1980s has been affected by the slow growth of the world economy, particularly the European economy, which has historically been the market for Turkey's exports. Unemployment in Europe has created problems for Turkish guest-workers in the European Economic Community. Each community government, particularly the West German government, encourages Turkish workers (with cash bonuses) to leave. According to the *Financial Times*, European unemployment had reached 18.1 million (10.6 percent) by the end of 1983.[25]

Turkey has been trying to re-orient her exports from the developed industrialized countries to the oil-rich Middle East and African countries. But declining oil prices and the continuing Iran–Iraq war dampened the prospects for expanding exports to this region.

Rapid economic growth in Turkey in the 1960s and 1970s did not solve her joblessness, and the slowed-down rate of growth in the 1980s made it worse. The industrialization policy pursued has not created jobs fast enough to meet the growth in population. According to the World Bank, Turkey's population grew at an annual average of 2.5 percent in 1960–70, 2.3 percent in 1970–82, and is expected to grow at 2 percent in 1980–2000.[26] The labour force growth rates during these periods are 1.4 percent, 2.0 percent, and 2.3 percent, respectively. Turkey's employment grew 11.9 percent from 1970 to 1982, which is about one-half the labour force growth rate (24.3 percent). The rate of unemployment rose from 5 percent in 1970 to 18 percent in 1982. (See Table 4.4).

As Turkey has adopted export-oriented industrialization her reliance on transnational corporations (TNCs) has significantly increased with the liberalization of her foreign investment regulations to attract direct investment.

Table 4.4
Turkey: labour force statistics, selected years
(in thousands)

	1970	1975	1980	1982
Civilian Labour Force	14,544	16,040	17,180	18,081
Total Employment	13,820	14,698	15,310	15,467
Unemployment Rate (%)	5.0	8.4	10.8	18.1
Labour Force Participation Rate (%)	72.7	68.4	65.3	63.5

Source: OECD Economic Surveys: Turkey (various years).

As a result, foreign direct investment in Turkey has tripled since 1980 – from $300 million prior to 1980 to over $900 million in 1983.[27] The problem with foreign direct investment, as opposed to foreign loans (or portfolio investment), however, is that it requires a higher rate of return (and a higher amount of profit-repatriation as opposed to interest payments). As foreign direct investment accumulates, the total amount of profits to be repatriated increases. In addition, foreign direct investment does not necessarily bring in fresh new capital; often capital is created in the host country.

The availability of external funds, through direct investment rather than loans, presents another problem. The control of decision-making shifts from the host country (Turkey) to the home base. As a result, the TNCs become the main actors that decide what to invest and where to invest as they pressure the country to provide economic concessions and establish tax free 'free trade zones.' As Folker Frobel et al. point out, 'For the first time in centuries the underdeveloped countries are becoming sites for manufacturing industry on a vast and growing scale. Concomitantly the new international division of labour entails a growing fragmentation of the production process into a variety of partial operations performed worldwide at different production locations.'[28]

The free trade zones opened in Turkey for the TNCs' plants do not solve Turkey's problems of unemployment and foreign exchange shortages as indeed they have failed elsewhere. The export-oriented production in free trade zones requires considerable raw material imports. In addition, export oriented facilities in free trade zones require infrastructural investments, and these investment projects are completed usually with external loans which have to be serviced. The net gain comes from the wages paid and is not significant. Since profits are to be transferred abroad, the companies resort to transfer pricing mechanisms beyond the legal limit imposed by the host country. Turkey's debt service as a percentage of its total exports increased from 8.4 percent in 1967–69 to 16.7 percent in 1970–79 and 40.9 percent in 1980–83. As the decade closes, the percentage is expected to go to well over 50 percent. Hence, the success of the ELI (Export Led Industrialization) strategy, as it is being implemented, is highly questionable.

The unfolding class struggles

Lopsided capitalist industrialization has caused immense dislocations in Turkey, uprooting many people from their homes in rural villages and towns and forcing them to urban centres. Urbanization has increased as a result of massive emigration from the hinterland. Rural migration has continuously changed the composition of the population. Many people have travelled great distances for the first time, lived in far-away places, seen different people, places, and ways of life. Many have gone to Europe and come back. Feudal institutions are being replaced by capitalist ones. There is a class-conscious industrial proletariat and a progressive student body and intelligentsia. Turkey now has a population which is more mobile, more knowledgeable and more aware of the changing world.

Until the mid-1960s, the activities of the working class were under the complete control of the government. Although labour was organized around trade unions, and later was represented by TURK-IS (Confederation of Turkish Trade Unions – established in 1953 with a strong affiliation to AFL-CIO), it did not have much power against private capital and the state, because it lacked legal and political protection. Thus, labour left its fate to the state. Trade union membership was limited due to the small size of the working class, as Turkey was predominantly an agrarian society with a large segment of the population engaged in self-employed subsistence farming. Lacking the legal right to collective bargaining and the right to strike, and without a political party of its own,[29] the working class was forced to accept whatever the government granted. When the late 1950s hit the workers with rising inflation and unemployment, the working class was absolutely defenceless, having no legal or political muscle.

The decade of the 1960s witnessed a gradual tendency of the working class to move towards organizational, political, and ideological independence from both bourgeois parties and the state.[30] As the industrialization and ensuing urbanization proceeded, industrial workers and union membership increased significantly. The trade unions intensified their struggle by staging mass demonstrations against the government in power when Parliament failed to pass the Labour Law granting workers' rights, including the right to strike. The working class continued to press its demands, and these rights were finally won in 1963. Soon after the new labour legislation was passed, there were many strikes throughout Turkey by unions demanding economic benefits and political freedom. The workers' struggles occasionally turned bloody when the government used police and military force to suppress the strikers. As the agitation of the workers continued to increase, the trade union leadership fell behind the rank and file movement, and the leaders in TURK-IS adopted a more conciliatory attitude towards the government and the bourgeoisie. The resulting political vacuum was partially filled by the Workers Party of Turkey (WPT), founded by radical trade unionists in 1961. Later, in 1967, several progressive unions broke away from TURK-IS and formed the Confederation of Revolutionary Trade Unions, called DISK. For the first time in Turkey, many progressive publications emerged, Marxist literature was translated into Turkish and widely distributed, and Marxism–Leninism and socialism were openly discussed. The working class and the intelligentsia criticized fascism and US imperialism and debated on the nature and prospects of alternative social systems.

The workers' struggles through strikes, street demonstrations, and factory occupations, led by DISK and supported by the WPT, were unseen before in Turkey. As the 1960s came to a close, the number of strikes and of workers involved in strikes increased significantly. Gradually, the working class improved its economic lot and put the bourgeoisie on the defensive for the first time. Even though there was no challenge to the bourgeoisie's political power, the economic position of capital was threatened. In 1970, over 100,000 workers marched to protest against the government's curbs on trade union rights. According to Taylan, 'this event was a watershed of decisive importance in the history of class struggles in Turkey.'[31]

In 1970 and 1971 strikes reached their peak, paralysing many sectors of the economy. The government of Suleyman Demirel declared martial law in order to suppress the workers' strikes, control militant trade unions, and halt urban guerrilla activities. But soon the military intervened and forced Demirel to resign and appointed its own government to curb the left. The military controlled civil strife with brutal force, arresting left-wing intellectuals, students, trade union leaders, and other progressives. The working class, supported by the intelligentsia, students and other progressive groups, struggled hard to undo the post-coup military government's new laws. When in the mid-1970s the government openly sided with right-wing terrorists against the leftists, and advocated new stringent legislation to control the left, the working class fought the government in the streets by staging large demonstrations. In 1976, DISK protested against the establishment of the State Security Courts by declaring a general strike, in which more than 100,000 workers participated. The working class struggle was an important factor blocking the establishment of the State Security Courts. DISK workers, with the participation of hundreds of thousands of other workers, celebrated May Day for the first time in Turkey's history. Over 200 strikes were declared by the trade unions. Workers were joined by progressive organizations of students, teachers, engineers, technicians, architects, and lawyers. This class battle continued in the late 1970s despite the fact that the government declared martial law in many provinces. The martial law commanders, ignoring the terror unleashed by the right, fought against the leftists and the Kurdish militants, and terrorized the communities which had become sanctuaries for these groups.[32]

As government repression and terror by the right increased, the response by the left was equally strong. The left paid a heavy price; its leaders were gunned down; 37 people were machine-gunned during May Day demonstrations in Istanbul and over 100 people were killed and many homes burned in Kahramanmaras by right-wing commandos. Armed clashes between the left and the right continued until the military coup on September 12, 1980 – a coup that decimated the left and eliminated all the progressive institutions and movements which had been the legacy of the 1961 Constitution.

The Junta banned all political parties and expropriated their property following the coup. The leaders of the two main parties, Suleyman Demirel (JP) and Bulent Ecevit (RPP) were banned from political activities and from making (or writing) political statements. The leaders of all the other parties were arrested, later prosecuted, convicted, and sentenced to prison for several years, the left-wing leaders drawing heavier prison sentences.[33] The junta made mass arrests, killed thousands of people in search-and-destroy missions, and tortured tens of thousands of political prisoners. Many were kept in detention centres for years without any charge against them. The junta also shut down DISK, the left-wing trade union confederation, imprisoned its leaders, and prosecuted them with the death penalty. The junta purged nearly all dissent from Turkish universities, firing about 40 percent of all university professors and expelling many graduate students studying under them, while at the same time establishing new universities under strict government control. Under the rubic of educational reform, the junta has controlled the Turkish universities directly since 1982 through the newly formed Higher Education Council. Council Members are appointed by the junta; the council appoints university presidents who then appoint deans. Previously, faculties elected their own presidents and deans. Several of the new appointees have direct connection or association with the neo-fascist Nationalist Action Party. A tight, conservative, ideological conformity is exerted upon teachers, textbooks, and course syllabi.[34]

Labour laws have been rewritten to constrict sharply the scope of labour activities. There is an attempt to remake industrial unions into company unions and to limit union demands and activities to economic issues.[35] Union leaders are banned from participation in partisan politics. The 1983 labour law, while not making strikes completely illegal, makes them exceedingly difficult. Strikes can only be against one company, lockouts are legal, and the Supreme National Arbitration Board, the tripartite government-dominated body, is stacked against labour. There are only two labour representatives on the board of nine members. Recently a new press law has been passed which permits the seizure of newspapers, the closing down of press offices, and the imprisonment of journalists and editors (television and radio stations are not a concern since they are government-owned and operated).

Even the Society for Peace, legally founded before the coup, and organized for disarmament activism rather than any partisan political purpose, was not spared persecution. The founders of the society, all prominent professionals, have been held in prison for nearly three years. Their trial, which lasted over a year and ended in November 1983, resulted in the conviction of 23 of the 28 defendants who were sentenced to prison terms of five to eight years.

The Turkish state, under military control, is an authoritarian state. The government owns and runs the radio and television stations, and the press is under various forms of censorship; the state controls the diffusion of information. The educational system, from primary school through college, is under tight government control. Textbooks have been rewritten and course syllabi have been revised to reflect the reactionary position of the government.

The class struggle in Turkey has been continuing below the surface since 1980, despite the power of the repressive state, and it will intensify and become more violent as Turkey moves on to the next stage of her transition to democracy. Preparing for the impending confrontation, the right has already begun regrouping its forces, and the left is attempting to forge a unity among its own ranks, as alliances similar to the 1980 pre-coup periods develop on both sides of the political spectrum.

Notes

1. The Republican People's Party held power from 1923 until 1950 and was Turkey's only party until a RPP splinter group formed the Democrat Party in 1945.
2. See Dogan Avcioglu, *Turkiye'nin Duzeni*, vol. 2, Istanbul, Cem Yayinevi, 1973; Korkut Boratav, *Turkiye'de Devletcilik*, Istanbul: Gercek Yayinevi, 1974; Berch Berberoglu, *Turkey in Crisis: From State Capitalism to Neo-Colonialism*, London: Zed Press, 1982; Fikret Ceyhun, 'Economic Development in Turkey since 1960: A Critique,' *Economic Forum*, Summer 1983; Z. Y. Hershlag, *Turkey: An Economy in Transition*, The Hague: Uitgeverij van Keulen N.V., 1958; Ozlem Ozgur, *Sanayilesme ve Turkiye*, Istanbul: Gercek Yayinevi, 1975.
3. When examining the data for the founding dates of all private businesses from 1923 to 1960, we find that 60 percent of them were established during 1946–60. See Dogan Avcioglu, *Turkiye'nin Duzeni*, vol. 2 (Istanbul, 1973), p. 725.
4. International Monetary Fund, *International Financial Statistics Yearbook*, 1972 and 1981. OECD, *National Accounts of OECD Countries: 1950–1979*. Vol. 1 (Paris, 1981). Rates of growth in investment and GDP were calculated for 1950 to 1980. The 1954 decline in GDP was the largest in the last 30 years. The next largest declines were 3.5 percent and 3.8 percent in 1979 and 1980, respectively. For the most recent data, see OECD, *Economic Surveys 1981–1982: Turkey* (Paris, 1982).
5. For number of strikes, strikers, and strike days lost, see Ronnie Margulies and Engin Yildizoglu, 'Trade Unions and Turkey's Working Class,' *MERIP Reports*, no. 121 (February 1984), p. 18. There was a significant increase in the number of strikers and work days lost from 1969 through to the March 12, 1971 military coup.
6. Prime Minister Demirel ruled Turkey from 1965 to 1980, with brief interruptions by the military in 1971 and the RPP coalition governments in 1973–74 and 1978. Hence, the period 1950–80 marks its imprint in Turkey as conservative, pro-private enterprise, and pro-US.
7. Turkish workers, who, in 1961, began immigrating to Western Europe to obtain jobs, reached one million in 1981. The workers' remittances also climbed as emigration from Turkey continued. By 1981, the workers' cumulative earnings repatriated to Turkey exceeded $15 billion – an average of over $2500 per worker per year. See: Is ve Isci Bulma Kurumu Genel Mudurlugu, *Istihdamda 30 Yil* (Ankara, 1976), pp. 11 and 15, and *Yurt Disindaki Turk Iscileri ve Donus Egilimleri*, Yayin No. 114 (Ankara, 1974), p. 4; Turkish Industrialists and Businessmen's Association, *The Turkish Economy 1982*, pp. 56 and 219.
8. Labour agitation reached its peak in 1980. The number of strikes, strikers, and work days lost reached a historic high. See Margulies and Yildizoglu.
9. 'Since the military intervention of 1980, the Ministerial Turkey–EEC Joint Association Council and its parliamentary counterpart have not met. . . . From the Community's side, human rights issues are seen as a major sticking point. A number of controversial trials have ensured that $530 million of economic aid, due under the Fourth Financial Protocol has been blocked since 1981.' *Financial Times*, Section III, Financial Times Survey, 'Turkey: Trade and Industry,' December 24, 1984, p. 6.

10. David Tonge. 'Turkish Industry: New Scope for Investment,' *Financial Times*, December 19, 1983, Section III, p. 1.

11. David Tonge, 'Labour: Unions Tied Hand and Foot.' *Financial Times*, December 19, 1983, Section III, p. 5.

12. Ibid.

13. *OECD Economic Surveys: Turkey*, various years.

14. David Tonge, 'Labour: Unions Tied Hand and Foot.' p. 5.

15. *Financial Times*, Section III, Financial Times Survey, 'Turkey: Trade and Industry.' December 24, 1984, p. 8.

16. As Feroz Ahmad points out, 'The NSC [National Security Council] permitted the formation of new political parties to contest the General Election in November, it vetoed hundreds of "new" politicians, apart from the 723 ex-politicians who had already been barred from the election.' See Feroz Ahmad, 'The Transition to Democracy in Turkey,' *Third World Quarterly*, vol. 7, no. 2 (April 1985), p. 214.

17. *Financial Times*, December 24, 1984, p. 8.

18. *Yanki*, no. 666 (January 2–8, 1984), p. 32.

19. *Yanki*, no. 674 (February 27–March 4, 1984), p. 20.

20. *Ibid.*

21. *Ibid.*

22. *Ibid.*

23. David Tonge, 'Economy: Competitiveness the First Priority.' *Financial Times*, December 19, 1983, section III, p. 2.

24. During the period 1973–82, Turkey's foreign debt grew by 417.4 percent and interest payments by 903.5 percent. See *World Debt Tables*, 1983–84 edition.

25. *Financial Times*, 'World Economy,' September 17, 1984, Section III, p. 2.

26. *World Development Report*, various years.

27. OECD, *Foreign Investment in Turkey: Changing Conditions Under the New Economic Programme* (Paris, 1983), p. 7. The 1954 foreign investment law no. 6224 was updated by government decrees: Decree 17 in 1983 and Decree 30 in 1984. These decrees made foreign investment economically attractive through tax concessions and subject to less bureaucratic controls. Among the benefits given to foreign investment are 'exemption from customs taxes and duties for the importation of machinery and equipment; exemption from taxes and duties from medium and long-term credits; an investment allowance (up to 100 percent of fixed investment is deductible from corporate taxes); exemption from consumption tax and cash rebate made by the central bank out of fixed investment expenditures up to 20 percent. . . . Foreign companies can repatriate all of their profits and there is no bar to repatriation of capital over time.' See *Financial Times*, May 20, 1985, special section on Turkey, p. 7.

28. Folker Frobel, Jurgen Heinrichs, and Otto Kreye, 'Export-Oriented Industrialization of Underdeveloped Countries,' *Monthly Review*, vol. 30, no. 6 (November 1978), p. 23.

29. In earlier years, prominent leftists, among them Sabahattin Ali, Nazim Hikmet, and Hikmet Kivilcimli, endured long prison sentences, and the entire leadership of the Communist Party of Turkey was murdered in 1921. More recently, many left-wing intellectuals and left-wing party leaders, like Cetin Altan, Sadun Aren, Behice Boran, Yalcin Kucuk, Aziz Nesin, and Dogu Perincek have served prison sentences.

30. Turgut Taylan, 'Capital and the State in Contemporary Turkey.' *Khamsin*, no. 11 (1984), p. 18.

31. Ibid.

32. After the 1980 coup, the military concentrated its war activities in the eastern provinces where the ethnic Kurdish minority predominates. The military established checkpoints in many towns where outsiders (Turkish or foreign) are not allowed to enter. Military concentration is so heavy in these provinces that, for instance, in Tunceli Province – the second least populated – there are three soldiers per local resident. See *Yeni Gundem*, vol. 2, No. 41 (February 21–March 9, 1986), p. 10.

33. The leaders of the NSP were freed in 1985 and the conviction of the NAP's leaders is on appeal.

34. Feroz Ahmad, 'The Transition to Democracy in Turkey,' *Third World Quarterly*, vol. 7, no. 2 (April 1985), p. 216.

35. According to the 1982 Constitution, labour unions cannot 'pursue a political cause, engage in political activity, receive support from political parties or give support to them, and they shall not act jointly for these purposes with associations, public professional organizations and foundations.' See *Financial Times*, May 20, 1985, special section on Turkey, p. 11. The Constitution and the labour legislation enacted thereafter provided the government legal means to declare any strike illegal or postpone it indefinitely.

5. Political Power and the Saudi State[1]

Ghassan Salamé

The absence of a central political power has been a prominent feature throughout the history of the Arabian peninsula. The focus through most of early Muslim society shifted rapidly from Mecca and Medina in the western part of the peninsula, to Damascus and then Baghdad, and in its wake the web of tribal authority reasserted itself. Power was exerted primarily from the outside, or by local forces sustained from the outside. But more often than not, authority was restricted within the tribe. Foreign forces were reluctant to control with a direct physical presence this huge, barren heartland of the peninsula. The Ottomans (as well as European powers) largely confined themselves to its perimeters.

The Saudi regime, in this setting, is noteworthy for its indigenous Najdi character. Subdued by Muhammad 'Ali of Egypt in 1818, and then by an alliance between the Ottomans and various eastern tribes late in the 19th century, Saudi power rose again when 'Abd al-Aziz Ibn Saud conquered Riyadh at the beginning of the 20th century. A few years later he moved successfully against the Shammar tribes to the north, consolidating power in central Arabia. During and after World War I he collaborated with the British, and after the war he granted oil concessions to more recent arrivals in the area – the Americans. The indigenous 'authentic Arabian' origins of the Saudi regime have allowed it a margin of independence from the British and the Americans, and substantial 'legitimacy' when compared with other Arab rulers (such as the kings of Iraq and Transjordan) who were directly installed on their thrones by the British.

It is remarkable in a tribal society that one tribe has been able to gain the degree of hegemony attained by the Sauds. This can largely be attributed to the crucial Wahhabi connection which gave the Sauds a supra-tribal ideology to manipulate in their drive to establish a permanent principality, rather than one of those numerous volatile and short-lived tribal confederations. Saudi access to revenues from the Mecca pilgrimage after 1926, and from oil exports after World War II, has enabled the family to add money to its religious, military, and other (notably, politically arranged marriages) means of maintaining hegemony.

Control over urban areas posed a more complex problem for the Sauds. Outright military occupation was appropriate in the small oases of the interior, but a more sophisticated method was required in the coastal Hijazi cities. There, after some hesitation, Ibn Saud permitted a certain degree of local autonomy and some continuation of local laws. But this autonomy was gradually whittled away and, in 1932, the country's name was changed from the Kingdom of Najd, Hijaz, 'Asir, Hassa and Their Dependencies to Saudi Arabia. Provincial names were replaced by geographical nomenclature – for example, Hassa became the Eastern Province, and Hijaz the Western Province. Wherever threats to Saudi power might arise, large military installations and garrisons sprang up, such as in Dhahran, Khobar, and Khamis Mushayt in the 'Asir area.

In the late 1920s, Ibn Saud himself disbanded the *Ikhwan*, the military religious brotherhood of mainly Bedouin warriors who had helped the family reconquer four-fifths of the Arabian peninsula. More and more Ibn Saud came to rely on alliances and a family presence throughout the territory. One element which he assiduously maintained, though, was the intimate connection of the regime with the *ulama*, the religious leaders charged with interpreting Muslim law, who are still consulted today on many public issues. For a long while, religious power was centralized in the al-Sheikh family, the descendants of 'Abd al-Wahhab; this power is now more widely distributed among generally Najdi-born *ulama*, however.

From Saudi power to Saudi state

The time when Ibn Saud could govern his kingdom with the help of a few Syrian scribes and tribal councillors is past. Today the Saudi state has a council of ministers, ministerial departments, an army, an official newspaper – all features common to most modern political states.

The emergence of the Saudi state apparatus was much less an internally generated transformation of a tribal power than a response to systematic external pressure. The first challenge facing the regime was the absorption of the Hijaz province after the defeat of the Hashemites in 1925–26. The integration of this province into the kingdom posed two series of problems. First, the government had to avoid provoking the population of Hijaz – a largely urban, commercial, educated people prone to flaunting their superiority over the fanatical, warrior–nomad people of Najd who had defeated them. Hijaz had a constitution, municipal councils, and a regular army – things the conquering Sauds knew almost nothing about. In addition, as a result of foreign trade and pilgrimage activity, this province had long-standing ties with other countries, notably with Egypt.

To attack the historic administrative structures of Hijaz would have risked rebellion; allowing these structures to remain intact threatened a progressive detachment of the Hijaz from the Saudi orbit. The choice between these alternatives was all the more difficult because it came at a time when Ibn Saud was barely able to restrain his *Ikhwan*, who wanted to impose their simple, tough and fanatical worldview on more sophisticated Hijazis. He settled on an intermediate solution: permitting Hijaz to keep some of its laws and institutions from former times, while naming his own son, Faisal, vice-regent of the province to ensure a Saudi presence at the head of governmental structures left by centuries of Hashemite–Ottoman rule. Consequently, the Hijaz administration was considerably better organized than that of the central government.

On September 18, 1932, the country was unified under the name Saudi Arabia. Following the example of Hijaz, Ibn Saud named governors to the different provinces, giving them considerable latitude, in view of the large area of the country, the lack of modern communications, and the very peculiar conditions of each of the various provinces. Whereas in Hijaz Faisal regularly consulted local notables, in Hassa 'Abdallah Ibn Jiluwi governed in the patriarchal manner of Ibn Saud, with scarcely matched severity.

The vice-regency model developed for Hijaz indirectly established the notion of the delegation of power. Gradually, this concept was extended to the various sectors of governmental activity. Although under Ibn Saud such activity was rudimentary, it was already clear that the king could not involve himself in every little administrative detail. He developed the practice of delegating personal representatives, both in the central administration and in the government of the provinces.

Faisal, situated in Hijaz with easy access to foreign communications, was made responsible for diplomacy. He served as a sort of diplomatic jack-of-all-trades – at once minister of foreign affairs, representative to the United Nations and roving ambassador. The foreign ministry, then at Jeddah, was integrated with the personal secretariat of Faisal, the vice-regent of the province. The kingdom responded very slowly to requests from other countries to open embassies, with only five or six established instead of the 30 expected. Poor finances, a good deal of chauvinism, and lack of interest in routine diplomacy explain this reluctance.

The Ministry of Finance was also created in 1932. Here the problems were more serious: the sovereign's personal expenses were not separated from the state budget, and remained so until the end of the 1950s. Maintenance of the currency (whose parity had to be set) and a minimum of bookkeeping were essential. 'Abdallah al-Suleiman, an old client of the king, was appointed to distribute sacks of rice or flour, and later dollars, to the allies and clients of Ibn Saud. For a long period of time he monopolized the title of *wazir* (minister), and he was indeed the only one.

Even this modest organization, however, could not develop further as long as Ibn Saud was alive. Jealous of his royal prerogatives, he did not hesitate to involve himself in very trivial issues, – arbitrating between individuals or tribes, drafting diplomatic dispatches, personally receiving visitors. The king did not like the ministerial organization tolerated in Hijaz. But just as exchanges with other countries compelled him to name a minister of foreign affairs, relations with the petroleum companies forced him to establish a Ministry of Finance.

In 1944, the American decision to install a base at Dhahran prompted the king to establish a Ministry of Defence as well. But these offices, arising purely as a result of external pressure, did not affect his personal power in the slightest, and he often ignored them. Finally, just a few weeks before his death in 1953, he agreed to establish a Council of Ministers in order to have certain of his sons and councillors share in the power of his heir, Saud, and because he was finally convinced that this was a requirement for all states. The main motivating factor was that Ibn Saud did not want to transmit to only one of his 37 sons a power as absolute as that which he himself had exercised.

Besides the death of Ibn Saud, the other factor that hastened the emergence of a state apparatus was oil. Saudi crude was only produced in major quantities after 1945, but its development then became very rapid. Oil revenues were spent in the most careless manner, despite the anxieties this created for ARAMCO, fast becoming a kind of state-within-a-state upon which the royal power was growing increasingly dependent. In return for royalties the government had nothing to offer ARAMCO but its signature at the bottom of a contract – no armed forces to defend installations, no administration capable of handling complex negotiations, no skilled labour, no educated personnel, no real infrastructure of any sort, much less a governmental body capable of regulating the corporate giant at the heart of the kingdom.

As a result, ARAMCO engaged not only in all phases of Saudi oil production, but also built housing, airports, hospitals and schools, laid down roads, founded educational centres, dug for water, launched agricultural research and, above all, encouraged the US government to install a military base near the oil fields that would protect them and the people who worked there. This activity posed a double challenge to Riyadh; it stimulated the Saudi government to improve its negotiating position vis-à-vis the foreign power, and also to prepare itself to rival and replace it in the domain of oil as well as the many sectors of civil life where it was now involved. In 1953, at the death of Ibn Saud, the kingdom found itself in an absurd situation: oil, its principal resource, was formally nationalized, but there was no state apparatus capable of administering it.

The Council of Ministers met for the first time on March 7, 1954, in Riyadh. Ministries of the interior, education, agriculture, health, industry and commerce, and information were added to defence, foreign affairs and finance. Rivalries between ministers, as well as inexperience, caused numerous problems. The Ministry of Economy was created in 1953, but closed the very next year. The governor of Hassa province in the east categorically refused to submit to the minister of the interior and continued to organize the police of the province in his own way. Committees, supreme councils and special commissions came and went like the wind, sometimes becoming ministries, but more often falling into oblivion.

It was not until much later, mainly under the influence of Faisal, that an organizational framework began to emerge from this chaos. A royal decree clarifying the duties of the Council of Ministers, issued on May 12, 1958, remains a cornerstone of government. According to this document, the council is responsible for the budget and internal affairs, but only the king can legislate and issue laws, treaties and concessions. The king can oppose a proposition of the council, but he has to justify his veto. The regional organization of the kingdom is based on a decree of October 1963 which divides the kingdom into six provinces (*muqata'a*), which are further subdivided into a number of regions (*mantika*). Each governor is appointed by royal decree. A vice-governor and a 30-member provincial council, chosen by the Council of Ministers, assist him.

The royal family and its allies

From the composition of the government, little has changed since 1975, and it is easy to see that the sons of Ibn Saud occupy all the important posts: first and second deputy prime ministers, defence and aviation, public works and housing, interior and municipal and rural affairs. Foreign affairs has fallen to a member of the third generation (Saud, son of King Faisal and nephew of the present king) as has the position of deputy minister in all these (and other) departments.

Outside the council this nepotism is only increased. When he was only a crown prince, Fahd was at the head of a series of supreme councils that brought under the direct authority of the Saud family sectors formally entrusted to non-family officials: national security, education, universities, oil affairs, youth, pilgrimage, and industrialization. These councils thus extended the personal imprint of Fahd and his so-called 'Sudayri' clan over the whole administration. Provincial government is entrusted only to near relatives of Ibn Saud. His sons are governors of Medina, Mecca, and Riyadh, and his nephews and grandsons are at the head of other provinces. In 1986, King Fahd named his own son to be governor of the oil-rich Eastern province, breaking a tradition of uninterrupted rule of this province by the Jiluwi branch of the family, and clearly showing an inclination to re-concentrate provincial government in the hands of the king.

From the beginning, the power of the Saudi monarchy has depended on alliances with other forces inside the kingdom. The new governmental apparatus also permits the ruling family to repay these faithful supporters through co-optation. The al-Sheikh, descendants of the founder of Wahhabism, are one of the most well-known of such allies. Their influence has been cemented by their permanent presence in the Council of Ministers. Other traditional tribal allies include the Sudayris, a tribe from which Saudi princes often choose a wife, and the Thunayyan, who brought to the family administrative experience gained in the service of the Ottoman Empire. Within the family itself, certain branches are given more influence than others, depending on the goodwill of the king. While Khalid once had Jiluwis as advisers, King Fahd has reopened the corridors of power to the descendants of King Saud and the now pardoned renegade branch which fought against the family in the 19th century. Loyal but less prominent tribes are accommodated through financial transfers and the national guard, where the sons of the chiefs naturally serve as officers, and their clients as soldiers.

Clan and state: the officer-princes

The mineral wealth of the country has increased its vulnerability. The kingdom must have a strong armed force to cope with many formidable threats. These armed forces number about 70,000 and are men, equipped increasingly with sophisticated weapons. But the military has some severe handicaps. A military career holds little attraction for young Saudi men, despite very attractive incentives for the recruit and his family. At best, only 2 percent of the population is in the army, and the ratio of personnel to territory is even less impressive: one for every 16 kilometres. Nor does the quality of the Saudi army's training readiness compare favourably with that of neighbouring states, even poor ones. Nevertheless, in 1982, the defence budget was $26 billion, of which a considerable proportion went to the US as payment for arms, equipment, and services. Today, the kingdom spends more on defence on a per capita basis than any country in the world, with a per capita expenditure of $2,500 (compared with $520 for the United States). Despite improvements since 1975, particularly in weaponry, Saudis remain sceptical about the military's prowess.

One detects in the royal family itself a reluctance to undertake major development of the armed forces. The monarchy, anxious to defend its wealth, seems to fear the potentially high political price of a strong army. Too many dynasties and civilian regimes in the immediate vicinity of the kingdom have already paid it. Even aborted coups prove to be expensive. One attempt in 1969, originating in the Air Force, triggered renewed doubts about its officers' loyalty.

The dilemma between defending the country and defending the regime shows how limited the institutionalization of power remains. The insistence on 'protecting the cities against the enemy' leads to posting garrisons close to the principal urban centres. This is only one sign of how much the regime fears the army and how adamantly it intends to keep this force under its thumb as an insurance against a sudden uprising.

Another sign is the regime's reliance on two military corps – the army and the national guard – which were for a time almost equal in size. This is no mere holdover from the past, or a formal division with no practical meaning. The United States, responsible for the formation of both, considers them as two distinct forces, complementary certainly, but possibly antagonistic in case of conflict.[2]

The guard is an extension of loyalist tribal groups, while the army is an outgrowth of the Hijazi troops inherited from the Sharif of Mecca. They are commanded differently: the Ministry of Defence and Aviation is a stronghold of the Sudayri clan, represented by Sultan, the brother of the king. The guard is under the authority of 'Abdallah, probably the strongest counterweight to the influence of the Sudayri clan (the king and his six full brothers). The armed forces are charged with defending the borders and helping to put down internal rebellion. The guard is principally charged with the protection of the cities and oil wells. Both were used to quell the Mecca rebellion in 1979.

Although the armed forces of the kingdom share the same commander-in-chief – the king himself – the large size of the royal family allows it to place a great number of princes in positions of command. It is difficult to provide an exact count of these officer-princes, but they are generally estimated to be in the hundreds. Prince Bandar, the ambassador to Washington and Prince Salman, the astronaut, both belong to this category. This holds true as much for the national guard, the air force, and other services. As a rule, princes who have not received a military education abroad fill the higher posts in the guard or the army, whereas graduates of Lackland, San Diego, or Fort Leavenworth serve as officers in the other armed services.

The National Defence sector is not reserved for Saudis alone; but the regime is very reluctant to supply information on who the many foreigners are or what role they play in the Saudi army. The information that is available indicates three categories of people serving in the armed forces:

1.   Contracted foreign officers serving in an individual capacity. About 1,500 of these are of Pakistani origin. Officers of Jordanian origin number in the dozens. There are also Syrians, Iraqis, Palestinians, Bengalis and Egyptians. These officers are treated like nationals; they seem to be most active in training and logistics.
2.   Officers sent to the kingdom by virtue of bilateral agreements between the kingdom and their country of origin. The United States, French, British, and Pakistani governments, among others, are represented by such missions. It is possible that a full-fledged Pakistani division has been stationed in the kingdom.
3.   Employees of foreign firms involved in Saudi military projects. The greatest number of military-related foreigners working in the kingdom belong in this category. American companies clearly predominate in this sector, employing at least 6,000 United States citizens. French and British number in the hundreds.

The presence of these foreigners poses many problems. Their political role is rather obscure, and one wonders whether their presence is due wholly to Saudi deficiencies. Is this not a mercenary type of force? Will these soldiers be more active in the concrete concerns of internal politics than in the hypothetical defence of the nation's borders? The fact that French gendarmes, and possibly American soldiers, participated in the repression of the Mecca rebellion is no more disputed, and this is only one example among many. One could also question the real role played by the American-manned AWACS stationed in the kingdom since 1980.

Property and wealth

At the birth of the kingdom, 80 percent of what was to become Saudi territory was the property of nomadic tribes. In this pastoral subsistence economy, founded much more on movement than on the settled holding of land, the concept of private property was certainly primitive. Only afterwards did these lands come to be considered the collective property of the tribes who inhabited them in the past; indeed, they were once the source of an unlimited number of intertribal conflicts.

Thirty percent of all cultivated land, notably in the non-Saudi regions of Hijaz and 'Asir, belongs to the private sector. In other cases, inheritance rights are based not on ownership, but on usufruct. Some *miri* lands were given as *iqta'* (fief) to military chiefs who had supported the dynasty, but a decree of 1957 forbids these 'owners' to register their lands without the authorization of the king. Once registered, the land become *mulk* (property), a rare development outside of 'Asir. Other lands belong to tribes or sedentary communities in the east. These are *musha'* lands. *Waqf* (religious land) constitutes close to 10 percent of the cultivated land. Members of the royal family have accumulated fortunes by selling to the state the land they were allocated by this same state.

Table 5.1
Land holdings and cultivated land (in hectares)

Emirate	No. of Villages	No. of Holdings	Total of Cultivated Land
Eastern	111	11,372	6,947
Riyadh, Afif & al-Khasira	374	9,668	35,064
Gassim	284	6,695	21,046
Hail	241	6,645	5,669
Jawf, Qurayyat & Northern Boundaries	95	2,655	597
Medina	264	7,815	2,832
Mecca	2,423	37,000	32,808
Asir	1,317	31,302	11,905
al-Bahah	961	19,534	3,988
Jizan	1,406	34,802	387,066
Majran	71	2,389	3,067
Bisha & Ranyah	258	10,912	13,737
Totals	*7,805*	*180,789*	*524,726*

Source: Saudi Ministry of Planning. *Second Development Plan. 1975–80.* p. 119.

Even more important in the Saudi system of land tenure are the property rights that the state holds over the subsoil. The state appropriated the right to displace entire tribes in order to facilitate the exploitation of mineral wealth. Thus, Ibn Saud initiated oil agreements by simple royal decrees.

The financial structure was dominated after 1952 by the Saudi Arabian Monetary Agency (SAMA). In 1954, the Ministry of Economy and Finance was created to supervise the country's revenues and fiscal activities. The statutes of the Council of Ministers of 1954–58 charged this agency with approving the annual budget published by royal decree. The emergence of these bureaux, along with new ministries of agriculture, commerce, industry, planning and oil, accompanied a net reduction by two-thirds of the sums annually allocated to the princes of the royal family.

Institutionalization of the financial sector continually runs up against the same obstacles encountered by the administration in general – the exclusivity of political power, the personalized division of power among members of the royal family, and the lack of a skilled workforce. No one knows how much money is distributed to members of the royal family under diverse and vague categories. Because the royal family holds the political power, it 'directs and is able to appropriate Saudi national income to itself, and has the last word in the investment policies.'[3] It is estimated that some $300 million is allocated to the princes of the royal family individually, not including the large tracts of land they personally possess. The amount the budget officially allocates to members of the royal family occupying official posts, and which they may spend almost arbitrarily, must be added to this already considerable sum. Habits of easy income and luxurious spending were, however, curtailed in the mid-1980s due to a decline in oil revenues. The necessary readjustments led to tensions within the ruling circles in the kingdom, as well as in the smaller oil countries of the Gulf.

The people of Saudi Arabia

The five million people of Saudi Arabia[4] presently experience the contradictions that naturally arise when an extremely traditional society becomes, almost overnight, intimately linked with the international capitalist system.

Has the tribal nomadic life become a simple memory for the people who came from it? Nomads are now an estimated 6 percent of the population – 'an essentially precarious, nonmonetary, socially-particularized subsistence economy, in the face of a hypermonetary economy based on oil and related only to a small part of the population.'[5] This gap cannot endure indefinitely. Today, the bedouin are 'in a state of cataclysmic transition.'[6] This transformation is not due solely to oil. Greatly fearing the hostility of the cosmopolitan cities, the Saudi regime has, since the beginning, relied on the bedouin. Between 1912 and 1927, Ibn Saud tried to settle a number of them to form the backbone of his troops, the *Ikhwan*. Tribal loyalties were to prove much stronger than the new supra-tribal identity which the regime tried to foster in them, and tribal cleavages were too obvious when the *Ikhwan* rebelled and were defeated by the settled tribes which remained loyal to the king – with some help from the Royal Air Force.

Today, the government seeks to settle all the nomads. The government's intervention seems to have a double aim: to forestall the formation of an urban *lumpenproletariat* which could, sooner or later, pose a threat; at the same time, to take advantage of this potential workforce to stem the tide of immigrant workers. In addition, of course, it is easier to exercise political control over a settled population than over groups perpetually on the move.

The transition to sedentary life is occurring very rapidly, and the government seems incapable of mastering this development, which is largely independent of its will. Communications have had a great deal to do with this transition, which has been speeded up by the collapse of the old desert economy. The nomadic economy is disappearing, while tribal loyalties remain. Yet the regime fears them less than it does the disillusionment and sense of betrayal caused by rapid urbanization. The nomad problem does not disappear with their seden- tarization. It only changes form.

The Saudi regime owes its survival and expansion to the combination of a Najdi thrust and a Wahhabi religious current. This combination of regional and religious expansionism imposed itself through systematic recourse to raiding, war and enforced tribal alliances. Resistance to this political and religious hegemony was considerable. Today that resistance is weaker, due to the political unification of the country, the diffusion of the benefits of oil revenues and, of course, more efficient tools of repression. But the hegemony of the clan in power is not equally accepted with enthusiasm by the whole population. Indeed, the tribal, geographical and religious heterogeneity of the population holds the potential for revolt of a traditional sort.

Tribal factors
The increasingly exorbitant privileges awarded to the members of the royal family and their near relatives are difficult to justify to the rest of the population. They are, first of all, contrary to Islam, especially to the egalitarianism of Hanbali and Wahhabi schools, based on a fundamentalist, literalist interpretation of the Qur'an. Invoked as the exclusive ideology of the state, Islam also does not sanction the practice of hereditary succession, and favours personal aptitude as the criterion for choosing the leadership. Are the Saudi princes thus fit to govern? Or, posing the question differently, are there not other people just as capable outside the Saudi family?[7]

The hegemony and these privileges, moreover, are recent. Only two centuries ago the Sauds were notables in a small oasis of Najd, like so many other families who have since disappeared or who today perpetuate the memories of a 'fief' destroyed by the Sauds. The Shammar, that illustrious tribe of the Arabian north-east, fought against the central power until the 1930s, and had to see their centuries-old *imara* around Ha'il satellized by the Sauds. The Mutayyir of the same region, the Harb of Hijaz, the Baun Khalid of Hassa, the Zahtans of southern Hijaz, and others have been conquered or neutralized by marriages, money, and the commissioning of their chiefs, but they have hardly, in themselves, been broken apart. The experience of *hijra*[8] demonstrated the unrealistic nature of inter-tribal integration schemes, especially in a society where political power is maintained by internal tribal cohesion. The royal family has been content to institute a supra-tribal order that does not profoundly affect traditional alliances and that could one day turn against the royal family itself.[9] One could easily find signs of tribal solidarity in all protest movements known to have occurred in the kingdom, including the 1979 rebellion in Mecca, where a young 'Utaybi succeeded in drawing his brother-in-law (designated as *al-Mahdi*, or the Messiah) and several members of his tribe into a confrontation with the authorities.

Regional factors

Regional heterogenity is no less an issue. In Saudi Arabia everyone is aware that the present power is, essentially, a Najdi power. The names of the provinces have been replaced by geographical terms. The existence of a single bureaucracy and the obvious economic interdependence of the provinces of the country have largely helped diminish provincialism, at least on the political level.

Provincialism has not disappeared and, given favourable circumstances, it could give rise to attempts at secession. All political opposition must be tempted to appeal to this sentiment. Saudi Arabia extends over 1.5 million square kilometres. Between one city and another, one province and another, the emptiness of the desert is often complete. At one time, this emptiness constituted a barrier, if not a boundary. The eastern region, separated by the Nafud, has been historically as intimately connected with Iraq, Bahrain, and even Iran and India, as with the Najd hinterland. In the western part of the country, ever since the emergence of Islam, the cities of Hijaz (Mecca, Medina, and Jeddah) have acquired renown, autonomy, and enviable contacts with the world at large. 'Asir was the locus of the autonomous Idrisi rule, and was marked by a certain way of life and a religious tradition different from that of its Najdi conquerors. Jizan and Najran had much stronger links to Yemen than to Najd. From oil-rich Hassa to commercial Hijaz, through bedouin Najd and the 'bread basket' of 'Asir, the history, traditions, accents and ways of life differ. In fact, they differ radically, especially with the tribal heterogeneity that further increases their specificity. For example, it is now beyond doubt that Hijazi merchants were involved both in the 1969 air force coup attempt as well as in the 1979 Mecca rebellion. To a large extent, Shi'i dissatisfaction with the regime has strong local roots, since it is confined to areas around Qatif which were historically autonomous vis-à-vis the Najd.

Religious factors

It seems likely that dissidents would channel their discontent into a lack of enthusiasm for the Wahhabism that the Najdi conquerors have imposed upon them as a 'state religion', for by no means all Saudis share 'Abd al-Wahhab's interpretation of the Qur'an, more compatible with the traditional customs and harsh life of the Najdi bedouin than with the urban ways of the Hijazi Sunni or the Twelver Shi'a of Hassa. Indeed, the Shi'a, some 200,000 of whom live in the eastern region, will not soon forget the Wahhabi fanaticism which has oppressed them for two centuries, nor their own religious affiliation, which has frequently cost them their lives. This stimulates them to maintain strong ties with the Shi'i centres, such as al-Najaf in southern Iraq, Qum in Iran, or Bahrain, where their co-religionists make up the majority of the population and enjoy a relatively better status.

The Sunnis, although they constitute the overwhelming majority of the population, are by no means unified. Despite the constant pressure of Wahhabism, the four recognized Sunni schools continue to exist in the country. Malekis and Hanafis are numerous in Hassa, while Hijaz and 'Asir respond to Hanbalism – in the Wahhabi version imposed upon them about 50 years ago – through a secular attachment to now Egyptian-centred Shafeism.

These variations would probably mean very little if the fundamentalist Wahhabi doctrine did not appear so inappropriate to the 'spirit of the age' that now chaotically pervades the kingdom. If Islam and modernity are reconcilable, Wahhabism certainly does not offer Islam's most supple or innovative interpretation. On the contrary, it seems to widen the gulf between traditional lifestyles and the new social forces that 'development,' whether chaotic or controlled, inevitably creates. And religious fundamentalism can be a refuge for those who have been left behind by the social and economic evolution of the country, as the events of Mecca have shown. These events have demonstrated that you can be more genuinely Muslim than the rulers in this Muslim country *par excellence*, where ritualistic and official Islam has largely lost its appeal. They have also shown that Hanbali Wahhabism, a politically quietist school of interpretation, could not be overly used to legitimize a status quo power.

Foreign workers

Official figures for 1975 claimed that 314,000 non-Saudis were working in the kingdom. The government anticipated an annual increase of 21 percent over the five following years, to a total of 813,000. This cumulative increase of 159 percent was well above the 18 percent growth in the Saudi labour force.

But these figures cannot be trusted. The 1975 figure was clearly underestimated. Wells thinks it should be doubled to 600,000 foreign workers (against 900,000 nationals), while *Le Monde* puts the figure at one million for the same year.[10] Just a year and a half later, Eric Rouleau made an estimate of 1.5 million. He mentioned the case of an industrialist employing 1,040 workers, of whom only four were Saudi. The Mercedes assembly plant near Jeddah employs no Saudis, except for the chairman; it is managed by 15 West Germans, and employs 250 Turks on the assembly line.[11] Until 1972, a large number of Yemenis were able to enter the kingdom without a passport, and they alone made up approximately one million workers. These individual estimates suggest that the foreign workforce passed the two million mark around 1980–81, far from the official figure of 813,000 foreign workers in 1980.

These figures have enormous impact; the departure of immigrant workers would completely paralyse the country's economy, whether they were the European pilots of Saudi Airlines or the Yemeni port workers. They also constitute a gamble for the future because 'the fate of every attempt at industrialization will depend on the ability of the government to absorb the foreign workers.'[12]

Although the kingdom does not publish precise figures, available information indicates that, in the early 1980s, over one million Yemenis were

Table 5.2
Saudi Arabia: employment by economic sector and nationality, 1975

Sector	Saudi Arabian No.	%	Non-national No.	%	Total	Saudi Arabians' share of all employment %
Agriculture and fishing	530,700	51.7	54,900	7.1	585,600	90.6
Mining and petroleum	15,400	1.5	11,600	1.5	27,000	57.0
Manufacturing	21,550	2.1	94,350	12.2	115,900	18.6
Electricity, gas and water	7,200	0.7	13,150	1.7	20,350	35.4
Construction	35,900	3.5	203,400	26.3	239,300	15.0
Wholesale and retail trade	60,600	5.9	131,500	17.0	192,100	31.5
Transport, storage and communications	72,900	7.1	30,950	4.0	103,850	70.2
Finance and insurance	5,150	0.5	6,950	0.9	12,100	42.6
Community and personal services	277,100	27.0	226,600	29.3	503,700	55.0
Total	1,026,500	100.0	773,400	100.0	1,799,900	57.0

Source: J. S. Birks and C. A. Sinclair. *International Migration and Development in the Arab Region*. International Labour Organization. (Geneva. 1980) p. 160. These figures tend to understate the number and proportion of non-Saudis in the workforce.

employed as unskilled manual labourers; colonies of immigrant Sudanese, Egyptians, Palestinians and Libyans, each ranging from 100,000 to 300,000, work in government offices, schools, or other 'white collar' positions. A large number of Indians, Pakistanis, South Koreans and Malaysians work in occupations as diverse as doctors, technicians, and unskilled manual labourers. Close to 40,000 Americans, and some 20,000 Western Europeans, are engaged in different aspects of modern technology or finance.

Such a large number of non-Saudis constitutes a real danger to the kingdom. Jeddah, the commercial centre of the country, is like Kuwait – approximately 50 percent of its 800,000 inhabitants are foreigners. Large salaries attract foreign workers – an unskilled worker can make at least $5,000 a year. A Sudanese MD is better paid as a nurse in Jeddah than as a surgeon in Khartoum, and an Egyptian unskilled worker in Saudi Arabia can earn a better salary than a cabinet minister in Cairo. Some 2,000 people who entered the country illegally, mostly on the *hajj* pilgrimage, are repatriated every month, and South Koreans who tried to strike were immediately deported.

In an effort to impose restraints on a situation threatening to get out of control, and despite strong opposition from neighbouring countries, the government in March 1976 issued a decree requiring foreign firms with a major contract (involving more than $28.5 million, more than 50 employees and lasting more than three years) to import the necessary workers, provide housing, and guarantee their loyalty. This policy favours Asian firms controlling cheap labour, especially Koreans, which ensure the success of their firms by sending ex-army officers as foremen to maintain order among their nationals. The decline in oil prices and revenues in the mid-1980s is not expected to lead to less reliance on foreign workers, as clearly shown by Roger Owen[13] and others. Unemployment in Europe has not led the French unemployed to replace the Senegalese in clearing the streets, and the observation would be all the more pertinent in a rentier economy like Saudi Arabia where work ethics are very poorly rooted. The decline in oil prices will, however, mean lower pay and more competition as far as the foreign workers themselves are concerned.

Rich and poor

There are important pre-capitalist features in the way wealth is distributed in Saudi Arabia.[14] The most impoverished in Saudi society are the bedouins (settled or nomadic), the non-Saudis (especially Yemenis), and the Saudis who have no access to the ruling clan – no family ties, no community or faith, no ancient nobility capable of selling its support.

Although the present phase of economic growth encourages increasing social mobility, individual success stories are real but too few to be considered a general trend in social mobility. Oil revenues remain in the hands of the state or, to be more precise, in the hands of influential members of the royal family who dominate the state.

Important urban families have infiltrated the state structure and established close ties at the highest levels. Thanks to a system of sponsorship and partnership, this comprador bourgeoisie profitably concentrates on mixed industrial projects with the state, on franchises for the most powerful Western firms and, more recently, on large public works and consulting projects. This symbiosis of the traditional power and the urban bourgeoisie flourishes amid persistent and reciprocal suspicion. It has led to the bourgeoisification of the royal family through the increasingly open involvement of the princes in business.

The relationship is clearly unequal; a prince can become a businessman more easily than a Jeddah merchant can become a minister. This sort of transformation is limited to a small circle difficult to enter for persons outside the royal family, its close allies, or the traditional merchant families of Hijaz or Hadhramawt. The population as a whole remains dependent upon state assistance and is increasingly feeling the effects of the concentration of wealth as an automatic corollary to the concentration of power. Neither under-development nor tribalism, nor a hegemonic religious superstructure can slow down, or even camouflage, the rapid emergence of increasingly distinct social classes. This fact became more evident when, faced with the difficulties of a new era marked by a sharp decline in state revenues, the ruler's appeals for 'economic patriotism' fell on deaf ears among the new comprador class. The large merchants, besides their own difficulties in adapting to the new, more competitive circumstances, were unwilling to invest in long-term projects, like so many of their colleagues across the Third World who have always preferred the safety of Zurich and city banks to investments in their own countries. On the other hand, some of them were reluctant to engage in such a 'patriotism' without receiving concessions from the royal family on the power-sharing issue. Political decision-making is still denied them despite the repeated and as yet (mid-1986) empty promises to give the country a constitution and a non-elected consultative council.

Men/women

The public Saudi society which confronts this colossal transformation is composed almost exclusively of men. Women benefit widely from the new wealth in the form of household appliances and other conveniences now at their disposal, but their voice is never heard in politics or business. A Saudi woman can now obtain a passport in her own name, but she cannot yet travel without a close relative. She cannot drive an automobile, visit a museum, nor with few exceptions, choose her own husband. Although women have been admitted to the University of Riyadh since 1962, they take courses separately through closed-circuit television, and are rarely able to enter professions other than teaching, or nursing in women's hospitals.

The segregation of the sexes is profound. At home, at school, and in the street, the barriers are strictly preserved. The regime has encountered many obstacles in establishing education for women. The first girls' school dates back only to 1960, and the first secondary school to 1969. Traditional groups were firmly opposed to women's education, and they currently frustrate any attempts to introduce women into more active social roles. In 1975, 27,000 women worked in the few areas open to them compared with 1.2 million men in the same professions. The government hoped to bring the number of working women up to 48,000 by 1980 by increasing the number of posts in the fields already reserved for them, rather than by allowing them to enter other sectors such as office work.

The minister of information speaks of the necessity of 'utilizing this enormous potential which would otherwise be a great waste of labour,' but he runs up against the intransigence of traditionalists who insist that the Institute of Public Administration be reserved for men, and who instruct Saudi ambassadors to forbid women students abroad to enrol in the faculties of engineering, education, business, economics and politics out of a 'concern for the preservation of the dignity of women.'

The Saudi woman faces more than the well-known rules of traditional Islam: she faces the precepts of the fanatical Wahhabi sect upon which the legitimacy of the Saudi regime is based. The kingdom which so desperately needs labour absurdly excludes half of its population from public life.

Such discrimination could lead eventually to protests, but more than feminist opposition groups will be needed. The country must wait for the growth of the social and political opposition groups which place the liberalization of mores prominently on their agendas. Such a process would accentuate the dilemma of the regime, since liberalization could not be limited to the domain of morality. The film *Death of a Princess*, by invoking so much controversy has shown the vulnerability of the regime at this point, the revolt of a woman having unveiled the general hypocrisy of the system. Following the Mecca rebellion of 1979, the freedoms and social-professional activities of Saudi women were major casualties in the reassertion of traditional values (notably by Sheikh 'Abd al-Aziz Ibn Baz, the highest religious authority in the country).

The contradictions emerging from the Saudi social transformation have yet to produce marked effects on the evolution of the political regime. The regime's short-term stability is aided by a number of factors: internal cohesion of the family in power, despite clan divisions and princely rivalries; the favourable regional context since the June 1967 war, the demise of Nasser, and the general defeat of Arab nationalist regimes and forces; financial resources more than adequate to fund a policy of appeasement and allegiances, both internally and regionally; Washington's fervid commitment to the regime's survival; an organized and efficient repressive apparatus; the clear majority of Sunni Muslim Arabs (thus avoiding divisions like those of Lebanon, Iraq, Sudan); and the weakness, disorganization and disunity of the opposition.

The political opposition

A royal decree of June 11, 1956 (No. 217/23) imposes a penalty of at least one year in prison for striking, or incitement to strike. The decree of 1961 forbids the profession of any ideology other than Islam, or the formation of political parties. It calls for the execution of anyone who 'engages in violent action against the state or the royal family.' The state completely controls the radio and television media, and films are forbidden. The Ministry of Information was created in 1962 to monitor the press, and a 1964 code drastically restricted the right to start a periodical, and accorded the ministry the right to shut down newspapers and veto editorial candidates or demand their resignation. In 1971 the state established an information agency to feed the media 'selected' material. All this at least partially explains the low profile of political parties and their weakness.

The Saudi Communist Party originated in the National Reform Front, which was founded following the 1953 ARAMCO strike. By 1958, the front no longer satisfied the militants who disagreed with its practices and its reformist title. It became the National Liberation Front. In 1963, the NLF entered the Arab National Liberation Front, associated with the dissident Prince Talal and his brothers. The ANLF's programme sought to transform the country into a constitutional regime and to leave to a referendum the choice between monarchy and republic. The programme also included revision of the agreements with the oil companies and an international policy of active non-alignment, but the ANLF suffered from a very heterogeneous membership, which included, in addition to the four rebel princes, Nasserites, Ba'thists, and Shi'i religious leaders. Nasser, who supported the front, is said to have told its leaders to form a liberation army – a rather unrealistic proposal. The front also had some support from Iraq.

The communists decided it would be more to their advantage to maintain a presence at the heart of the ANLF, while acting autonomously through a secret group formed in Beirut – the Organization of Saudi Communists. The NLF and the OSC disappeared very quickly, and the few Saudi communists who remained used the name of the NLF until August 1974, when the leadership of the front appointed a 'preparatory commission for the first congress of Saudi communists.' The congress took place in August 1975 and adopted several resolutions, including a programme and a change of name to the Communist Party of Saudi Arabia. The congress also elected a central committee, which elected a political bureau and a first secretary.

The tenets of the CPSA do not appear to be very innovative.[15] Internationally, the alignment of the CPSA is unconditionally pro-Soviet: it believes that 'certain symptoms of liberalism are beginning to appear in the superstructure of the quasifeudal and capitalist social system;' it claims to be favourably disposed towards 'a patriotic, democratic and republican regime' which would establish a constitution, guarantee public liberties, parliamentary procedure, and the freedom of political parties and labour unions, institute citizen equality, re-establish diplomatic relations with the USSR, and move towards the nationalization of mineral resources and the industrialization of the country. In spite of its efforts, the party does not seem to have attracted much mass support.

There are innumerable other Saudi opposition groups – all with scant followings – which emerged from the fringes of Arab nationalism and are closely related to the Ba'th party, the Arab Nationalist Movement, or Egyptian Nasserists. The Union of the People of the Arabian Peninsula, founded in 1959 and supported by Cairo, was the most important and the most heterogeneous of these groups. The UPAP, led by Nasir al-Said from the Shammar capital of Hail, defines itself as 'a revolutionary Arab organization, believing in scientific socialism, and struggling to bring down the corrupt monarchy.' The UPAP is committed to the total unification of the Arabian peninsula.[16]

The Socialist Front for the Liberation of the Peninsula was, contrary to its name, a Hijaz group preaching the autonomy of that province. The Democratic Popular Movement constituted a local splinter of the party. There was also the aforementioned Arab National Liberation Front, led by Prince Talal. These groups on the whole experienced very brief lifespans, limited membership and severe repression. In the mid-1980s, Prince Talal was still convinced that 'only democracy and political participation' could lead to real development of the country.

The Organization of the National Revolution, founded by one-time members of the Arab Nationalist Movement, tried to revitalize the opposition towards the end of the 1960s, but without success.[17] The Saudi branch of the Ba'th was founded in 1958. Support from Baghdad from the late 1960s to the mid-1970s gave it the means to spread its views – means which did not accord with its actual strength.[18] An independent Marxist group, the Democratic Popular Party, took over the Democratic Popular Movement and continues to publish *Al-Jazira al-Jadida* irregularly. But the secession and regrouping of part of the group around another publication, *An-Nidal*, has weakened this party.

The Saudi opposition, whether the potential opposition of the new middle class or the organized opposition of this or that political group, cannot expect a substantial change in the situation except through developments largely independent of its will, without which any initiatives appear suicidal. This was clearly shown in the fervently utopian and poorly organized Mecca rebellion in 1979, when the regime, after some confusion, successfully defeated the rebels and hanged 63 of them without visible negative reactions from the population.

The opposition could try to exploit to the fullest the few conflicts within the royal family. The most serious challenges to the regime originated in these conflicts – the Saud–Faisal struggle, Talal's dissidence, the assassination of Faisal in 1975. In the absence of some degree of disaffection in the royal family, it is reasonable to conclude that an alternative to the regime is very difficult to establish.

The Saud family holds an incontestable position – an opening to the population, a martial tradition, secular alliances, modern means of repression, a thorough infiltration of the armed forces. The Saud family, moreover, has developed a system of consensus-making formulae to circumscribe, at least up until now, the consequences of its undoubtedly numerous internal quarrels. The informal consultative assembly of influential princes organized the peaceful transitions which permitted Faisal to dethrone Saud in 1964, Khaled to succeed Faisal in 1975, and Fahd to succeed Khaled in 1982. It is evident that if these formulae were to be weakened or fall apart, the regime could be very seriously threatened. Politics is at least as important among the small constituency of approximately 5,000 Saud princes as it is in the general Saudi constituency.

In this more general framework, it has often been predicted that the new middle class will ask for political power, be denied this power, and consequently be led to topple the regime. This model, although verified in many Third World countries, presupposes different important conditions, such as the existence of a full-fledged civil society, a unified national market, and a certain amount of class consciousness. The Iranian revolution has clearly shown that this model may easily be altered by forces allied to this 'middle class,' but eager to dominate it rather than represent it. In Saudi Arabia it is still difficult to state that this class now exists as such. Hundreds of millionaires living on the fringe of the regime do not make a class, especially when tribal and regional cleavages remain so strong. If an alternative to the regime is to be found, it is more likely to originate in a mixture of grievances made up of political, economic, tribal, and regional frustrations, with possible Arab references and support. But even then, it is going to be difficult to dispense with the monarchy, which has been, to date, the most important factor linking the country. It remains to be demonstrated that the so-called new 'middle-class' can play this unifying role, or is ready to risk its interests in a game which could destabilize the regime to the extent of threatening the country's territorial unity. It is difficult to think of such a development in the foreseeable future, although through careful co-operation a gradual opening to the élites outside the royal family has become inevitable.

Notes

1. An earlier version of this article appeared in *MERIP Reports*, no. 91 (October 1980). Reprinted with permission.

2. Report of the Staff Survey Mission to the US House of Representatives Committee on International Relations. *US Arms Policies in the Persian Gulf and Red Sea Areas* (December 1977) p. 22. In April 1978, the National Guard signed a billion dollar contract with a British firm for an electronic communications system independent of that of the army.

3. J. Malone, *The Arab Lands of Western Asia* (Prentice-Hall, 1973).

4. The figure is hotly disputed; however, experts agree that the kingdom substantially inflates its population figures so as not to be unfavourably compared to neighbouring countries (North Yemen and Iraq), and to veil the crucial role played by foreign manpower in its economy.

5. *Le Monde Diplomatique*, May 1975.

6. M. M. McConohay, special report in *International Herald Tribune* (February 1978) p. 14.

7. The question at least poses itself on the provincial level. In a state otherwise highly centralized, there are no local allies on whom the ruling family can confer local government.

8. *Hijra* – literally 'migration' – refers to the break with the nomadic past which every *Ikhwan* believer must make; in the words of al-Rihani: 'leaving the abode among the unbelievers and moving to the realm of Islam.'

9. The assassin of King Faisal and numerous pro-Iraqi enemies of the king are linked to the Shammar tribes. The Union of People of the Arab Peninsula is also an organization almost exclusively tied to the Shammar tribes.

10. Wells, p. 10; *Le Monde*, June 21, 1975.

11. On January 24, 1977, Senator Mike Mansfield, during his visit to the kingdom, noted that there were as many Yemini workers living there as adult Saudi males.

12. Wells, p. 10. The problem is not new. In the early 1960s an observer noted that 'the Saudi government would not be able to function without oil revenues and technical aid. Without the Egyptians and the Palestinians there would be no administration, and no schools.' A royal decree of August 31, 1954, had stated that 75 percent of a firm's employees must be Saudi. This has clearly remained a dead letter.

13. Roger Owen, *Migrant Workers in the Gulf* (London, Minority Rights Group, 1985).

14. P. Bonnenfant, 'Utilisation des recettes pétrolières et stratégie des groupes sociaux dans la péninsule arabique,' *Machreq-Maghreb* no. 82, pp. 60–69, and no. 83, pp. 61–72.

15. See the documents of the first congress in *Watha'iq al-Mu'tamar al-Awwal 'al-Hizb ash-Shyui fia-Saudia* ('Documents of the first conference of the Saudi Communist Party'), August 1975.

16. Author of a violently harsh, poorly documented, and highly subjective book against the Saudi royal family, Nasir al-Said was successfully kidnapped from his Beirut refuge – reportedly with Palestinian help – into the kingdom where, according to Arab media, he was rapidly executed.

17. See the analysis of the Saudi situation in *al-Hurriya* (Beirut), June 10 and 17, 1968, and H. Lackner, *A House Built on Sand* (London, Ithaca Press, 1978), pp. 98–106.

18. This group enjoyed many hours of air time on Radio Baghdad and published some 20 issues of *Sawt al-Tali'a*. The Saudi branch of the Ba'th was founded in 1958.

6. Class Struggles, the State, and Revolution in Iran

Farideh Farhi

For Iran, as for many other Middle Eastern countries, the 19th century marked the beginnings of economic and social transformation associated with the expansionism of the capitalist West. In contrast to Turkey, Egypt, and Syria, however, the Iranian integration into the world economy came at a relatively slow pace.

Historical background

Several facets of the Iranian socio-political arrangements have been identified as the cause of this gradual integration.[1] First, Iranian geography and its criss-crossing mountain ranges made central control difficult, while the existence of independent nomadic tribes (comprising half the population in 1800 and a quarter as late as 1914) aggravated the situation. Second, although Iranian society was saved from direct control, it nevertheless became an arena of conflict between two great powers: Britain and Czarist Russia. This conflict did not prove to be very conducive to change, as various development schemes proposed by one side were rejected by the other.[2] Finally, the political structure of the country also stifled change. Characterized by a weak and disintegrating central government unable effectively to thwart the challenges from minorities, nomadic tribes, and urban classes, it became increasingly dependent on foreign powers for its survival. Ultimately, the state found itself more interested in survival and domination of civil society than promoting development.

Despite the inhibition of change, social transformation did occur with consequences for the Iranian social structure.[3] The slow incorporation of the Iranian economy into the world capitalist system manifested itself in trade treaties with both Russia and Britain (Commercial Treaty with Russia in 1827, Anglo–Persian Treaty in 1841). With the development of trade, the role of large merchants – dealing in products such as silk, rice, and opium – increased in importance.[4] There were other social groupings that also benefited from this foreign trade: landowners involved in cash crop production for export, money-lenders in an increasingly monetized society, and the bureaucrats and members of the court and royal family who always managed to find personal use for foreign loans. Many members of intermediate classes were negatively affected by foreign trade, however. The old petty bourgeoisie – smaller merchants and artisans traditionally organized in self-regulating guilds of the bazaars – were especially hurt by the encroachment of foreign trade. The importation of British textiles began to undermine Persian handicraft production, for example.[5]

This increasing foreign penetration of the economy, therefore, set the stage for a series of confrontations between the old petty bourgeoisie aided by the Islamic clerical leaders (*ulama*) and the Qajar dynasty, which culminated in the Constitutional Revolution of 1905. In this confrontation, the religious community was particularly instrumental as Islam became a voice against Western penetration. The alliance between the old petty bourgeoisie and the *ulama* has been a recurrent theme in Iranian history. It essentially arises from their close integration, which includes financial support for mosques and religious schools by the bazaris in return for commercial adjudication and religious schooling on the part of the *ulama*. Secular forces (mainly intelligentsia), however, were also quite effective as the revolutionary coalition was forged in response to a corrupt central government with ominous ties to foreign powers. Accordingly, the constitutional document that resulted in 1906 limited the power of the Court, and granted representation in the parliament (*Majlis*) to the social groupings that participated in the revolution.[6] Despite cosmetic changes, however, the power structure did not really change. Neither of the foreign rivals found the extensive mobilization much to their liking. By 1907, the country was effectively divided into spheres of influence (Britain in the south, Russia in the north), with a neutral zone across the centre to be ruled by a new monarchy. Despite impressive opposition which deposed the Shah, the Qajar dynasty was ultimately saved by the military intervention of Russian forces in 1911.

The following ten years were essentially characterized by internal factionalism and disruptions associated with World War I. The major event, however, was the Russian Revolution of 1917, which removed from the Iranian scene a major power contender and the main supporter of the Qajar dynasty. Amidst internal confusion and the outbreak of local rebellions in Gilan, Azarbaijan, and Khorasan, a colonel from the Russian-instituted Cossack Brigade by the name of Reza Khan rose to power. It is generally admitted that the Khan's rise to power was backed by the British, who found themselves in a situation of sole dominance after the Russian withdrawal.

Reza Khan's tenure as the founder of the Pahlavi dynasty (1926–41) marked a new era in Iranian history.[7] His reign was the most concentrated period of political centralization and economic development that Iran had yet experienced. This was made possible by the creation of a modern state that no longer rested 'on the sands of tribal contingents and communal manipulations, but on three stone pillars of a standing army, a modern bureaucracy, and extensive court patronage.'[8] This modern state was far from being a mere agent of the owners of capital in Iran. The national bourgeoisie was too weak to exercise such a domination over the society or the state.[9] Given this weakness, the state became the principal agency through which the dominance of the capitalist mode was established. It assumed the role of organizing relationships among various propertied classes, and mediating between those classes and the propertied classes in advanced capitalist countries.[10]

This newly acquired role of the state was very significant in terms of both class formation and capital accumulation. In terms of the latter, under Reza Shah, Iran witnessed the emergence of the structure of an interventionist state. Attempts were made to encourage a small private industrialization programme financed mainly through tariffs, taxes, and small oil revenues. The state also built railways and roads, and established the first institution of higher learning.[11] The state's efforts to build the infrastructure and to promote private industries were, however, inhibited by meagre resources largely caused by Reza Shah's unwillingness to attack the structure of agrarian relations.[12]

Nevertheless, by creating the seeds of an interventionist state, Reza Shah was able to transform the Iranian social structure. The powerful bureaucracy and military created an important social grouping independent of traditional power contenders. Also associated with the rise of state and industrialization policies, a new group of professionals – lawyers, judges, doctors, engineers, and teachers – joined the ranks of the intermediate classes. State-sponsored industrialization also gave rise to an important industrial working class. On the other hand, there were consistent attacks against the traditional intermediate classes associated with the bazaar. These also included attacks on the religious community which, as mentioned, had always been closely integrated in the bazaar's structure. Perhaps the most successful effort was directed against the nomadic tribes whose leadership was greatly weakened. Finally, while the landlords retained their local power and wealth, their composition changed. Large land-ownership was legitimized and encouraged, while small landholders were stripped of their land as their holdings were confiscated by Reza Shah and other large landlords.[13]

In short, Reza Shah set the stage for full-fledged capitalist development under the guidance of a centralized state; however, World War II interrupted his effort. His alleged opposition to the Allies' desire to send supplies to the Russian front gave the Allies the pretext to invade Iran in August 1941. Reza Shah was forced into exile, and his son, Mohammad Reza, became the Shah. The post-war task of rebuilding the economy and reasserting Pahlavi dominance was a formidable one. The Allied invasion had discredited the Pahlavi dynasty, and this had unleashed social forces – already festering under Reza Shah's dictatorial rule – which were quite difficult for the young, inexperienced Shah to control. Indeed, the next thirteen years were marked by tremendous turbulence that constituted the underlying dynamics of change for years to come.

Nationalist interlude and class struggles

With the collapse of Reza Shah's autocracy, Iran entered one of the most agitated periods in its political history. The stage was set by the occupation of

Allied forces, which weakened the regime and at the same time afforded liberties to the opposition forces.[14] Attention focused on a nationally based and highly ideological communist movement committed to mass mobilization. The Tudeh Party, which spearheaded this movement, was formed in 1941. In an excellent analysis of the class bases of the Tudeh Party, Abrahamian credits the modern intermediate class (which included professionals, intellectuals, and salaried personnel) with forming 'the major proportion of the party's top, middle, and lower echelons.'[15] The intriguing question is why the modern intermediate class was attracted to a party that openly questioned bourgeois values and existence. Abrahamian's answer is very instructive:

> The Tudeh's attraction for the intelligentsia resulted chiefly from the country's class structure. In the eyes of the intelligentsia . . . the destruction of Reza Shah's autocracy had heralded not a true democracy but a corrupt oligarchy of feudal landlords, tribal magnates, robber barons, grasping courtiers and dangerous generals. Moreover, the snobbish attitudes of the traditional upper class irritated the modern middle class.[16]

Accordingly, the Tudeh Party, as the only real organized challenger to this oligarchical dominance, and not as a harbinger of communism, became the platform from which some members of the modern intermediate class attempted to change the dominant structure. This can also explain why the Tudeh Party even managed a foothold within the Iranian military.

The Tudeh Party's most important constituency, however, was the industrial working class. Since the turn of the century, the Iranian industrial workforce had been growing steadily. This growth reflected not only the increasing importance of oil production, but also the industrialization policies followed by Reza Shah in the previous two decades.[17] The post-war relaxation of political control, high inflation rates, and labour shortages created a fertile ground for unionization.[18] Not surprisingly, most of the experienced labour organizers were from the top echelons of the Tudeh Party.[19] Between 1944 and 1946, the Central Council of the Federated Trade Unions of Iranian Workers and Toilers (CCFTU) led many major strikes, and pressured the government into decreeing a new progressive labour law which promised to set minimum wages, control local food prices, abolish child labour, and to limit the work day to eight hours.[20]

The rise of the Tudeh Party and the trade union movement also coincided with organized minority movements seeking autonomy from the central government. In 1945–46, two autonomous administrations were set up in Azarbaijan and Kurdistan with the support of the Soviet Red Army, which occupied these areas. These experiments in autonomous rule came to an abrupt halt as the realities of great-power rivalry, set within the context of the emerging Cold War, exerted themselves. Due to pressures from the United States and Iranian pledges for a joint Iranian–Soviet oil company, the Soviet Union pulled its troops out, thereby abandoning the Azarbaijani and Kurdish republics to destruction by the Shah's army. The defeat of the two republics proved disastrous for the entire communist movement. A rejuvenated central government, buttressed by improved economic conditions, slowly pushed the communist movement onto the defensive.[21] The Tudeh Party was declared illegal after an assassination attempt against the Shah in 1949. Martial law was declared in the hope that the Shah could start to consolidate his power.

The temporary taming of the Tudeh Party did not signal stability in Iranian politics. As mentioned earlier, the Tudeh Party spearheaded an extensive mass mobilization effort.[22] Opposition to the Pahlavi regime and its Western supporters was not limited to the lower ranks of the society, however. During this period, Iranian politics were also characterized by considerable dissension between the Pahlavi regime and the intermediate classes. The context of this conflict harked back to the disagreements that characterized the Constitutional Revolution: constitutionalism and nationalism.[23] Once again, the monopoly of power by the monarchy and its relationship to foreign powers was at stake. Lacking the mass base which characterized the Tudeh Party, the nationalist and constitutionalist politicians staged their fight to revive the 1906 constitution from the Majlis. Hence, in this period Iranian politics also became characterized by constant manoeuvring between the Majlis and the Court. Lack of organization prevented the nationalist forces from presenting a unified front against the Shah's increasing power. The declaration of martial law and the subsequent arrest of nationalist leaders in 1949, however, set the basis for the emergence of the National Front under the leadership of Dr Mohammad Mossadeq.[24]

As a united force, the front continued its challenge of the monarchy, as well as its objections to imperialist encroachments. The issue of the nationalization of the Anglo-Iranian Oil Company epitomized both of the above struggles. Iran had given the earliest oil concession in the Middle East to a British national in 1901. The discovery of oil in 1908 and the British Navy's conversion from coal to oil induced the British government to buy the majority of shares in the Anglo-Persian Oil Company – Anglo-Iranian after 1935, now British Petroleum.[25] The ownership of Iranian oil by foreign powers had always been problematic to the nationalist forces. This foreign ownership meant a determination of Iranian income by the needs of outside forces, in addition to low revenues for the Iranian government. The patently exploitative nature of this foreign extraction was reflected in the fact that the Iranian government received only 16 percent of the company's *net* profit (allowing the Anglo-Persian Oil Company to deduct income taxes paid to the British government from gross profits) until 1933. The 1933 agreement, negotiated by Reza Shah, replaced the old 16 percent formula by a flat royalty rate of four shillings to be paid to the Iranian government for every ton of oil sold in Iran or exported. The tangible results, in terms of financial gains, were not much better, however. Of course, meagre revenues for the Iranian government do not reflect the amount of Iranian oil that was furnished to the British admiralty at a very low price for 40 years.[26]

It is, therefore, not surprising that the oil concessions became a sensitive nationalist issue; they also created a platform from which to attack

Mohammad Reza Shah's increasing power. This became possible because of his refusal to challenge Britain on the oil issue. Accordingly, once the leader of the oil protest movement, Mohammad Mossadeq, became prime minister in 1951, he began to challenge the Shah's authority.[27] The Iranian oil industry was nationalized a few months later; however, the triumph of nationalist forces was shortlived. The nationalization of the Iranian oil industry led to the closing of the oil refinery, the withdrawal of all British technicians, an embargo on parts and equipment needed to maintain oil facilities, and an almost universal shipping boycott of Iranian oil. As the fiscal situation deteriorated, Mossadeq found it difficult to keep his National Front coalition together. Ultimately, Mossadeq was overthrown 'by a coalition of forces within and outside Iran – just as the Constitutional Revolution had been.'[28]

Clearly, on the most general level, Mossadeq's ousting was made likely within the context of what Hamza Alavi has called the 'structural imperative' of peripheral capitalism.[29] This notion essentially allows for actions of a capitalist state to be out of line with the logic of the international capitalist economy and its objective needs. Such deviations cannot, however, continue without negative consequences for the state which promulgates such an action. The economic dislocations that ensued after nationalization were directly linked to this structural imperative. In this sense, it was not at all surprising that international capital's boycott of Iranian oil was terminated once the reinstated Mohammad Reza Shah corrected the previous policy and allowed the logic of the international capitalist economy to reimpose itself upon state policy.[30]

While the structural imperative set the stage for the downfall of Mossadeq, it was the internal class struggle that ultimately finished him. Mossadeq's social base had always been organized around contradictory interests. The deteriorating economic conditions amplified these contradictory interests and undermined Mossadeq's original base of support. The major split was between the parties representing the old petty bourgeoisie, led by the *ulama*, and the secular parties representing the modern intermediate class and the national bourgeoisie. Disagreements led to defections of the parties representing the bazaar. The revival of the Tudeh Party in 1950 also proved problematic.[31] The nationalist forces had always had a tenuous relationship with the Tudeh Party; while they both essentially agreed on their dislike of royalty, they were clearly incompatible in their social bases and their vision of the future. Mutual suspicions led to inconsistent policies on the part of both sides. On the one hand, the revived Tudeh became much more confrontational and held mass meetings to demand higher wages and protest against government restrictions. On the other hand, Mossadeq, while allowing the front organizations and demonstrations to continue, refused to form a broad alliance with the Tudeh to prevent a royalist military coup. Rejected by Mossadeq, the Tudeh failed to act against the US-backed military coup.[32] The coup was a severe blow to both nationalist and communist forces, as the reinstated Shah pursued an effective campaign against all nationalist leaders and the Tudeh organization. Ironically, but perhaps not surprisingly, the coalescence of contradictory interests to undermine a foreign-based state had once again given rise to a much stronger state. which owed its survival to US assistance and was even more intent on dominating society.

Return of the Shah and the politics of uneven development

The 1953 coup was a watershed in modern Iranian history. When Mohammad Reza Shah returned to the country, few guessed how dominant a leader he would become. The road to the Shah's consolidation of power had already been paved by the increasing presence of the United States, however. The United States government was not only implicated in the coup itself, it had set the stage for the emergence of one-man rule in the years prior to Mossadeq's downfall.[33] Furthermore, it continued to remain the backbone of the regime, militarily and financially.

The build up of US presence in Iran had been underway since the war; its military aid was especially noticeable in the reorganization of the Iranian army. After a short suspension of aid during the Mossadeq era, Eisenhower showered Iran with emergency financial aid and technical assistance. Under the direct supervision of the CIA and other security advisers from the United States, a new secret police named SAVAK (the National Security and Information Organization) was established in 1957. In 1959, a bilateral military treaty directly committed the United States to the defence of Iran. With American military aid (approximately $500 million between 1953 and 1963), together with substantial oil revenues resulting from the ending of the oil dispute with Britain,[34] the Shah was able to expand the armed forces from 120,000 men to over 200,000 by 1963. The annual military budget also rose from $80 million in 1953 to nearly $183 million in 1963.[35]

Despite solid support from the outside, the Shah's state did not emerge as a dominant and independent entity that pulverized society until 1963. In the interim, the question of internal class conflict had to be settled. Empowered with a new, sophisticated secret police, the Shah moved decisively against the working class and intellectuals. After a series of arrests from 1953 to 1958, the Tudeh Party was effectively neutralized. The SAVAK also repressed strikes, helped the creation of state-dominated unions, and expanded its network to monitor recruitment into the civil service, the universities, and the large industrial plants.

The Shah's reaction to the *bazaari* and landed classes was much more cautious. After all, as the National Front disintegrated a substantial segment of the *ulama*, allied with the merchants and landlords, supported the Shah, and the landed interests had never found the National Front's attempts to introduce land reform much to their liking. The Shah, therefore, paid lip service to Islam, and the Majlis continued to be dominated by the landed class. But. the 'dual policy of wooing the traditional classes and tightening control over the modern classes was suddenly disrupted in 1960–1963 by an acute economic crisis and by American pressures for land reform.'[36] The severe economic crisis antagonized the *bazaari* and working classes, who were adversely affected by the recession. Once again, the number of strikes increased. The severe economic crisis coincided with a change of administration in the United States. The Kennedy administration was intent on taking a more active posture in the pursuit of capitalist development in the Third World. As in programmes pursued under the auspices of the Alliance for Progress in Latin America, the break-up of the traditional system of land tenure was felt to be necessary for the vitality of capitalist economies in the Third World. The problem was seen from the point of view of inefficiency. Not only was rural output inadequate, but there remained intact a semi-feudal rural social structure which prevented the integration of the rural masses into the modern capitalist economy. It was imperative, therefore, that the government break up large estates, encourage more efficient land utilization, and bring the rural poor into the marketplace as producers and consumers.

The above thinking conformed with that of the progressive modernizers inside Iran. These elements were critical of the Shah, but initially found themselves supported by the Shah, whose interests lay elsewhere. Emerging from a period of intense power struggle, the Shah was now more secure in attacking the landed interests and pursuing a full-fledged capitalist model.[37] He was, however, also interested in land distribution as a policy which would enhance the power of the central government, in addition to generating political support.[38] In regard to the latter, the Shah hoped to placate the progressive modernizers by championing various social reforms which had been advocated by the National Front and others. He appointed a strong reform cabinet, headed by Dr Ali Amini, to promulgate a package of reforms, which included expansion in social services and education, extension of suffrage to women, and land reform, aggregately coined the 'White Revolution'.

The Land Reform Law of 1962 was the centrepiece of the White Revolution and significantly altered the economic structure of the countryside. The reform, which had three phases, limited landlords (in the Iranian case, largely absentee) to the ownership of only one village, while subjecting the rest of their holdings to redistribution.[39] The reform did not, and was not intended to, eliminate absentee ownership of agricultural land. It did, however, accomplish as intended the objective of reducing the power and influence of large landlords. Thus, by 1971 (the year land reform officially ended), the great and powerful landlords had virtually disappeared, but tens of thousands of smaller absentee owners continued to thrive.[40] On the other hand, the land reform did not redistribute land to traditional agricultural workers on the grounds that there was too little land to go around. Given the increasing mechanization of agriculture, this created a problem, as many agricultural labourers moved to the cities in search of jobs. The land reform did enable the overwhelming majority of peasants holding traditional cultivation rights (*nasagdars*) to become peasant proprietors. Unequal distribution of land, however, created a situation where a minority of peasants acquiring larger portions of land (new rural bourgeoisie) continued to exploit the majority of villagers comprised of subsistence peasant farmers and landless rural workers. In short, no radical restructuring of traditional relationships in the countryside was intended or achieved. From the state's point of view, the effects were positive, as government control of the countryside was enhanced; however, the long-term economic results were not as auspicious.

While the new social reforms ultimately assured the Shah's consolidation of power, the immediate response by various social forces was not very favourable. Sensing his complete consolidation of power, the Shah had already replaced the reformist cabinet of Amini with his own loyal supporters and was ready to tackle the opposition head-on. The opposition from landed interests was not very formidable, since larger landowners were given options to reintegrate these holdings into more favourable industrial or commercial projects, while smaller landlords were not undermined by the reforms. Opposition from the bazaar, the merchants, and the religious community was a different matter. Foretelling the increasing encroachment of the state to regulate private enterprise and commerce, in addition to religious activities, these social groupings reacted vehemently. Street demonstrations were held and objections raised to issues varying from land reform to female suffrage. The regime reacted with force. Many of the senior *ulama* were arrested, and a consequential future religious leader, Ayatollah Khomeini, was exiled. Ultimately, in a bloody showdown, the bazaar crowds were also tamed by the army. In short, the opposition was effectively defeated and the Iranian state was able to shake itself loose of class conflicts within the civil society. Presumably it could now dominate the existing social forces in its pursuit of new social and economic programmes.

The economic policy promoted in Iran foresaw the use of revenues generated from oil production to oversee a gradual expansion of Iranian industry. The assumption was that the internal market for Iranian products would grow as oil revenue 'trickled down' to the masses. In short, the idea was to use oil to diversify and develop industry and agriculture in such a manner as to make Iran ultimately independent of oil. This over-reliance on oil as the backbone of the economy had ironic results, however. While it promoted growth, it inhibited the intended consequence of growth: the reduction of the over-dependence of the country on one export product. In fact, the opposite occurred. Iran became increasingly dependent on oil, which represented 17 percent of the GNP in 1967–68, and 38 percent in 1977–78. In the latter years, it accounted for 77 percent of government revenue and 87 percent of foreign exchange earnings.[41] The reasons for this were multifaceted and entailed a combination of constraints imposed by the nature of oil as a commodity, and misguided policies pursued by a corruption-ridden state apparatus.

The oil industry, in general, does not contribute to the promotion of balanced growth in any underdeveloped country. Its capital-intensive nature means that thousands of dollars of capital must be invested in order to generate jobs. Furthermore, oil production is not conducive to industrial development by itself, as most technology and capital come from abroad. It does provide the much-needed foreign exchange for the government but, as many observers have pointed out, the actual spur for development depends on how the government disposes of that foreign exchange, or what some have called economic rent.[42] Unfortunately for the Iranian people, the economic policies pursued, despite superficial flashes of success, were inherently flawed and fragile.

The industrial policy promoted was based on import substitution (IS) for the newly generated internal market.[43] Like so many other underdeveloped countries, Iran used IS to encourage the establishment and growth of manufacturing firms producing goods which had previously been imported from abroad. High tariffs and import licensing were designed to give Iranian entrepreneurs, and increasingly their foreign partners, a strong competitive edge over foreign firms producing the same goods. At the same time, the government used internal licensing to restrict the amount of internal competition with which a new producer must contend. Unlike most other underdeveloped countries, however, the Iranian IS was originally geared towards the internal market. Most other countries who rely on IS promote manufacturing exports in order to pay for a proportion of their imports of capital and intermediate goods, which are in turn necessary for the continuation of IS. This was, of course, rendered unnecessary in the Iranian case, due to the reliance on oil exports. Oil exports made the progress of IS much more real. In fact, given the increasing revenues derived from the skyrocketing price of oil,[44] progress was so favourable that it allowed Iran to switch from import substitution of light industry to export promotion and the development of heavy industry (eg., steel, heavy metal plants, aluminium smelters, and petro-chemicals).[45] Plans were made for the exploration of the world's second largest known reserves of natural gas, for copper mining and processing, for car and other machine manufacturing industries, and for nuclear plants.

The realization of the projected policy of export promotion encountered many obstacles, however. First, these projections continued to depend on the uncertainties of the world market. While Iran benefited from the quadrupling of oil prices in 1973–74, she also suffered from the reduced demand for oil in the 1975–76 recession.[46] Second, the production processes of the fastest-growing sectors usually consisted of the assembly of imported parts, rather than manufactured components. In addition, given the high protective tariffs, these assembly plants were marred by inefficiency. Third, whatever was manufactured was likely to be consumed at home, due to the purchasing power generated by the petrodollars. The domestic demand was so high that the Iranian infrastructure (port facilities, roads, etc.) could not even handle the flow of Western merchandise to Tehran. Thus, the ambitious economic plan not only failed to strengthen exports, but conversely led to massive increases in imports. In turn, the growing dependency on imports created severe shortages and brought the economy to a standstill. Fourth, the Shah's obsession with military matters led him to invest more in foreign supplied armaments – the largest single increase in imports – than in domestic industry. Fifth, the inflation that accompanied the massive inflow of petrodollars diverted a significant part of accumulated money capital away from industry into real estate speculation, usury and hoarding. Finally, the whole situation was aggravated by extensive corruption (prevalent among the royal family and the cumbersome bureaucracy) which is bound to flourish in an environment that promotes personal profiteering.[47]

The prospect for agriculture was even more bleak. The change towards mechanized agriculture was not even satisfactory in terms of food production as internal demand for foodstuffs soared. Agricultural output increases (2 to 3 percent annually) could not keep up with the increasing demands generated by petrodollars, and it fell behind population increases (3 percent annually). Foodstuffs, therefore, became another source of imports and a drain on the much-needed petrodollars.

The uneven sectoral and regional development of productive forces created political tensions which were heightened by the oil boom. The sudden five-fold increase spurred the regime to make promises and claims, which in turn expanded the expectations of the people. At the same time, the oil-based prosperity made the regime much more confident in its attacks against the traditional economy represented by the bazaar. The regime extended its authority through price control, anti-profiteering campaigns, and the imposition of a state-sponsored guild to oversee all bazaar guilds. The regime even proposed the construction of an eight-lane highway directly through the Tehran bazaar. These attacks and the regime's proclamations (eg., that it would become the world's fifth industrial power, as the Shah used to say), which were clearly unreasonable, angered many and began to clash with the people's heightened expectations, as the world recession reduced the demand for oil and thus occasioned drastic cuts in Iranian foreign exchange receipts. In other words, the economic crisis of the mid-1970s accentuated the inherent contradictions of uneven development in Iran and set the stage for one of the most extensive anti-government mass mobilizations recorded in history. The underlying economic conditions cannot, by themselves, however, explain the organized opposition and the eventual collapse of the Pahlavi regime. Similar conditions have existed, and continue to exist, throughout the underdeveloped world, yet revolutions are rare phenomena. In order to understand the Iranian Revolution, we need to look at the nature of the state and how it interacted with social classes. The understanding of this interaction will also shed light on the revolutionary conjuncture which made oppositional politics possible.

The state and revolution

For more than a decade (1963–76), the Iranian state, personified by Mohammad Reza Pahlavi, dominated Iranian society. This was done through an elaborate repressive machinery and unprecedentedly large sums of money to buy off potential competitors. The abrogation of political rights, which included actions ranging from torture of dissidents by SAVAK to emasculation of parliament and the judiciary, helped Iran avoid some of the instabilities of other underdeveloped countries, and surely smoothed the path to economic growth, but it left the Shah without means for absorbing and deflecting popular protest. The Shah, as the personification of the state, and the SAVAK became perceived as the major sources of tribulation. The straw that broke the camel's back was the creation of the Resurgence Party (*Hizb-i Rastakhiz*) and the announcement of a one-party system in 1975. The previous two-party system was indeed a farce, but the negative proclamations in regard to the reluctance of many people to join further antagonized what might have been a loyal opposition.[48]

The Resurgence Party confirmed once again that the Shah would not tolerate political independence on the part of the high-ranking civilian leaders. Every decision had to be sanctioned from the top. This extreme centralization of the Shah's rule proved to be inefficient in coping with the huge increase in administrative demands created by the oil boom. The Shah's conscious refusal to delegate authority created fear and resentment among various bureaucracies unable to respond to the innumerable problems that suddenly faced them. This problem was evident even in the armed forces. Since the armed forces were the mainstay of the Shah's rule, he became almost paranoid about their loyalty. Financial rewards, in addition to opportunities for graft, assured the officers' dependence on the regime. Moreover, the Shah controlled military recruitment, personally approved important promotions, and regulated the size and organization of the armed forces. At the same time, fearing military collusion against him, he juggled commands, exposed those granted opportunities for graft, and then expelled them on charges of corruption. This kind of control over the military was very consequential in the armed forces' eventual unwillingness to continue repression or to carry out a coup once the Shah's position had weakened. Lacking any independent identity, the armed forces were unable to displace the Shah and save the state at his expense. As in other revolutions, this lack of direction on the part of the repressive machinery allowed a widespread popular resentment to become mobilized and explode into the Iranian political scene.

The Iranian revolutionary struggle was by far the most popular and broad-based agitation in modern history. Several special characteristics distinguished it from other successful revolutionary movements (with the possible exception of the revolutionary movement in Nicaragua). First, it was predominantly urban in composition. Many of those who participated in the struggle may have been of rural origin, but it was an urban event. Second, this overwhelmingly urban characteristic affected the means of confronting the regime – political confrontation as opposed to armed conflict – until at least the last stages of revolutionary confrontation. The general strike, which lasted more than six months, was extremely effective in unravelling a highly repressive and militarized regime. Finally, the events that culminated in the 1979 revolution were characterized by an almost unprecedented spontaneous, and amazingly rapid, forging of diverse social groupings. No political party or group commenced the uprisings. Most of the organizations (e.g., Revolutionary Guards and Islamic Republic Party) that came to dominate post-revolutionary politics were created after the fall of the Shah.[49] The participants in the revolutionary struggle came from different backgrounds, employed different tactics, and had different agenda for the future.

The earliest organized opposition to the Shah's post-1963 regime can be traced back to the guerrilla activities which began to germinate in the early 1970s. Two guerrilla organizations were especially troublesome for the regime as they embarked upon a series of largely ineffectual, but nevertheless well-publicized attacks on government and foreign properties and officials. The *Sazman-i Mujahedin-i Khalq*, usually known as the Mujahedin, was Islamic in orientation,[50] while *Sazman-i Cherikha-yi Feda'i Khalq*, generally referred to as the Fedaiyan, had a definite penchant for Marxism. The recruiters for both organizations were mostly drawn from the young generation of the intelligentsia.[51] The Mujahedin, however, came mostly from the lower ranks of the old petty bourgeois families, while the Fedaiyan were largely drawn from the offspring of the salaried professional intermediate class. These groups, due to their underground organizations which were equipped with publishing facilities and weapons, proved to be important in the last days of the revolutionary uprising, as they staged successful attacks on police stations and the barracks of the Imperial Guards. They also remained forces to be reckoned with in the post-revolutionary period, since they continued to be heavily armed.

In their armed uprising against the state, the Mujahedin and the Fedaiyan were joined by the once again rejuvenated Tudeh Party. While the Tudeh was effectively subdued inside Iran, after the 1950s it continued to survive abroad. Before its re-emergence, its exiled members had re-evaluated their earlier position in regard to the National Front and Mossadeq. They admitted their mistake and concluded that, as a representative of the national interest and as a force against imperialism, Mossadeq should have been supported. The evaluation was very consequential in Tudeh's later persistent support for the Islamic Republic and clerical rule.

Another rejuvenated organization was the National Front, which in late 1954 had re-emerged under the new name of the National Resistance Movement (*Nehzat-i Moqavemat-i Melli*). This movement continued to encompass diverse political orientations ranging from moderate socialist to moderate Islamic. Mehdi Bazargan, the post-revolutionary provisional prime minister, was a prominent member of the movement, and his religious tendencies were helpful in establishing close links with Ayatollah Khomeini. Along with Ayatollah Taleqani, a popular and progressive religious leader, Bazargan also created the Iran Freedom Movement (*Nehzat-i Azad-i Iran*). This movement was quite effective in bridging the deep chasm between the religiously inspired opposition and the secular reformers. The diversions between these two world views had been instrumental in reinvigorating the monarchy in 1953. Their alliance was, therefore, necessary to undermine the monarchy. The immediate post-revolutionary period reflected this alliance as many of the Freedom Movement's members (e.g., Bazargan, Bani Sadr, and Sadeq Qotbzadeh) rose to political prominence.

Finally, the clerical opposition to the regime was also diverse in composition and political outlook. There is no doubt that Ayatollah Khomeini's adamant opposition to the Shah ultimately made him the leader of the religious community and the revolutionary movement in general. His interpretation of Islam was not necessarily dominant, however. Unlike many religious leaders, Khomeini envisioned a society in which the Islamic clerical leaders (*ulama*) would actually gain control of the state, and interpret and implement the Islamic laws (*Shari'a*). Other religious leaders, like Ayatollah Shariatmadari, were mostly interested in reforming a clearly repressive political institution, but not necessarily controlling it. Yet others were mostly apolitical but ultimately became dissatisfied when the regime started to attack the bazaar and religious institutions.

Neither was the religious community monolithic in regards to its economic outlook. Given the strong financial links between the bazaar and the religious community, it was no surprise that Islam once again provided the ideological leadership for the *bazaari* elements. On the other hand, the merchants, wholesale traders and shopkeepers of the bazaars exerted a moderating influence on the economic outlook of the *ulama*. In fact, one of the basic reasons for the harmony between the bazaar and the *ulama* has been the fact that Shi'a Islam has never questioned the sanctity of private property and ownership. A much more radical version of Shi'a Islam, however, was germinating among the lower ranks of the religious hierarchy and among the youth of the intermediate and lower classes. The Islamic Mujahedin was a reflection of this radicalization. Influenced by the works of Ali Shariati, they shunned an ossified version of Islam based on inaction. Shariati himself was very critical of the established *ulama* for retaining monopolistic control over the Islamic scriptures. He called for a revolutionary version of Shi'a Islam that was based on equity, brotherhood and public ownership of property.

Despite the variety of social regimes and diversity of social and political outlooks, all these political forces coalesced under the leadership of Ayatollah Khomeini and a generalized version of Islam. This was made possible because all these forces had one thing in common: opposition to an increasingly corrupt, exclusionary, repressive, and seemingly anti-national state. The Islamic ideology was important insofar as it was a response to changing social and economic conditions, and gave form to already existing grievances against a foreign-dominated, repressive state. In this sense, Islam was a statement of Iranian nationalism. Islam was, of course, also important at the level of culture. As a value system already embedded in the traditional social structure, it became an important source of resistance to the dominant ideology disseminated by the Westernizing Shah and his presumed Western masters.

Islam was even more important on the organizational level. The traditional network and organization that existed for religious meetings and ritual celebrations of key Islamic holy days proved to be indispensable vehicles for mobilizing the masses against the regime. Of course, these were complemented with strikes by private and public sector employees. The oil workers' strike was especially devastating to the regime, as it incapacitated other industries and disrupted daily life in the urban areas. Nevertheless, without Islam's collective organizational capacities and the autonomous resources (mostly furnished through the bazaar), the co-ordination among various groups would have been impossible, and popular resistance could not have been sustained.

Finally, Islam was important because it was able to offer a charismatic leader behind whom all oppositional forces could close ranks. Khomeini's adamant refusal to compromise persuaded many National Front leaders not to compromise with the Shah when he was ready to do so. Khomeini's adamant posture also brought down the government of Shahpour Bakhtiar – the National Front leader who did compromise in exchange for the Shah leaving the country.[52] As has been the case with a number of other revolutions, however, Khomeini's charisma was not sufficient to keep the united opposition together after the common enemy was finally defeated.

Post-revolutionary struggles and the rise of the theocratic state

Like other great revolutions, the Iranian Revolution was marked by a power struggle among the divergent interests that had coalesced earlier against a common enemy. The struggle was resolved in favour of the fundamentalist clergy and their political arm: the Islamic Republic Party (IRP). The human costs of this power struggle were extremely high. The political repression that ensued effectively disintegrated, or forced into exile, the moderate forces such as the National Front and Freedom Movement. More brutal was the way the regime dealt with national and ethnic minorities (such as Kurds) and the leftist (both secular and Islamic) organizations, such as the Mujahedin, who lost thousands of militants in a bloody wave of killings.

The immediate post-revolutionary discord resulted from the struggle for power among the representatives of various intermediate classes. As discussed above, the intermediate classes spearheaded the movement that overthrew the Shah. The post-revolutionary conflict occurred as different intermediate classes vied for hegemony over the lower classes. The state apparatus was originally dominated by moderate forces representing the salaried intermediate class. The socio-political agenda of these forces was essentially limited to political reform of dictatorial rule. They also suffered from organizational weakness which inhibited their attempts to establish hegemony over the lower classes. On the other hand, the popular organizations, such as revolutionary committees (*Komitehs*), Revolutionary Guard (*Pasdaran-e Engelab*), and revolutionary courts gained the support of the clergy-dominated Revolutionary Council,[53] which in turn was connected to the old petty bourgeoisie.[54]

The relationship between the popular organizations and the fundamentalist clergy was an important one. These popular organizations had spontaneously gained momentum in the revolutionary process; but the fundamentalist clergy acquired influence within these organizations by espousing their ideals and sanctioning their activities – which included the use of violence against political opponents. Ultimately, this sanctioning enabled the clerics to become fully entrenched as 'true' leaders of the revolution, and the Islamic Republic Party

(IRP), which was founded by the clerics of the Revolutionary Council, became the structure which gave ideological direction to the revolution.

Providing ideological direction has not been an easy task for the IRP. This is essentially because of the close relationship between the clerical community and the bazaar classes. The bazaar merchants contributed heavily to the revolution and the clerical leadership; but in supporting the revolution, they were acting out of mixed motives. In the pre-revolutionary period, they resented their loss of status, competition from foreign industries, and excessive concentration of economic power in the hands of the few. They were also weary of excessive government regulation of commerce and belated attempts to increase taxes. Their vision of post-revolutionary government was that which protected private property, freed them from government restrictions and controls, provided them with greater business opportunities, and taxed them lightly. The clerics, however, found it difficult to subscribe to this vision, since their post-revolutionary success was due to their ability to generate support from popular organizations. Also, in order to maintain their hegemony over the urban poor, they created a number of populist organizations to administer and pursue social welfare and reconstruction programmes. Once instituted, these organizations began to generate demands representing their constituency.

In their attempt to maintain the support of popular organizations, the IRP articulated a state ideology imbued with populism; it advocated redistributive policies and sought to antagonize the lower classes against the *mostakbarin* (predators).[55] The consequence of this populist strategy was a very peculiar relationship to the bazaar community. Clearly, many members of the community were absorbed into the revolutionary organizations and the government. But because of the objective position they occupied as members of a populist state, they began to act in contradiction to the interests of the stratum or class from which they came.[56] Their actions were detrimental to the interests of large merchants, and even middle traders and artisans. At the same time, however, the regime was unable to rid itself of its *bazaari* roots. The result was, and continues to be, a power struggle within the government and the IRP.

Notwithstanding the fact that any categorization does injustice to the complexities of the real world, two opposing views of Islam, representing real interests, can be broadly identified as the main adversaries in this power struggle.[57] One view essentially promotes moderation, or even conservatism, on economic issues; while it proposes vast changes in legal–cultural areas (like an overhaul of the judicial system), it opposes land reform on grounds that Islam protects the rights of private property. The more radical view is less concerned with legal–cultural issues and is more interested in land reform, redistribution of wealth, and stringent controls on the bazaar. Most observers of Iranian politics agree that, after a brief period of radicalization, the moderate/conservative view began to dominate.[58] Reflecting the views of the majority of high-ranking clerics, the moderates'/conservatives' confirmation of the sanctity of private property also confirmed the close relationship with the *bazaari* classes. This should not be interpreted as the total demise of the radicals. While the radicals do not enjoy the support of the majority of high-ranking clerics, they carry considerable weight within ruling circles because they are well organized and continue to be influential within the revolutionary organizations. Khomeini's departure may give them the upper hand.

While the vacillation between its *bazaari* base and the popular organizations that support it introduces some ambiguity about the class nature of the post-revolutionary regime, there is no doubt as to how the new state has responded to political forces representing the working class and the peasantry. The regime has perceived any independent attempt to organize on the part of the workers as a threat to its consolidation of power. Accordingly, it has cut the formal wages of workers, purged the oppositional workers' councils (*shuras*) and individual workers, and has extensively used force and repression to undercut worker militancy.[59] The regime's response to peasant militancy has been similar; the government clearly opposed land seizures.

> Units of newly formed Revolutionary Guard often intervened forcefully on the side of the landlords. Peasants were evicted from land they had, and in some cases their leaders were jailed or even killed. The crackdown was particularly harsh in the national minority areas, where landlords allied themselves with the new regime and successfully presented peasant actions as threatening the unity of the state as well as challenging the 'Islamic' social order.[60]

More importantly, the workers and the peasantry have suffered from the regime's economic policies. Initially, the Islamic Republic maintained a faltering economy by drawing from the infrastructure inherited from the pre-revolutionary regime and relying on oil revenues to import necessities. But the inability to institute genuine land reform, combined with promises of inexpensive housing and other amenities in the urban areas, have exacerbated mass migration from the countryside to the cities. Urban economic life, on the other hand, has also become increasingly difficult with the deterioration of workers' purchasing power as a result of high inflation, direct wage cuts, and high unemployment. The workers' grievances have materialized in such forms as sabotage, slowdown, and waste. But, in reality, the reign of terror that has been unleashed against the Iranian people has effectively undercut organized opposition. The IRP has also penetrated the workers' syndicates and imposed the Islamic ideology from the top.

The war with Iraq has been the best pretext for monopolizing political power and the Islamicization of the society. All secular laws have been declared illegal, and all women have been forced to wear religious clothing in public. In addition, the war has solidified certain post-revolutionary institutions. For instance, the Revolutionary Guard (now the Ministry of Revolutionary Guards), has experienced expansion of its ranks, improved training, and strengthening of its command structure. It is now numerically larger than the regular army and has a permanent place in the regime's security apparatus. But the Gulf war has also had its costs. The need to import vital military goods has meant that Iran has been willing to sell crude oil for less than the official OPEC price to whichever country is willing to buy, including the West and Japan. This is a reversal of two of the major premises of the revolution: the conservation of Iranian oil by curtailing production, and the reduction of Iranian trade with the West.[61]

The continuing dependence on oil exports to the West and, hence, the inability to combat cyclical fluctuations that characterize the world capitalist system, point to a fundamental failure of the Islamic regime. The post-revolutionary leadership has made no systematic effort to articulate, let alone implement, a comprehensive revolutionary programme of economic and social reform. In fact, they have approached the economy on an *ad-hoc* basis. Some of the reasons for this can be traced to the Gulf war, but explanations must also accord significance to the divisions that exist within the regime.[62] These divisions have led to an incapacity to establish an alternative economic structure, and this in turn has prevented the weakening of ties to international capital and its particular political, social, and ideological interests.[63] This means that the Islamic Revolutionaries have produced a new political form based on the guardianship of Islamic jurists, without fundamentally altering the economic structure or finding other means to generate surplus. This is a contradiction that must necessarily be dealt with by the regime, because without the production of material wealth, the very existence of the Islamic state will be endangered.[64]

Conclusion

After seven years, the Iranian Revolution and the theocratic state it gave rise to remain an enigma. On the one hand, Iran continues to be in revolutionary turmoil, manifested in domestic political agitation and economic difficulties, in addition to international conflict. On the other hand, the regime has exhibited an uncanny ability to dodge potential threats to its survival. In fact, in comparison with the political turmoil of its earlier years, the regime has even managed to introduce a surface calm to the Islamic Republic. Nevertheless, the regime does face serious challenges.

First of all, it has not been able to reconcile the contradictory interests which constitute it. There is no doubt that the Islamic regime has destroyed the power structure associated with the Shah's regime and created a ruling bloc within which the lower petty bourgeoisie has a pre-eminent place. Yet, given the structure of the Iranian bazaar and its connection to the clergy, the regime has also had to contend with rich merchants. It is within this context that one must look for the roots of conflict between the conservatives and radicals inside the government and the IRP. Given the deteriorating economic conditions caused by the Gulf war, decreased oil revenues, lack of effective management, and corruption, this conflict is bound to worsen, and it will be the most important factor in shaping Iranian politics in the near future. In all likelihood, it will be unleashed fully once Khomeini is no longer present to act as an arbiter.[65] The intensity of this conflict will depend on the popular energy the radicals can muster in order to launch an attack against the already well-entrenched moderate/conservative forces.

The second problem facing the regime relates to its inability to convince a large part of the population that its socio-economic vision is correct. This part of the population includes the politically repressed opposition forces, such as the Mujahedin and Marxist groups, as well as some members of the religious community. While the government has effectively disoriented the Mujahedin, the latter continues to maintain a foothold inside Iran. The Mujahedin leaders were expelled from France and now reside in Baghdad where they regularly broadcast into Iran and have formed an Iranian Liberation Army which sporadically engages Iranian troops and Revolutionary Guards in Kurdistan. The Marxist organizations, on the other hand, have been less successful in maintaining their credibility, as well as visibility. The loss of credibility has been a major problem for the Tudeh and the Fedaiyan (Majority). These organizations originally supported the Islamic regime on the basis of the regime's proclaimed anti-imperialist stance and the need for unity against the threat of counter-revolution. The Tudeh Party even became the only Marxist party to have been officially legalized by the Revolutionary Council. Nonetheless, the regime continued to persecute and imprison many of the Fedaiyan (Majority) leaders and cadres, and by 1983 had arrested the Tudeh leaders as well. Needless to say, their oppositional stance today is received by the public with scepticism. The Fedaiyan (Minority), a splinter organization composed of the Marxist revolutionaries who rejected the pro-regime stance of their original organization, did not compromise its position by collaborating with the regime, but its small size has never allowed it to become a significant public force. The same holds true for other small leftist groups, such as Paykar.

There is, however, another important group of opponents that may become politically significant in the future. The members of this amorphous group are devout Muslims from within the Shi'a community, as well as the now sizeable Sunni community (ten million people) in Iran. They consider the anti-democratic nature of the regime to be anti-Islamic. Islam, they argue, is a religion that respects diversity of opinion and action. Furthermore, the conversion to the Islamic code of conduct should come through persuasion, and not terror. The position of Islamic reformers is quite different – although their socio-economic vision may ultimately be the same – from the royalist and secular liberal positions that tend to blame Islam in general for all post-revolutionary problems in Iran. The Islamic reformers argue for reform within the context of Islam and, in this sense, they are much more in tune with contemporary Iranian politics and its likely development in the period ahead. Political differentiation and changes of allegiance in Iran have occurred, and will in all likelihood continue to occur, within the Islamic discourse. The realization of this is fundamental for the successful operation of any opposition group. The salaried/professional intermediate class may have learned to abhor Islam after the revolution, but the rest of the population has more faith and is willing to experiment with different versions of it.

At this point, there is a very precarious situation in Iran. Despite the fact that the opposition is organizationally weak and does not threaten the immediate survival of the regime, the government has had to rule by suppression. It continues to prevent the publication of opposition newspapers, break up rival political meetings, and imprison and execute people who are only remotely associated with the opposition. This is because the ruling clergy realizes that, while not a single opposition group is strong, there is a general feeling of opposition, which is vague and undefined, but prevalent. The regime seems determined to prevent any kind of political opening that would allow these undefined grievances to become transformed into political organization. Yet, there is no doubt the Iranian crisis is not yet over. Under the surface calm, Iran remains a country in turmoil, hoping to survive the possible eruption once the foremost leader of the revolution is no longer present.[66]

Notes

1. N. Keddie, 'The Economic History of Iran, 1800–1914, and Its Political Impact: An Overview,' *Iranian Studies*, vol. 5 (Spring–Summer 1972), pp. 59–61.

2. F. Kazemzadeh, *Britain and Russia in Iran: 1864–1914* (New Haven, Yale University Press, 1968).

3. For an excellent survey of the economic history of Iran from 1800 to 1914, see N. Keddie, 'The Economic History of Iran, 1800–1914, and Its Political Impact'. See also, C. Issawi, *The Economic History of Iran: 1800–1914* (Chicago, University of Chicago Press, 1971).

4. C. Issawi, *The Economic History of Iran: 1800–1914*, p. 43.

5. N. Keddie, 'The Economic History of Iran,' p. 71.

6. E. Abrahamian, *Iran: Between Two Revolutions* (Princeton, Princeton University Press, 1982), pp. 86–92. See also, H. Bashiriyeh, *The State and Revolution in Iran: 1962–1982* (New York, St. Martin's Press, 1984), pp. 8–10.

7. Reza Khan toppled the constitutional government in 1921. With the Qajar dynasty in ruins, the Majlis proposed the creation of a republic in 1924. Opposition from the religious community and merchants in the bazaar paved the way for Reza Khan to declare himself king and found the Pahlavi dynasty. The support for the creation of the monarchy by these conservative nationalist elements was premised on the hope that Reza Shah would strengthen Iran against radical threats.

8. E. Abrahamian, p. 149.

9. See A. Ashraf, 'Historical Obstacles to the Development of a Bourgeoisie in Iran,' in M. A. Cook (ed.), *Studies in the Economic History of the Middle East* (London, Oxford University Press, 1970). Ashraf cites three obstacles to the growth of an independent bourgeoisie: 1) strong Shahs and centralization of political authority; 2) the existence of powerful tribal groups, and 3) colonial penetration.

10. A. Ahmad, 'Class, Nation, and State: Intermediate Classes in Peripheral Societies,' in D. L. Johnson (ed.), *Middle Classes in Dependent Countries* (Beverly Hills, Sage, 1985), pp. 48–49.

11. While some financing of private enterprise was attempted, it is important to note that these state interventions were restricted mostly to investment programmes for the public sector. In this sense it was very different from the post-World War II planning attempts to spur private enterprise throughout the world.

12. F. Halliday, *Iran, Dictatorship and Development* (New York, Penguin, 1979), p. 23.

13. M. Zavareei, 'Dependent Capitalist Development in Iran and the Mass Uprising of 1979,' *Research in Political Economy*, vol. 5 (1982), pp. 143–44.

14. F. Halliday, *Iran, Dictatorship and Development*, p. 24.

15. E. Abrahamian, *Iran*, p. 236.

16. *Ibid.*, pp. 340–41.

17. Oil production in Iran began in 1908. By 1951, the industry boasted an Iranian contingency of approximately 55,000 workers, most of whom were skilled or unskilled labourers. Halliday reports that another 15,000 worked for 'employers who received contract work from the oil company.' F. Halliday, *Iran, Dictatorship*, p. 177. By the 1940s, a comparable number of workers were employed by the private sector. See A. Ashraf, 'Historical Obstacles,' p. 329.

18. Labour shortages were due to the employment of larger numbers of Iranian workers by the Allies. This clearly improved labour's bargaining position. In regard to inflation, Abrahamian points out that the cost-of-living index more than doubled from 1942 to 1945. By 1946, the Central Council of Federated Trade Unions of Iranian Workers and Toilers (CCFTU) boasted 186 union affiliates and a total membership of 335,000, which constituted 75 percent of the workforce. See E. Abrahamian, *Iran*, pp. 351–53.

19. *Ibid.*, p. 348.

20. *Ibid.*, pp. 352–5.

21. The power of the Iranian state was enhanced by Western, and especially US, economic and military assistance.

22. This extensive mobilization was mostly limited to the urban areas; the peasantry was generally left alone. The reasons for this are complicated and are essential to the general purpose of this essay. In general, the Iranian peasantry has not been very revolutionary. For an interpretation of why this is so, see F. Kazemi and E. Abrahamian, 'The Non-revolutionary Peasantry of Iran,' *Iranian Studies*, vol. 2 (1978). See also E. Abrahamian, *Iran*, pp. 375–82.

23. H. Bashiriyeh, *The State and Revolution in Iran*, pp. 16–18.

24. The National Front was a coalition of parties and included the Iran Party, the Pan Iranist Party, the Mujahedin-i Islam Party, the Toilers' Party, and the People of Iran Party. It brought together sets of interests representing the national bourgeoisie, the old petty bourgeoisie (which allied with the religious community), and some of the modern intermediate class. As mentioned above, the modern intermediate class was also attracted to the Tudeh Party. See Abrahamian, *Iran*, p. 259.

25. N. Keddie, *Iran: Religion, Politics and Society* (London, Frank Cass, 1980).

26. F. Fesharaki, *Development of the Iranian Oil Industry: International and Domestic Aspects* (New York, Praeger, 1976), p. 9.

27. It is important to note that the Shah had begun consolidating his power prior to the declaration of martial law; however, he started to lose his grip due to his unwillingness to challenge Britain. Two other factors were also important in the Shah's decline. First, his increasing domination of the system reminded people of his dictatorial father. Second, while he increasingly depended on US military, technical and economic aid, the US government was not as forthcoming as he would have liked.

28. F. Halliday, *Iran, Dictatorship*, p. 25.

29. H. Alavi, 'State and Class Under Peripheral Capitalism,' in H. Alavi and T. Shanin (eds.), *Introduction to the Sociology of Developing Societies* (New York, Monthly Review Press, 1982).

30. The new agreement was signed in 1954, and the Iranian oil industry was nationalized; but effective control over output and price remained in the hands of a newly created international consortium. The major consequence was the break-up of British monopoly. This international consortium now also included American, Dutch, and French capital. The National Iranian Oil Company gained control over distribution within Iran, and servicing.

31. The revival of the Tudeh Party was not based on legalization of the party; Mossadeq retained the 1949 ban. The Tudeh gradually emerged as a major force during 1951–53, however, by setting up clandestine presses, a secret network within the armed forces, and front organizations. These were made possible by the suspension of police controls under Mossadeq.

32. The CIA's involvement in the coup has been chronicled by B. Rubin, *Paved With Good Intentions: The American Experience in Iran* (New York, Oxford University Press, 1980).

33. H. Ladjevardi, 'The Origins of US Support for an Autocratic Iran,' *International Journal of Middle East Studies*, vol. 15 (1983).

34. Fesharaki reports more than a tenfold increase in oil revenues – from \$34 million in 1954–55, to \$358 million in 1960–61. F. Fesharaki, *Development of the Iranian Oil Industry*, p. 133.

35. Quoted from *World Armaments and Disarmaments Yearbook for 1972*, in E. Abrahamian *Iran*, p. 420.

36. *Ibid.*, p. 421.

37. For an interesting discussion of the land reform as a means of destroying the economic and political power of pre-capitalist forces in Iran, see P. Clawson, 'The Internationalization of Capital and Capital Accumulation in Iran and Iraq,' *Insurgent Sociologist*, vol. 3, no. 2 (Spring 1977).

38. E. Hooglund, *Land and Revolution in Iran, 1960–1980* (Austin, University of Texas Press, 1982).

39. For an excellent recent analysis of land reform and its effects, see *Ibid.* See also A. K. S. Lambton, *The Persian Land Reform: 1962–1966* (London, Oxford University Press, 1969).

40. E. Hooglund, *Land and Revolution in Iran*, p. 78. This does not mean that the old landowners effectively lost their wealth. As an influential class, they were broken up, but as Halliday succinctly points out, '[w]hatever the specific class destinations of the old landowners, there is no doubt that whilst their power in the village was broken by the intervention of the state, they themselves were reintegrated into the new Iranian ruling class as capitalist farmers, state employees, merchants or shareholders in industry.' F. Halliday, *Iran, Dictatorship*, p. 134.

41. *Ibid.*, pp. 138–9. See also F. Halliday, 'Iran: The Economic Contradictions,' *MERIP Reports*, vol. 8, no. 6 (July–August 1978).

42. For a discussion of oil revenues as economic rent, see H. Mahdavi, 'The Patterns and Problems of Economic Development in Rentier States: The case of Iran,' in M. A. Cook (ed.), *Studies in the Economic History of the Middle East*. See also H. Katouzian, *The Political Economy of Modern Iran: Despotism and Pseudo-Modernism* (New York, New York University Press, 1981).

43. Walton points out that the basis of import-substitution industrialization strategy must be found in the government's attempt to solve the country's balance of payment problems through the restriction of non-essential imports. 'The policy of import controls was later complemented with generous fiscal incentives, exclusive industrial licensing, low or non-existent project taxes and easily accessible low-interest loans in the manufacturing sector. The rather haphazard planning methods inherent in the first two plans were also modified in favour of more comprehensive five-year plans so that public and private sector investments could be better coordinated.' T. Walton, 'Economic Development and Revolutionary Upheavals in Iran,' *Cambridge Journal of Economics*, vol. 4 (1980), p. 278.

44. Additional revenue from petroleum was first achieved (1960–70) through an increase in the rate of reserve depletion. The spectacular rise in petroleum prices was a phenomenon of the 1970s.

45. Between 1963 and 1972, Iran reported an average annual GNP growth rate of approximately 8 to 9 percent, and a GNP per capita growth rate of from 5 to 6 percent. This growth was not even throughout the economy. Manufacturing, non-oil mining, and construction grew at an average annual rate of from 10 to 11 percent, and services at an annual rate of from 8 to 9 percent. During the same period, agricultural growth averaged only 2 to 3 percent. The post-1973 oil boom not only led to much higher (short-term) growth rates, but also magnified the above unevenness. Services and construction jumped astronomically, while agriculture remained on the fringes. See H. Katouzian, *The Political Economy of Modern Iran*, p. 256.

46. The increase in oil prices in 1973–74 led to the immediate doubling of most targets of the 1973–78 fifth five-year plan, and Iran became an immediate paradise for international investment. Shortly afterwards, however, the regime was forced to delay or completely withdraw major projects due to lack of funds.

47. For an elaborate discussion of the misuse of money capital and the reasons behind it, see

B. Jazani, *Capitalism and Revolution in Iran* (London, Zed Press, 1980).

48. In the announcement creating the Resurgence Party, the Shah branded those who were reluctant to join the party as 'Tudeh sympathizers.' He also gave these people the options of going to prison or leaving the country.

49. Although a committee of Khomeini's supporters began organizing a plan for a nationwide uprising against the Shah in December 1977, including those who later formed the core of the Revolutionary Council. See A. Taheri, *The Spirit of Allah: Khomeini and the Islamic Revolution* (Bathesda, Md., Adler and Adler, 1986), esp. p. 180ff.

50. The Mujahedin developed mainly from the religious wing of the National Front in the 1960s. Their revolutionary interpretion of Islam led the majority of these leaders to abandon Islam in favour of Marxism in 1975. This ideological change ultimately divided the Mujahedin into two factions: one Islamic, and the other Marxist. During the Revolution, the Islamic Mujahedin developed a much larger popular base, while the smaller Marxist Mujahedin re-emerged as *Sazman-i Paykar*. See E. Abrahamian, 'The Guerrilla Forces in Iran, 1963–1977,' *MERIP Reports*, vol. 10, no. 3 (March–April 1980).

51. E. Abrahamian, *Iran*, p. 480.

52. The Shah left on January 16, 1979. Shahpour Bakhtiar headed the government and unsuccessfully attempted to negotiate with Khomeini. Bakhtiar was expelled from the National Front for accepting the Shah's offer. On February 1, Khomeini returned to Iran and pronounced Mehdi Bazargan the head of a rival government. After a series of confrontations between February 9 and February 11, the military collapsed. Bakhtiar officially resigned on February 11, 1979, and went into hiding. Bazargan replaced him as the head of the provisional government. On March 30, a referendum proclaimed Iran to be an Islamic Republic.

53. The Revolutionary Council was established by Khomeini as the monarchy fell. It originally included representatives of both salaried and traditional intermediate classes. With the formation of the provisional government, however, Bazargan and six of his colleagues left to form the cabinet. The overall effect was the strengthening of the clerical position. For a detailed analysis of post-revolutionary power plays, see S. Bakhash, *The Reign of the Ayatollahs* (New York, Basic, 1984). See also, *MERIP Reports*, vol. 13, no. 3 (March–April 1983).

54. This is not to suggest that all of the bazaar merchants, shopkeepers, and clerics supported these forces. Many coalesced around the more moderate Islamic People's Republican Party (PRP) associated with Ayatollah Shariatmadari. On the other hand, the Revolutionary Council had strong support from the bazaar.

55. H. Bashiriyeh, *The State and Revolution in Iran*, p. 171.

56. For this observation, I am indebted to A. Ashraf's interview on the 'Bazaar and Mosque in Iran's Revolution,' *MERIP Reports*, vol. 13, no. 3 (March–April 1983), p. 17.

57. On the post-revolutionary power struggles, see *Ibid.* See also N. Keddie and E. Hooglund (eds.), *The Iranian Revolution and the Islamic Republic: Proceedings of a Conference* (Washington, D.C.: Middle East Institute, 1982). Most observers seem to agree that the conflict within the IRP began to intensify with the assassination of Ayatollah Beheshti in June 1981. As the undisputed leader of the IRP until his death, he was able to sustain an impressive show of unity in the heterogeneous leadership of the IRP.

58. See *MERIP Reports*, vol. 13, no. 3 (March–April 1983), notably the articles by Fred Halliday and the interview with Ahmad Ashraf. The handling of land ownership by the regime is generally referred to as a sign of moderate/conservative ascendancy to power. After land seizures in several areas, the government announced its own land reform. After eliminating the leftist groups, however, the government started to erode the stipulated limitations on land ownership.

59. A. Bayat. 'Workers' Control After the Revolution,' *MERIP Reports*, vol. 13, no. 3 (March–April 1983).

60. J. Paul, 'Iran's Peasants and the Revolution: An Introduction,' *MERIP Reports*, vol. 12, no. 3 (March–April 1982) p. 22.

61. Initially, determined to reduce its economic links to the West, the Iranian oil ministry attempted to strike barter deals with socialist and Third World countries. The Gulf war, however, created pressures to generate hard currency in order to buy military goods.

62. Many of these divisions may be explained in terms of Moaddel's analysis of the class divisions within the *ulama*. See M. Moaddel, 'The Shi'i Ulama and the State of Iran, *Theory and Society*, vol. 15, no. 4 (1986), pp. 519–56.

63. It is important to note that the regime has pursued policies which emphasized welfare spending and distribution of goods and services. In fact, perhaps the only difference from the Shah's period was a change in priorities away from capital investments and towards redistributive policies. This means, however, that the expansion/contraction of social services has become dependent on the expansion/contraction of demand for oil, since no alternative source of funding has yet been discovered.

64. This is not to underestimate the importance of the new political arrangement. This new political form is by itself significant, since it has vehemently promoted, in rhetoric and in practice, a reaction to the cultural hegemony of Western values and practices. It has also enabled Iran to choose her trading partners with greater freedom than before. But the fact remains that this relatively independent form is not in harmony with its dependent and unproductive material basis.

65. The Assembly of Experts has already chosen Ayatollah Montazeri as Khomeini's successor. Most observers agree that he does not have the authority and charisma of Khomeini that would enable him to arbitrate successfully between these conflicting interests. For a comprehensive discussion of the divisions within the regime, see Eric Hooglund, 'Iran and the Gulf War,' *MERIP Reports*, vol. 17, no. 5, (September–October, 1987), pp. 12–18. See also Ashraf, op. cit.

66. This essay was written in 1986. A number of developments have occurred during the past few years which have affected the course of events in Iran. These include the disbanding of the Islamic Republic Party (IRP), the winding down of the Iran–Iraq war, and the death of Ayatollah Khomeini in 1989. (Editor.)

7. Riot and Rebellion in North Africa: Political Responses to Economic Crisis in Tunisia, Morocco and Sudan

David Seddon

The year 1984 began in a bloody fashion in North Africa. Violent demonstrations erupted in the impoverished south-west and south of Tunisia at the very end of December 1983 and spread throughout the country during the first week of January. These followed the Tunisian government's introduction of measures to remove food subsidies. Bread prices suddenly doubled.

The state's response to the demonstrations was violent. As the unrest spread, security forces opened fire on crowds in several towns, including the capital, Tunis. The government declared a state of emergency and a curfew on January 3, and banned public gatherings of more than three persons. On the morning of January 6 President Habib Bourguiba appeared on television to rescind the price increases and promise the restoration of food subsidies, an announcement greeted with pleasure and relief by the crowds in the street. Three weeks later, after a period of relative calm, the curfew was lifted.

As Tunisia's social unrest subsided, students in Morocco initiated strikes over fee increases during the first week of January, and social turmoil increased rapidly as large numbers of unemployed workers in the towns of the south and north-east joined the students. Heavy news censorship prevented timely publication of details. The newspaper of the Istiqlal Party, *l'Opinion*, reported that troops from the Western Sahara and Sidi Ifni had been brought in to quell the disturbances.

The proposals for further price increases in both countries followed the recommendations of the International Monetary Fund. As in Tunisia, Moroccan demonstrators were met with massive state violence. On January 25, after relative calm had been restored, officials announced that 29 people had been killed and 114 injured during the previous weeks; press reports suggest that at least 100 were killed (as many as 400 according to some sources) and many more injured and arrested. King Hassan appeared on television in the evening of January 22 to announce that there would be no further increases in the price of basic goods after all. This, together with the repressive measures taken against the demonstrators, ensured that 'law and order' were restored within a few days. By the end of the month it could be said that Morocco, like Tunisia, had returned to 'normal.'

Just over a year later, at the end of March 1985, mass demonstrations in

Khartoum initiated a series of events which culminated in the overthrow of President Numairi's regime in Sudan by the Sudanese military. What began as popular protest against increases in the price of basic commodities was transformed within a week into a movement of political opposition. The violence with which the state met the early street demonstrations was an important factor in the development of an organized movement of opposition to the regime, although the 'bread riots' themselves lasted only a few days, and the total number killed was small in comparison with the number in Tunisia and Morocco. As in Tunisia and Morocco, the official response blamed the troubles on agitators, but as in Tunisia and also Morocco, the regime was obliged to recognize, after continued mass demonstrations revealed the popular character of the protest, that the removal of food subsidies and the resulting increase in prices lay behind the riots, and offered to rescind the price increases. Unlike the situation in Tunisia and Morocco, however, these offers came too late to have any substantial effect on what had rapidly become a much more orchestrated campaign of political opposition to the regime. 'Law and order' were not restored; a general strike was called and implemented, and eventually a state of 'civil rebellion' was declared. Before the disparate social forces involved in the campaign were able to construct an agreed political platform and programme, the army intervened and seized power. Since the military coup in April 1985, the civilian movement has continued to struggle for the restoration of civilian democracy and civilian rule.

'Enemies of the people': official explanations for the riots

Governments commonly identify mass demonstrations of popular anger and resentment as the work of highly organized small groups of agitators – preferably foreign-inspired and supported. To accept that large numbers of ordinary citizens may be so desperate as to act openly and violently together would be to admit that deep-seated and intractable problems exist.

In Tunisia, official explanations played down the doubling of bread prices and stressed the role of agitators with political motives. According to the governor of Kebili, foreign-inspired agitators were involved in the demonstrations there and in Douz and Souk al-Ahad – all small southern towns to the east of the great salt depression of Chott el-Djerid. In Gafsa, 'capital' of the south, the governor identified Libyan and Lebanese-trained Tunisians leading the demonstrations.[1] Late on the evening of January 3, 1984 Prime Minister Mzali declared on television that 'there has been manipulation. The young people have been enticed and misled into demonstrations which appear spontaneous, but behind which lies a plan for destabilization and elements more or less inspired by certain influences whose declared objective is the overthrow of the regime.'[2] He evidently had Libya in mind as the 'influences.'[3] In Paris, the Tunisian ambassador assured the French television audience that the price increase 'had very little to do with the rioting,' and blamed 'uncontrolled elements.'[4] A few days later, after President Bourguiba had publicly cancelled the food price rises, Mzali reiterated his conviction that 'we found ourselves faced with veritable insurrectionist commandos, well organized and coordinated.'[5]

Moroccan official statements likewise tended to lay the blame for the trouble at the door of agitators of various kinds. King Hassan, in his television speech of January 22, referred to three distinct categories of agitators: Muslim fundamentalists; communists and 'Marxists–Leninists'; and 'Zionist' secret services.

In Sudan, students referred to as 'ideologists' (an official euphemism for the recently banned Muslim Brotherhood) were initially blamed for the riots, and the authorities issued a list of Muslim Brothers wanted for questioning for inciting job-seekers from the provinces stricken by drought. The government also announced it would 'start forthwith emptying the capital of all elements responsible for sabotage,' 'tramps and vagrants' in particular. Between 1,500 and 2,000 people were arrested between March 26 and 28, 1985 – mainly the homeless and unemployed, many of them refugees from the countryside.[6]

Meetings were held over the last weekend of March to plan a mass rally early the following week; the demonstration had the backing of various professional associations. The president of the students' union stated that 'even the judges' committee has declared its support. The air is quivering.'[7] The Sudanese authorities were aware of the danger posed by these meetings. On Saturday, March 30, the secretary and the acting president of the Union of Academic Staff at the University of Khartoum were arrested at the same time as four leading doctors – two of them members of the central committee of the Sudan Medical Association. These followed the arrest earlier in the day of thirteen students and four others attending a meeting of the Khartoum University Student Union.[8]

On Monday, April 1, 1985, the authorities announced that the students arrested over the weekend were members of the banned Communist Party. The secretary of the Sudan Socialist Union promised that Communists, Ba'thists, and Muslim Brothers would all be hunted down; he also stated that the majority of demonstrators were not Sudanese. He accused Libya, Ethiopia, and the Soviet Union of involvement in anti-government activities, and stressed that the doctors arrested during the weekend were graduates of universities in the Soviet Union and other socialist countries.

On Tuesday, April 2, between 2,000 and 3,500 people attended a pro-government rally organized by the Sudan Socialist Union in Khartoum to demonstrate against Communists, Ba'thists, and Muslim Brothers – the alleged instigators of the opposition to the Numairi regime. In a message to the crowd, President Numairi condemned 'traitors and agents' for the previous week's riots and declared that 'the enemies of the revolution will end up in disgrace and destruction.'

Organized opposition or spontaneous protest?
(Tunisia and Morocco)

But if the identification of such elements as scapegoats is not surprising, it must nevertheless be asked whether there was any basis for the conception of a threat to the regime from politically motivated and organized groups; for it could be argued that such a threat, if it existed in reality – or was even genuinely perceived to exist – might provide an explanation for the violent response by the state to the demonstrations, even at their outset.

In Tunisia, the disturbances broke out in a region where political opposition has been openly manifested in the recent past. Only a few years ago, Libyan-trained Tunisian dissidents attacked and held for over a week the southern town of Gafsa. Since that time, economic co-operation between the two countries has increased significantly, and relations are, in general, more cordial. But the majority of the 60,000 Tunisians who work in Libya come from the south and south-west, and there was evidence of at least tacit support for the dissidents from the inhabitants of Gafsa. Furthermore, Colonel Qadhafi's attitude towards the Tunisian regime under Bourguiba is equivocal, to say the least. Qadhafi was at some pains to assure the Tunisian regime that he had no part in the organization of the demonstrations in the south; after a telephone conversation with Mzali, Qadhafi decided to send a delegation to Tunis to emphasize the point and to encourage 'coordination and cooperation aimed at overcoming the present situation.'[9] But concern about possible Libyan connections was reinforced when a pipeline carrying oil from Algeria to Tunisia was blown up on January 7, allegedly by a four-man commando group from Libya.

In Morocco, the north – and particularly the north-east where the disturbances were most violent and most prolonged – has been regarded since independence as potentially volatile. This is partly because of the long-standing connections between this region and western Algeria, and partly because of the more recent experience of social unrest. King Hassan certainly recalls the revolts of 1958 and 1959 in the vicinity of al-Hoceima and Nador. He himself – as crown prince – brutally put these down with the aid of 20,000 troops and full air support in January 1960.[10] We may even bear in mind the earlier republicanism of the northern mountain regions under the rebel 'Abd al-Krim during the 1920s. There was no suggestion officially of any influence, direct or indirect, from Algeria on those occasions. This, combined with the total lack of any evidence of Israeli involvement, removes the basis for any suggestion of a direct foreign influence on the course of events in Morocco.

In both Tunisia and Morocco, there was evidence of agitation by Muslim fundamentalist groups; but the Muslim fundamentalists in Morocco are divided into as many as 20 different groups, and their capacity to orchestrate large-scale demonstrations of the kind experienced in January is extremely questionable. In Tunisia, some commentators have suggested that growing Islamic fundamentalism enabled agitators to encourage violence against property representing 'the symbols of luxury, corruption, and foreign influence' and to adopt slogans such as 'there is but one God, and Bourguiba is the enemy of God.'[11] In 1983, a group of junior army officers stood trial on charges of propagating religious ideas in the armed forces, while another group of young fundamentalists was imprisoned for allegedly planning to blow up foreign cultural centres in Tunis, but this is extremely circumstantial evidence as far as the January disturbances are concerned.[12] The only direct indication of the involvement of Muslim fundamentalist groups, apart from the existence of some pamphlets and the use of certain slogans, was the fact that the minarets of the mosques were used, particularly in Tunis, to chant *Allahu akbar* ('God is great') and other religious declarations during the course of the demonstrations. In neither Tunisia nor Morocco is there reliable evidence that Muslim fundamentalists were significant in orchestrating the demonstrations, although there is little doubt that they were involved and active. Most local sources in the south of Tunisia, where the earliest disturbances broke out, appear to agree that the role of Muslim fundamentalists – or of pro-Libyan or other political groups – was in fact extremely limited.[13]

Despite the manifest involvement of political activists in the demonstrations, there is little concrete support for the notion that these played a key role in orchestrating the social unrest. They – like so many others – were taken by surprise by what was essentially a popular uprising. The *Mouvement d'Opposition Nationale Tunisien* (MONT) claimed responsibility, from Brussels, for the demonstrations in Tunisia, and denounced 'the repression' by the Tunisian security forces of the 'hunger rioters' (*les insurgés de la faim*);[14] but the recognized left-wing parties clearly intervened only after the outbreak of mass protest, and then only to call on the government to resolve the crisis. The Tunisian Communist Party, for example, wrote to Prime Minister Mzali demanding that there should be 'consultations' with all national forces to find a solution to the situation, and otherwise confined itself to condemning the violence.[15] The *Mouvement des Démocrates Socialistes* (MDS) and the Communist Party both criticized the state's recourse to the army and laid the responsibility for the troubles at the feet of the government.[16]

Yet, despite the flimsy evidence, there is little doubt that both the regimes perceived a threat from small groups of organized militants. They both initiated a systematic policy of arrest and interrogation of known activists. In Morocco, not only the left-wing revolutionary groups like *Ilal Alam* were targets, but even the *Union Socialiste des Forces Populaires* (USFP) was suspect, despite the fact that its leader, 'Abderrahim Bouabid, was a member of the King's cabinet. The Communist Party in particular was harassed, and its newspaper *al-Bayane* seized for several days running. In Tunisia, known activists from both Muslim fundamentalist and left-wing groups were taken in for questioning. Even the trade unions – which in Tunisia had organized numerous strikes in 1977–78,[17] and in Morocco in 1981 had certainly orchestrated the strikes and public rallies which preceded the bloody riots in Casablanca – were not evidently involved this time. In Tunisia, the *Union Générale des Travailleurs Tunisiens* (UGTT) had sought to negotiate concessions for the poor and a wage review, before prices were increased;[18] but its discussions were with the government at top level and did not involve the union rank and file, let alone the organization of rallies and strikes. In Morocco, there is no evidence that the trade unions played any part in increasing the pressure on the government to reverse the decision to raise price gains, even at the level of discussions with government ministers, as in Tunisia. In Casablanca and Mohammedia, industrial centres with the greatest concentration of organized labour in the country, there was little sign of disturbances, despite the fact that unemployment runs particularly high among the skilled and semi-skilled manual workers.[19]

One social category clearly and importantly involved in the demonstrations in both countries was that of high school and university students. In Morocco, school strikes helped generate the open protest that gradually transformed growing social unrest into overt opposition to the government's economic and social policies. By January 3, students in Tunis were throwing stones at buses, shouting anti-government slogans, and marching in the streets in solidarity with the demonstrators in the south.[20] During the next few days, as the students took to the streets, the authorities closed down the schools and the university. In both countries those most vocal in their criticisms of the regime during the demonstrations were the children of the middle classes, whose standard of living has improved substantially as a result of the economic policies of the past decade or so. But graduate unemployment, combined with the effective suppression of political opposition to the regime in both Tunisia and Morocco, ensure that significant numbers of the young, even from the relatively privileged social strata upon whom the regimes so crucially depend, are disaffected and highly critical.[21]

The social elements involved in the demonstrations of January 1984 were various and diverse. According to Godfrey Morrison, the Tunisian disturbances 'were caused mainly by the young unemployed, a section of society who until now have been largely ignored by both President Bourguiba's government and political analysts.' 'Right until the moment when President Bourguiba made his *volte face*, cancelling the increases,' Morrison wrote, 'it was the rage of the unemployed which dominated the protests, and it was they who alarmed the government.'[22]

In Tunisia, the social unrest evolved in two relatively distinct phases. It first broke out in the impoverished areas of the south and south-west, where the population depends heavily on food subsidies. It started as a series of small local uprisings and gradually spread throughout the southern interior. In the second phase, when unrest developed in the north and coastal areas, political orchestration appears somewhat more credible as a factor. Certainly new social elements were involved. Even there, the majority of those involved in the demonstrations were young, unemployed people from the 'popular' quarters and the shanty towns. In Morocco, it is also possible to identify two stages. In the first, students were predominant and the demonstrations had a limited focus; in the second, students were joined by large numbers of the unemployed and seasonal workers in provincial towns in some of the most disadvantaged regions of the country.

In both countries, the specific immediate causes of the demonstrations opened up deep feelings of resentment and anger that stemmed from underlying problems of inequality, unemployment and poverty, and a sense of political and social marginalization and impotence. The social unrest was essentially 'spontaneous' – significantly different from the organized rallies and strikes of 1977–78 in Tunisia and 1979 and 1981 in Morocco. In both Tunisia and Morocco, the demonstrations were first concentrated in remote and underprivileged regions. As they spread to other areas, they mobilized the deprived and disadvantaged of the popular quarters and shanty towns above all.

Organized opposition or spontaneous protest? (Sudan)

In Sudan, the riots that took place between March 26 and 28, 1985, appear also to have been essentially a form of 'spontaneous protest;' but, by contrast with the disturbances in Tunisia and Morocco, they very soon gave rise to a more organized and orchestrated movement of political opposition to the Numairi regime. On Tuesday, March 26, the day before the departure of President Numairi to the United States for a personal medical check-up and talks on aid for Sudan's ailing economy, demonstrations broke out in the streets of Khartoum. These were directly related to increases in the prices of bread and sugar-based commodities over the previous few days, following a 75 percent rise in fuel prices a couple of weeks before. On Wednesday, students and predominantly young unemployed persons clashed with riot police, as a mass demonstration began around nine a.m., when students congregated near the university, shouting anti-government and anti-Numairi slogans.

The demonstration attracted increasing numbers as it moved towards the city centre, and rapidly grew to well over 1,000 participants. Demonstrators smashed shop windows and car windshields, overturned vehicles and set them on fire, and blocked the streets with chunks of concrete and other heavy objects. Three buildings suffered particularly heavy damage: a branch office of the official Sudanese Socialist Union (the only party permitted under Numairi), the Faisal Islamic Bank (preserve of the Muslim Brotherhood), and the luxury Meridian Hotel. Students chanted, 'We will not be ruled by the World Bank, we will not be ruled by the IMF,' as the unemployed urban poor in the crowd protested at the increasing cost of living. Truckloads of riot police eventually arrived on the scene, firing tear gas and making sorties into the crowd. Sources in contact with hospitals reported that more than six – and perhaps as many as 18 – rioters were killed by police gunfire. Several hundred were arrested, and the government immediately set up special tribunals to try rioters.

Over the next two days violence continued in the streets as demonstrators confronted state security forces. Troops and police used batons, tear gas, and gunfire. Shops and government offices were shut, and part of the city centre closed down. Major clashes took place near the university and around the railway station, while troops posted outside the United States Embassy fired tear gas and live rounds to disperse a crowd – variously reported as 100- and 2,000-strong – marching on the embassy building. At least five people were reported killed in Khartoum. There were also reports of rioting in the west of Sudan, in Nyala, al-Fasher, and al-Geneina; Atbara in the north and Port Sudan in the east were the scenes of demonstrations as well.

After the third day of street violence had filled the Khartoum teaching hospital with the victims of army and police intervention, 600 hospital doctors met and voted for immediate strike action. The move was designed to press the national doctors' union and other professional bodies to call for a general strike. The doctors were also protesting against the extraordinary brutality shown by the security forces during Wednesday's and Thursdays's demonstrations. More than fifty people had been shot, some of them at close range; eight were dead on arrival at the hospital.

On Friday, March 29, Khartoum returned to relative quiet, with troops on full alert strategically positioned around the town. Reports were coming in of disturbances in the western provincial towns of al-Geneina and al-Obeid. Railway workers (organized by one of the country's strongest trade unions) went on strike in Atbara, a key industrial centre in the north.

Hospital doctors, now on strike, distributed leaflets on the streets of Khartoum describing the Numairi regime as 'a regime of hunger,' accusing the president of 'insulting the people of Sudan,' and referring to those who had died in the three days of rioting as 'martyrs.' During the course of Friday, while troops maintained heavy security in the streets outside, a secret meeting took place of the heads of organizations representing doctors, lawyers, engineers, academics, and students. This meeting decided to call on other professional and workers' bodies to join them in a general strike and campaign of civil disobedience, starting the following Monday.[23]

Over the weekend, government troops maintained a state of alert. Security police announced that all those on the streets of the capital should carry identity cards at all times, and said that there were as many as 60,000 'vagrants' in the city who would need to register for deportation to the provinces. The number arrested during the previous week was reported as 2,642; 851 had been sentenced and the remainder (the majority from the western Sudan provinces) detained prior to deportation back home.

Meanwhile, leaflets distributed secretly in Khartoum in the name of the outlawed police officers' association indicated that some sections of the police force were prepared to join actively in the campaign to bring down the regime. The leaflets argued that 'the police have been a tool in the hands of the dictator, Numairi,' and stated that 'from now onwards, the Association of Police Officers will do all it can to disobey any order to use force against the people of Sudan.' 'We say "no" to Numairi and "no" to dictatorship.' They concluded, 'the spirit of October is still alive,' referring to the popular uprising of October 1964, when a national strike led to the downfall of the military government of General Abboud.[24]

At the same time, the Free Army Officers' Organization distributed a statement to foreign news agencies in Khartoum. This declared that 'the Sudan Armed Forces side with the popular revolt against hunger, ignorance, and misrule, and for social justice and equality.' It condemned the existence of 'the rich, the war-profiteers, and the opportunists inside the armed forces.' It called on the people to demonstrate, but cautioned against damaging public property. It emphasized that the army also had suffered the effects of the rising cost of living and the cancellation of subsidies on essential goods.[25]

In Omdurman town, a part of greater Khartoum, hundreds of women took to the streets in a large demonstration to protest against raising food prices; many were shouting 'Down, down with the IMF.'[26]

On Monday, April 1, police used tear gas against demonstrators in the popular market of Khartoum. Meanwhile, Khartoum's doctors – including those from private clinics – continued their strike, refusing even to deal with emergencies; they were joined by the Lawyers' Association. Seven hundred doctors from Omdurman and Khartoum North joined the strike; the Medical Doctors' Association called on the people of the Sudan and the political organizations representing them to institute a campaign of civil disobedience, and suggested a mass demonstration and march on the presidential palace to demand the resignation of Numairi.[27] From outside the capital there were reports of continuing disturbances in Atbara.

The regime arrested leaders of the doctors' union, whose strike now effectively paralysed hospitals in the capital. The total number of those detained by the security forces was reported to have reached over 5,000. Despite this harassment, several other professional associations agreed to support the doctors' call for a general strike on Wednesday, and for mass demonstrations against the regime. Some sections of the police backed the proposed action.

In an attempt to forestall growing organized opposition, the Minister of Labour announced that wages would be increased between 20 and 40 percent. The largest increases went to the lower paid workers in order to offset the effects of the recent devaluation of the Sudanese currency and the removal of subsidies on certain commodities.[28]

According to a report brought out by messenger, all telex and telephone links to the outside world were cut early on Wednesday morning, April 3. Vast crowds took to the streets:

> Thousands of middle class Sudanese protestors flooded the streets of Khartoum on Wednesday. Diplomats estimated about 20,000 in the centre of the city. In contrast to the destruction during food riots the previous week by students and unemployed street dwellers, the demonstration was mainly people in their 30s and 40s and peaceful, if vociferous, and extremely well planned.[29]

The demonstration was led by the professional associations (doctors, lawyers, engineers and accountants) and joined by bank workers, shop staff, academics and students. The protest was predominantly directed against the

Numairi regime, but there were also shouts of 'Down, down USA' and 'We say no to World Bank policies.' Lines of riot police began firing tear gas into the crowd just after nine a.m., but in general the police and the army acted with restraint. Some police appeared even to support the demonstrators, who lifted one or two policemen onto their shoulders, chanting 'The police go with the people.'[30] Senior military officers apparently met First Vice-president Omar al-Tayib before the demonstration to insist that troops should not be used to back up police unless the protest became violent. They also said that only NCOs should be deployed, as they could not guarantee the loyalty of ordinary troops to the regime.[31]

At eleven a.m., as the crowd of some 20,000 began to march on the presidential palace, the judiciary declared a civil rebellion. The demonstration remained well organized and non-violent. Omar al-Tayib promised that 'popular committees' would study the increases in food prices.

Meanwhile, large numbers of workers and salaried employees joined those members of the professional associations already on strike. Shops and offices closed and transport, telecommunications, electricity, and water services were all seriously affected.

On Thursday, April 4, Sudan remained cut off from the outside world. In addition to the closure of telegraph and telephone facilities, the airports were closed and radio stations stopped transmitting. In Omdurman, police used tear gas to disperse stone-throwing demonstrators.[32] The strike became, in effect, a general strike, paralysing the economic and social life of the capital and affecting other cities also. President Numairi, still in the United States, announced at a press conference on April 4 that he had decided to return to Sudan on Saturday, April 6, to 'struggle from there.'[33]

Throughout Friday, April 5, the scale and extent of demonstrations and civil disobedience increased. Police and troops maintained heavy guard on government buildings and other strategic installations in Khartoum, but riot police were reported unwilling to confront the large crowds of protesters. The strike extended to affect every sector of the economy, including power and water supplies. In a letter to President Numairi, the executive of the doctors' association called on him to go: 'It is our patriotic duty to ask you to step down from the leadership of the Sudanese people and leave the national and democratic popular movements to make their destiny.'

At 9.35 on Saturday morning, Minister of Defence and army Commander-in-Chief General Siwar al-Dhahab spoke over Omdurman Radio:

The Sudan Armed Forces have been observing the deteriorating security situation all over the country, and the extremely complex political crisis that has affected the country over the past few days. In order to reduce bloodshed and to ensure the country's independence and unity, the Armed Forces have decided unanimously to stand by the people and their choice and to respond to their demands by taking over power and transferring it to the people after a specified transitional period.[34]

In a second statement, al-Dhahab declared the removal from power of President Numairi, his deputies, assistants, consultants, and ministers. The commander-in-chief suspended the constitution, declared a state of emergency all over the country, closed the border, and halted air traffic into and out of the country.

Immediately after the announcement of the military takeover, tens of thousands of rejoicing people filled the capital's main streets. A large crowd went to the notorious Kober prison, where hundreds of political prisoners were held, and freed them all. The following day, the new rulers formally announced the release of all political prisoners throughout the country. The Sudan People's Liberation Army (SPLA), whose military operations had shaken Numairi's regime in the southern part of the country, declared a cease-fire.[35]

The economic roots of social unrest

All of the evidence suggests that increased prices for basic goods, either actual or prospective, played a crucial role in triggering the violent upsurge of social unrest in the Maghreb in early 1984, and in the Sudan in Spring 1985. But price rises were only the trigger; the economic roots of social unrest in North Africa lie deeper than that.

In Tunisia, the unrest began in the Nefzaoua, a semi-arid region south-east of the Chott al-Djerid – the salt depression that separates the Saharan south from the industrial north and north-east. The south-west is historically the poorest region in Tunisia. It has the highest unemployment rate, and many workers leave in search of jobs in the more prosperous towns of coastal Tunisia; some 60,000 are employed in Libya. It suffered severely from drought during the winter of 1983–84; in the area south of the Chott al-Djerid, the date harvest was disastrous. Poor households in the small towns of Douz, Kebili, el-Hamma and Souk al-Ahad, who live close to the bread line at the best of times, were particularly badly affected. Neglect of agriculture in the south, combined with the relatively rapid development of industry and tourism in the north and north-east over the past decade, had accentuated the historical regional division between north and south, coast and interior. The districts of the interior, such as Sidi Bou Zid, Kairouan, Gafsa and Kasserine, received only 3.6 percent of the new factories established during the 1970s. Of the 86,000 or so jobs created between 1973 and 1978 in Tunisia as a whole, around 46,000 were in Tunis and the north-east; the number barely exceeded 4,000 in the south.[36]

In the south of Tunisia, after the demonstrations of January 1984, one local observer in Kebili remarked that 'it was not for bread that the young demonstrated, but because they were the victims of unemployment.'[37] In the impoverished regions of Tunisia and Morocco, the lack of investment in the rural areas has stimulated a massive rural exodus, but in the absence of any real growth in urban jobs, unemployment has grown there almost as rapidly as the population has grown.

Unemployment statistics are notoriously unreliable, but a figure often cited for the total unemployed in Tunisia is 300,000 (about 20 percent of the active labour force). This is almost certainly an underestimate. With a rate of population increase well over 2 percent a year, some 60 percent of Tunisia's 6.5 million inhabitants are under 20. A high proportion of the unemployed and underemployed are young. A large percentage of the young unemployed are in the poorer neighbourhoods and shanty towns which have mushroomed in the last ten years. Roughly 21 percent of the population of greater Tunis now lives in shanty town areas, and 12 percent inhabit housing projects. For example, the 'city' of Ettathamen, which had a population of 7,000 in 1975, had grown by 1979 to 28,000, and by 1983 had reached 65,000.[38]

In Tunisia, the vast majority of households rely on substantially less than the average annual per capita income of about $1,500. Income distribution is less unequal than in Morocco, but there are substantial inequalities. The recent downturn in the Tunisian economy has seriously affected the situation of the lower paid and the unemployed, who now amount to between 20 and 25 percent of the labour force. Wage rises of around 30 percent to basic wage earners in industry in 1981 and 1982 had little impact on those with only seasonal jobs or without employment, or on those working in the extensive 'informal sector.' Indeed, there is a significant divide between the organized industrial workers who benefit from wage increases, trade unions, and social legislation (health, safety, minimum wage, pensions, etc.), and the mass of casually or seasonally employed, and those without jobs at all. When the government proposed to compensate for the price increases by a raise of 1.9 dinars on the monthly wage of the most disadvantaged,[39] one local UGTT official remarked: 'But what can Mabrouk, with his eight children, do when a kilo of meat costs 4 dinars and the price of flour is doubled? For the poor, it means despair.'[40] The connection between economic disadvantage, large-scale unemployment, and social unrest in the south of Tunisia was undeniably close.

In Morocco, the earliest demonstrations also occurred in the south, particularly in Marrakesh. Here the drought of 1983–84 had seriously affected the availability of food and the cost of living. The condition of the poor and unemployed in Marrakesh had deteriorated markedly over the winter. Small wonder that the students were soon joined by others from the poorer quarters protesting at the prospect of further price increases.

The region in which mass demonstrations developed on the most significant scale, and generated the greatest violence, was the north-east. This region, and particularly that part of it that experienced Spanish colonial occupation between 1912 and 1956, has suffered considerable economic and social disadvantage in comparison with the rest of the country ever since independence. The integration of the old Spanish zone into the former French protectorate between 1956 and 1968 immediately caused great hardship and substantial increases in the cost of living for the population of the north. In 1958, and again in 1959, the region experienced massive social unrest as the people of the north-east expressed their resentment and anger at what they saw as discrimination, maladministration, and neglect. A commission of inquiry into the disturbances of 1958 in the central and eastern Rif mountains (the provinces of al-Hoceima and Nador) revealed exceptionally high levels of unemployment, lack of credit for agricultural development, inadequate economic and social infrastructures, and poor and corrupt administration.[41]

During the 1960s and 1970s, many Moroccans from the north sought employment outside the region. Historically, emigration had been east to Algeria, but after independence that route was closed and men from the Rif mountains either went west to the large cities of the Atlantic coastal areas (such as Casablanca), or to Western Europe.[42] For the last two decades, remittances from abroad have been the mainstay of the local economy, while agriculture and industry remained almost entirely underdeveloped. In 1971, when some 35 percent of the Moroccan population was recorded as unemployed, the province of al-Hoceima recorded a rate of 65 percent unemployment.[43] An evaluation of the 1973–77 national development plan shows that the north – notably al-Hoceima and Nador – received very little investment.[44] The development of irrigated agriculture on the left bank of the Moulouya River (which marks the southern boundary of Nador province) in the second half of the 1970s provided a boost to income among the minority owning land in the new irrigated perimeters, and a small increase in the local demand for labour. The north-east as a whole, and particularly the mountain areas, remained relatively disadvantaged and underdeveloped. The national plan for 1978–80 stressed the need for a reduction in spatial and social inequalities, but again concentrated investment in the most developed industrial and agricultural areas of the Atlantic littoral.

In Morocco, where income distribution is very unequal, the past two decades have witnessed a steady decline in the purchasing power of the poor. In 1960, the poorest 10 percent accounted for only 3.3 percent of the total value of consumption; by 1971 this had declined to a mere 1.2 percent. The introduction to the 1973–77 national plan recognized that 'the overall improvement in living standards from diminishing differentials in standards of living has to a certain extent accentuated the differentials.'[45] Between 1973 and 1977, food prices rose by an average of 11.1 percent a year, substantially faster than wages which, in any case, only marginally benefited the lower-paid and irregularly employed.[46] The rate of increase in the cost of living and in food prices slowed down somewhat in the period from 1977 to 1980 (averaging between 8.3 and 9.8 percent per year), but then accelerated dramatically again in the early 1980s: 12.5 percent between 1980 and 1981, 10.5 percent between 1981 and 1982, and 8.1 percent in the first nine months of 1983. Between 1973 and 1983, Morocco's cost-of-food index more than tripled. In the five months between July and October 1983, largely as a consequence of the August price increases, the food index rose 10.6 percent and the general cost-of-living index 8 percent.[47] For those able during the past 20 years to improve their incomes – certain sectors of organized labour, the better situated small businessmen, and the middle classes as a whole – the rising cost of living has been associated with improved standards of living. For those unable to keep pace with the rising prices – the 'unorganized' workers and some sections of the traditional petty bourgeoisie – the rise has meant declining living standards and pauperization.

Morocco has also experienced very rapid urbanization. With a demographic growth rate of some 2.5 percent a year, a large majority of the population under the age of 20, a massive expansion of the size and population of the popular quarters and shanty towns, and very considerable youth unemployment, the general features of the problem are similar to those of Tunisia, although arguably more serious. Even in 1971, the rate of unemployment and underemployment was estimated at around 35 percent of the labour force, and half of those recorded as unemployed were less than 24 years of age. The situation has worsened, if anything, since that time.[48] Within the more remote and relatively impoverished regions, rates of unemployment remain significantly higher even than in the shanty town areas of the big coastal cities.

Inequality, unemployment, and poverty are fundamentally social and not simple spatial problems. The 'poor' regions themselves exhibit major social inequalities, and the general lack of investment and economic development in these regions affects certain social classes more than others. In the north-east of Morocco, for example, it was clear even at the beginning of the 1970s that while foreign labour migration had increased the number of households with substantial incomes and had raised the average level of incomes within the region, it had also served generally to intensify economic and social inequalities. Those unable to obtain employment abroad were no more than before, from the working classes and small peasantry. The difficulty of finding reasonably paid jobs within the region ensured that their incomes were depressed both relatively and absolutely as the general cost of living rose.[49]

For the lower paid majority of workers in Tunisia and Morocco, and for the unemployed, the rising cost of living has had a devastating effect on their capacity to meet even their most basic needs. Only two and a half years ago, the World Bank suggested that well over 40 percent of the Moroccan population was living below the absolute poverty level.[50] In Tunisia, a very large proportion of households in the southern interior lives at or below the level of basic subsistence. In some of the shanty towns, conditions are at least as bad; infant mortality in the shanty town areas of Tunis, for example, ranges from 112 to 169 per thousand, compared with only 8 per thousand in the middle class residential area of al-Menzah.[51]

When President Bourguiba cancelled the price increases, he made some attempt to justify the original decision, remarking that bread was so cheap that some were feeding their cats on it. Such profligacy would be unthinkable for the majority of the population, and this comment reveals the yawning gap between the lived experience of rich and poor in Tunisia. When the price increase came in Tunisia at the end of December 1983, it was dramatic. The price of the 700-gramme flat loaf that is the basic staple for most poor people was raised from 80 millimes to 170 millimes. In the far south of Tunisia, it was the increase in the price of semolina (used for *couscous*) that created the main impact; as one local person explained, 'a sack of 50 kilos of semolina went from 7.2 dinars to 13.5, and a kilo of flour from 120 millimes to 295.'[52]

In Morocco, the major increases came in August 1983, when the 20 percent reduction in subsidies on basic commodities had its first impact: tea (much consumed by the poor) increased by 77 percent, and sugar by 14 percent, butter went up by nearly half, and cooking oil by 18 percent; on top of these came increases in the prices of soap and candles. At the beginning of January, virtually all basic foodstuffs (flour, bread, tea, sugar and cooking oil) went up by at least 20 percent, while cooking gas increased by 5 dirhams a bottle.[53] The budget for 1984 proposed further increases still. The *Financial Times* reported at the beginning of December that 'so far, the population has accepted the austerity measures and appears resigned to the lean years that lie ahead.'[54] But the second round of price rises, with the prospect of more to come, created an enormous sense of despair and anger which required only the trigger of the school strikes and demonstrations to burst out in an open, violent protest.

In Sudan, the bread riots in Khartoum and other towns during the Spring of 1985 were the culmination of more than five years of economic crisis and growing social unrest in the rural and urban areas.[55] Between 1978 (when the International Monetary Fund imposed an austere 'economic stabilization plan') and 1984, the value of the Sudanese pound declined from $2.87 to less than half a dollar. Exports slumped, and the cost of imported goods, including an increasing element of food grain, rose dramatically. The effect was a rapidly deteriorating balance of payments, a growing trade deficit, and a serious decline in the standard of living of urban workers and small rural producers as the cost of living soared. In 1979, there were mass demonstrations in the streets of Khartoum following increases in the price of several basic commodities – notably fuel, transportation, and food. Police eventually gained control after ten days of disturbances, but not without considerable violence and the eventual cancellation of the price increases by the government, and direct state intervention to ensure adequate supplies of bread and meat for the urban population.

Further implementation of 'the IMF package' during subsequent years – involving devaluations in 1980 and 1981 – failed to produce any increase in exports and was largely responsible for an upsurge of social unrest and protest throughout the country during December 1981 and January 1982. By the end of 1982, the Sudanese pound was devalued by 31 percent, and new austerity measures were declared. By 1983, after a series of poor harvests, the grain reserves in many provinces (including Kassala, northern and southern Darfur, and northern Kordofan) were virtually depleted, driving up grain prices to the extent that a bowlful of unprocessed sorghum could fetch as much as £6 Sudanese in the markets near Gedarif at the end of the 1983–84 harvest season. By January 1984, one bag of sorghum was selling for £140 Sudanese. People began to starve.

For months, the Numairi regime successfully covered up the existence of a growing famine, but in the meanwhile, there were incidents of hungry peasants attacking the granaries of merchants in al-Obeid and Gedarif, who responded by hiring armed guards to protect their hoards. Unrest mounted in the countryside, notably in the south, where the activities of the Sudan People's Liberation Army and Sudan People's Liberation Movement (SPLA/SPLM) were more effectively mobilized against the regime, and where guerrilla attacks on government forces and installations were increasing. Finally, early in 1984, during his visit to Washington, Numairi requested emergency food assistance from the United States. Approval in principle by the Reagan administration for some 70,000 tons of grain for the Sudan was delayed in practice, and by late 1984 the UN Food and Agriculture Organization (FAO) listed Sudan as one of the twelve countries hardest hit by famine, and estimated that over a million people were at risk of starvation.

In eastern Sudan in particular (where refugees from Eritrea and Tigray have been crossing the border for years as a result of protracted war, drought, and famine), the situation was extremely serious. In 1984, drought hit the eastern Sudan very badly (estimates suggest that more than 80 percent of the harvest failed) and contributed to a growing shortage of food and dramatic rises in the price of grain (from £30 Sudanese in 1984 to £140 Sudanese by January 1985) in the area. In addition, the price of livestock dropped as peasants sold off their animals to buy grain, thereby reducing their capacity to raise income, while wages for agricultural labour declined, as did the demand for farm labour itself. The result was rapid pauperization and immiseration of large sections of the rural population. One major consequence of this was an acceleration of the already substantial rural exodus to the urban areas, notably to Khartoum. In the town, however, conditions for the urban poor had also deteriorated as the government's austerity measures, combined with the economic crisis, ensured a reduction in employment opportunities and incomes. When in March 1985 the government introduced yet another round of price increases – first in fuel and later in sugar-based commodities and bread – the urban poor and the rural refugees joined together in a wave of mass demonstrations which lasted three days and provided the impetus for the rapid development of organized political protest and opposition to Numairi's regime.

Economic policy and economic crisis

Why in Tunisia, Morocco, and Sudan in 1984 and 1985 was the price of basic commodities, upon which the urban poor so crucially depend, increased? After all, the social and political repercussions of such measures are well known, and even in North Africa in the mid-1980s there was ample evidence that bread riots were a distinct possibility as a response to food price rises. In Egypt in 1977 and the Sudan in 1979, 'bread riots' were a reaction to major increases in food prices.[56] In Morocco, price increases in June 1981 for a range of basic commodities (sugar, flour, butter, and cooking oil) provoked a warning strike by the Democratic Labour Federation, founded in 1978 to protest against price increases in staple goods. In Casablanca, these turned into violent street demonstrations as workers in both the private and public sectors were joined first by small shopkeepers, and then by students and the unemployed from the shanty towns. The social unrest brought special police units, the national guard, and finally the army into action. In two days of clashes throughout the city, between 637 and 1,000 demonstrators were killed.[57]

In a period of increasing economic difficulties, the economic cost of maintaining subsidies on certain consumption items may appear too high to governments, and the social costs of removing these subsidies simply the price to be paid for improved performance. If those whose support for the government is essential can be convinced of this need for austerity, and if the most obvious sources of organized opposition can be either muzzled or co-opted by preferential treatment, the social and political repercussions of adopting a hard line on subsidies may appear manageable.

The annual report of Tunisia's central bank in Autumn 1983 warned of difficult years ahead. Clearly, it believed that an economic crisis was a possibility. In the last few years, lower output and prices for oil and phosphates (the two major foreign exchange earners), a decline in foreign tourists, and a slowing down of industrial growth have all affected the balance of trade and balance of payments. In 1983, the trade deficit grew by 24 percent, to 738 million dinars, during the first ten months. This led to the restriction of imports of certain raw materials and semi-finished goods to 80 percent of 1982 volumes. Agriculture, which has remained a low priority in Tunisia's development strategy, has virtually stagnated in terms of output since 1976, and grain imports have become increasingly necessary. Inflation has also risen significantly in the last five years reaching double digit figures in 1982. In 1983, the bread subsidy alone cost around 114 million dinars – about 2 percent of GDP. Subsidies on all cereal-based products (bread, couscous, and pasta) account for 60 percent of the total food subsidy of 259 million dinars.[58]

But this deterioration in the state of the Tunisian economy could not be said to have reached a crisis yet. The *Financial Times*, which reflects an economic philosophy close to that of the IMF, observed that 'the manner in which the Tunisian authorities set about reducing the growing budgetary burden of subsidies on basic foodstuffs provides an object lesson in how not to do the right thing.'[59] In its view, it was not the removal of subsidies that was at fault, but the suddenness and the size of the increases in the price of basic goods, and failure to consider seriously the social and political implications. It argued that 'neither the IMF nor the World Bank advocated, or would have advocated, the approach to subsidies adopted by the Tunisian government at the turn of the year.'[60] In fact, the IMF and World Bank have put pressure on numerous Third World countries, including Morocco and Sudan, to adopt austerity measures without delay and with little heed for the social, and even political, implications, as will be shown below.

It is significant that the former Tunisian minister of economic affairs, Azouz Lasram, who had overseen the gradual and relatively trouble-free removal of subsidies on energy prices since 1980, resigned in October 1983, precisely because he was aware of the implications of the sudden dramatic increase in basic commodity prices. Lasram argued that the poorer Tunisians should be protected; yet the price of the *baguette* (mainly consumed by the middle classes) increased by less than that of the popular flat loaf that is the staple for the urban poor, or of the *couscous* that is central to the diet of the far south. It is also of interest that the new draft budget presented to the Tunisian National

Assembly in Tunis in March 1984 included proposals to raise revenues by increased by less than that of the popular flat loaf that is the staple for the cut back on investment. Together, these measures would generate approximately 40 million dinars. Between March and July 1984, several small price increases were introduced for specific foodstuffs and public services and gave rise to no obvious social unrest. A slight increase – up to 10 millimes – in the price of bread, semolina, and other cereal products, on July 10, 1984, occurred without any particular reaction from the mass of the Tunisian population.

Why, then, the earlier decision suddenly to raise prices? Prime Minister Mzali stated that the potential saving was around 140 million dinars. 'If the government had relied on taxes,' he said, 'all prices would have increased as in 1982 and the government would not have raised a fifth of that amount.'[61] Another reason is the confidence of the government that they had the strong support of the middle classes and the tacit acceptance of organized labour. Finally, there was clearly a belief that the security forces could maintain control and prevent social unrest. In the event, it was not from organized labour that the protest came, and not from the middle classes, if one excepts the students, but from the mass of the poor and disinherited. The government seriously miscalculated both the response of the Tunisian people and the capacity of the state to implement its 'new' economic policies without repression.

If the Tunisian economy was in serious difficulties at the beginning of the 1980s, the Moroccan economy was already in crisis. Morocco's foreign debt is now over \$11 billion, and debt servicing alone rose from 700 million dirhams in 1976 to 2,500 million in 1980, and reached an estimated 5,000 million dirhams in 1983. The critical balance of payments situation results from internal problems, world price changes, increasing Common Market competition and protectionism, and the cost of the war in the Sahara. Industrial output has not increased significantly, and agriculture has remained generally stagnant in terms of output over the past decade, while the international price of phosphates declined in the second half of the 1970s. The overall value of exports has grown slowly – from 6,200 million dirhams in 1975 to 7,300 million in 1979 – but in the second half of the 1970s, the cost of imports rose steeply – from 10,440 million dirhams in 1975 to 14,300 million in 1979. The balance of trade deficit has steadily worsened.[62] In the 1950s, Morocco was a net exporter of cereals, but by the late 1970s, between 40 and 50 percent of the country's cereal requirements were imported. Earnings from remittances and from tourism have increasingly failed to cover the deficit, and Morocco has become even more dependent on aid and loans.

Efforts in late 1983 to reschedule about \$530 million of its debts owed to commercial banks (which fell due between September 1983 and the end of 1984) ran into considerable difficulties. In September 1983, the International Monetary Fund formally approved the programme of 'economic stabilization' that it had earlier recommended, and made it a condition for further loans. This was the programme which the Moroccan government began implementing in August. It included a creeping devaluation of the dirham, the rescheduling of part of the foreign debt, severe cuts in public expenditure (including investment), and the removal of subsidies on basic goods. August saw a 10 percent devaluation and a first round of price rises. At the beginning of December 1983, negotiations with major United States and European banks to reschedule part of the country's foreign debt were reportedly nearly complete; but the prospects for the next year or so looked grim even at that time. Just servicing the foreign debt would absorb at least 40 percent of Morocco's hard currency income, while the visible trade deficit – which the government reduced by around 27 percent during 1983, largely by restricting imports and stifling domestic demand – would remain uncomfortably high. Officials projected that the investment budget for 1984 would decline by roughly a third, compared with the 1981–85 Economic Development Plan projections. The figure for 1985 was thought likely to drop to 40 percent below initial projections.

Given this bleak outlook and the pressure from the IMF to maintain tight control over expenditure, the Moroccan government was inclined to reduce even further the burden of subsidies, and the draft budget for 1984 contained proposals to raise prices again.

Unlike the case of Tunisia, the pressure from the IMF to adopt extremely stringent austerity measures was great and immediate. With the recent experience of 1978–79 and 1981 clearly in mind, the Moroccan government must have approached the price increases of August 1983 with very considerable trepidation. There was no dramatic response at the time, for several reasons. First, the price increases came after two years of rapidly rising food prices, whereas in Tunisia the price of basic foodstuffs had been kept level for a long period of time. Second, the price increases in August were between 20 and 35 percent, compared with the 100 percent or more increase in Tunisia. Third, wage increases among certain sectors of organized labour had helped reduce the threat of union-organized strikes. But if the price increases did not immediately bring the Moroccan people onto the streets in open protest, they added considerably to the sense of desperation and frustration of the large majority whose living conditions have not visibly improved over the past decade, and particularly of those who have seen their standard of living deteriorate. A second round of price increases at the end of December set the stage for the January 'bread riots.'

In Sudan, the economic crisis was even more acute than in Morocco. Throughout the 1970s and into the early 1980s, reliance on export earnings to fund economic and social development, combined with policies which effectively starved the export sector, led to increasing balance of trade and balance of payments deficits and growing foreign debt. The external public debt rose from $308 million (15.3 percent of GNP) in 1970 to $3,097 million (37.2 percent of GNP) in 1980, and then to $6,300 million in 1982. Foreign reserves were insufficient to pay for even half a month's imports. IMF 'economic stabilization' measures imposed between 1978 and 1984 failed to resolve the acute crisis in the Sudanese economy and, indeed, arguably exacerbated it. By the beginning of 1985, the high hopes of a decade earlier – when the UN Food and Agriculture Organization described Sudan as a potential 'bread-basket of the world' – had turned to economic nightmare. Agricultural and industrial production had declined (in per capita terms) over the previous seven years; external debt had risen to over $9 billion, and even interest on the debt could be paid only by raising new loans; imports were three times the level of exports; the value of the Sudanese pound had fallen to less than 10 percent of its 1978 value (against the US dollar); and the 1984 grain harvest had failed to provide even half of the country's needs (1.5 million tons instead of 3.4 million tons).

In Sudan, as in Tunisia and Morocco, the logic of the economic 'liberalism' pursued over the previous decade has led directly to the growth of inequality, unemployment, and social deprivation, which themselves underlay the discontent and social unrest. Particularly in a period of world economic recession, the 'open door' strategy for economic development has proved a snare and a delusion. Ultimately, these economic policies and their social consequences derive from the distinctive class structure and dynamic of contemporary Tunisia, Morocco, and Sudan, and from the dominance of certain economic interests within the political sphere. The balance of forces in all these countries has enabled certain sections of the bourgeoisie to maintain their predominance in the political as well as the economic sphere. They thus could ensure that the government pursued 'liberal' export-oriented economic policies – over the past decade in Tunisia and Sudan and for roughly 20 years in the case of Morocco – to their very considerable advantage, but at the expense of the majority of workers and peasants. The struggle between the various sections of capital, and that between capital as a whole and organized labour, have marginalized a significant proportion of the population and perpetuated economic policies favouring big capital. These policies have created their own social and political contradictions and deepened the crisis of the national economy.

Even if the riots of 1984 and rebellion of 1985 do not oblige an immediate reassessment of the entire economic strategy on the part of the governments in Tunisia, Morocco, and Sudan, it may stimulate more serious consideration of alternatives among those whose interests are not best served by the 'open door' policies that have predominated hitherto. The opposition parties and trade unions may reconsider their own political strategies and recognize the potential for a broad-based popular movement to include the unorganized and unemployed, as well as the organized workers and disaffected members of the middle class.

Neither the repression of popular protest in Tunisia and Morocco, nor the military coup which replaced Numairi in Sudan, will be able for long to prevent further social and political unrest unless new economic policies and strategies can be developed which meet both the demands and the needs of the masses. Such policies and strategies, however, are unlikely to be pursued unless the social and political contradictions created by previous regimes give rise to a significantly new balance of social forces.[63]

134   *Power and Stability in the Middle East*

Notes

1. *Le Monde*, January 31, 1984.
2. *Ibid.*, January 5, 1984.
3. *Times* (London), January 4, 1984.
4. *Ibid.*
5. *Le Monde*, January 7, 1984.
6. All details from dispatches in British newspapers of March 29, 1985, including the *Guardian*, *Times*, *Daily Telegraph* and *Financial Times*.
7. *Times*, April 1, 1985.
8. *Guardian*, April 2, 1985.
9. *Le Monde*, January 6, 1984.
10. J. D. Seddon, *Moroccan Peasants* (Folkestone, UK, William Dawson, 1981) pp. 176–80.
11. *Le Monde*, January 6, 1984.
12. *Financial Times*, February 1, 1984.
13. *Le Monde*, January 31, 1984.
14. *Ibid.*, January 7, 1984.
15. *Ibid.*
16. *Ibid.*, January 4, 1984.
17. This period of strikes culminated in the violence following the general strike of January 1978, when the army intervened and large numbers (estimates vary between 46 and 200) were killed. See W. Ruf, 'Tunisia: Contemporary Politics,' in R. Lawless and A. Findlay (eds.) *North Africa* (New York, St Martin's Press, 1984) p. 109.
18. *Le Monde*, January 4, 1984.
19. These workers represent 47 percent of all unemployed, but only a quarter of the labour force. Anne M. Findlay, 'Geographical Patterns of Moroccan Emigration,' MA thesis, University of Durham, 1978, p. 60.
20. *Le Monde*, January 4, 1984.
21. A. Zghal, 'La Tunisie, dernière république civile,' *Jeune Afrique*, no. 1,205, February 8, 1984.
22. Godfrey Morrison in the *Times*, January 7, 1984.
23. *Times*, March 30, 1985; *Al-Sharq al-Awsat*, March 31, 1985; *Al-Rai al-Aam*, March 31, 1985.
24. *Times*, April 1, 1985; *Al-Sharq al-Awsat*, March 31, 1985.
25. *Al-Watan*, April 2, 1985.
26. *Al-Arab*, April 2, 1985.
27. *Guardian*, April, 2, 1985; *Al-Watan*, April 2, 1985; *Al-Sharq al-Awsat*, April 2, 1985.
28. *Guardian*, April 3, 1985; *Times*, April 3, 1985; *Daily Telegraph*, April 3, 1985; *Al-Sharq al-Awsat*, April 3, 1985.
29. *Times*, April 6, 1985; *Al-Anbaa*, April 4, 1985.
30. *Guardian*, April 6, 1985.
31. *Al-Watan*, April 5, 1985; *Al-Anbaa*, April 5, 1985.
32. *Guardian*, April 4, 1985.
33. *Al-Anbaa*, April 5, 1985; *Times*, April 6, 1985; *Al-Sharq al-Awsat*, April 6, 1985; *Times*, April 6, 1985.
34. *Al-Ahram*, April 7, 1985.
35. *Al-Watan*, April 8, 1985.
36. A. Findlay, 'Tunisia: The Vicissitudes of Economic Development,' in R. Lawless and A. Findlay (eds.) *North Africa*, p. 225.
37. *Le Monde*, January 31, 1984.
38. A. Zghal, 'La Tunisie: dernière république civile,' p. 35.
39. At the end of 1983, $1.00 equalled 0.73 Tunisian dinars.
40. *Le Monde*, January 31, 1984.
41. J. D. Seddon, *Moroccan Peasants*, p. 179.

42. J. D. Seddon, 'Labour Migration and Agricultural Development in Northeast Morocco, 1807–1970,' *The Maghreb Review* (1979).

43. A. Findlay, 'The Moroccan Economy in the 1970's,' in R. Lawles and A. Findlay (eds.) *North Africa*, vol. IV, no. 3 (May–June 1979).

44. P. de Mas, 'The Place of Peripheral Regions in Moroccan Planning,' *Tijdschrift voor Economische en Sociale Geografie*, vol. 69, nos. 1–2 (1978).

45. *Plan de Développement Economique et Social 1973–1977* (Rabat, 1973) vol. 1, p. 14.

46. A. Findlay, 'The Moroccan Economy in the 1970s,' p. 193.

47. Banque Marocaine de Commerce Exterieur, *Monthly Information Review*, no. 46 (November–December 1983) p. 26.

48. A. Findlay, 'The Moroccan Economy in the 1970's,' p. 210.

49. J. D. Seddon, *Moroccan Peasants*, pp. 247–48.

50. *Financial Times*, January 24, 1984.

51. A. Zghal, 'La Tunisie, dernière république civile,' p. 35.

52. *Le Monde*, January 31, 1984.

53. At the end of 1983, $1.00 equalled 8.0 dirhams.

54. *Financial Times*, December 1, 1983.

55. The following analysis of the roots of social unrest in Sudan draws on J. O'Brien, 'Sowing the Seeds of Famine,' *Review of African Political Economy*, no. 33 (August 1985); N. O'Neill, 'Recent Trends in Foreign Investment and Uneven Development in Sudan,' and an unnamed Sudanese economist, 'Sudan: A Policy of Increasing Denationalization of National Wealth,' both in *Review of African Political Economy*, no. 26 (July 1983); T. Niblock, 'Sudan's Economic Nightmare,' *MERIP Reports*, no. 135 (September 1985); and A. Abdelkarim, A. el-Hassan and D. Seddon, 'The Generals Step In,' *MERIP Reports*, no. 135 (September 1985).

56. For a discussion of these and the factors behind them, see M. G. Weinbaum, 'Food and Political Stability in the Middle East,' *Studies in Comparative International Development*, no. 15 (Summer 1980) pp. 3–26.

57. *Le Monde*, (English version) in *The Guardian Weekly*, July 12, 1981.

58. *Economist*, January 14, 1984.

59. *Financial Times*, January 9, 1984.

60. *Ibid*.

61. *Le Monde*, January 7, 1984.

62. P. Sluglett and M. Farouk-Sluglett, 'Modern Morocco: Political Immobilism, Economic Dependence,' in R. Lawless and A. Findlay (eds.) *North Africa*, p. 88.

63. Since the writing of this essay in 1987, similar riots and rebellions have taken place in Algeria in 1988 over rises in the price of bread and other staples, resulting in many deaths through repressive military action and the imposition of a state of emergency throughout the country. And on June 30, 1989, another military coup took place in Sudan, following continued unrest in that country. Details on the nature of the latest military action in Sudan are unavailable at press time.

8. Women and National Politics in the Middle East[1]

Julie Peteet

This essay examines the political activism of Middle Eastern women in the context of militant national liberation movements, incipient state formation, and state consolidation. The first part looks at women in a selective variety of Middle Eastern political settings with a view to ascertaining how they fared in the wake of state consolidation or in national movements. The second part is an examination of one specific case: the Palestinian movement in pre-1982 Lebanon.

Women and politics in the Middle East

The literature on women and politics in the Middle East is still in its infancy,[2] and a number of questions need to be posed. Why do some states and movements find it imperative to mobilize women and the domestic sector? How do women respond to this campaign? Why do groups of women focus their energies and organizational capacities on mobilizing women for national political endeavours? What are the implications of recruitment for changing the political consciousness of women? What classes and ages of women are mobilized, and what happens when extensive mobilization gives way to the task of state building? Finally, does the participation of women inform a transformation of assymetrical gender relations?

A cursory review of historical and anthropological literature sheds light on the current political behaviour of women, for women were politically significant and visible prior to the era of modern, national politics. As early as the 1960s, the literature on women in the region cast doubt on the universality of a gender-based, hierarchically arranged, ahistorical private/public dichotomy where women occupied a subordinate position distant from the political arena.[3] In a study of a Lebanese Druze community it was found that women played a significant role in 'crossing dangerous political boundaries' during political crises when male mobility was hindered, and actively gave their support to their menfolk in local disputes and political alliance-making; highly endogamous Druze marriages ' . . . tended to perpetuate the territorial continuity of Druze occupation. . . .'[4] Druze women are thus significant not only in the local sense, that is, in maintaining group cohesion, but play a critical role in sustaining the national structure of Lebanon and in the Druze community's position as a minority sect.[5] L. Sweet shows that with increasing integration into regional, national, and international capitalist economic structures and market relations, public/private separation intensifies. Women's role in production declines, and ideologies of their subordination are more easily realized.[6] For example, with migration to the West and the constant flow of remittances from abroad, '. . . the women of 'Ain ad Dayr are now more confined to the village and community home activities than they may have been in the recent past.'[7]

While exposing the limitations of the public/domestic dichotomy, research that highlights the political roles of women in alliance making and in informal power situations also indicates their limited access to the channels and personnel of the power structure, particularly where these channels have been transformed and integrated into larger regional or national entities. Among the Qashqa'i nomads of Iran, for instance, where sexual asymmetry is not marked, decisions concerning migration routes and encampments are made jointly by men and women, but political relations with external agencies are the exclusive concern of men.[8] State-enforced sedentarization, entry into regional capitalist markets and economic specialization, and state control over nomadic affairs '. . . tend(s) to erode women's status, because the very bases of status shift from the domestic camp arena to a wider arena.'[9] Cultural constraints that circumscribe the mobility of women beyond domestic confines are called into play as nomads attempt to compete with and assimilate into the urban socio-normative structure. The presence of strangers in the vicinity of now fixed domestic units further necessitates increased control over the activities of women.[10]

On the border region of Turkey and Syria, élite women controlled property in those instances where men were unavailable. Women were, however, unable to sustain such a relation to property when its management and the distribution of surplus entered the capitalist orbit of productive relations '. . . due to their inability to make major alliances in the male-dominated patron–client relationships external to the immediate village.'[11]

Although a sharp line of demarcation between the public and private worlds of men and women in the Middle East has been overdrawn, studies indicate that a more pronounced form of separation occurs during the process of tighter integration into regional political entities, state structures, and urban-based capitalist markets.[12] This process of integration can entail restriction of women's mobility, access to resources, and their ability to initiate and sustain economic and political relations beyond the kin group. It is at this economic and political juncture that limitations to the social participation of women and their ability to enter into social relations become clearest. Ideologies that define women domestically and limit their mobility rather quickly assume new, more restrictive dimensions as they are realized in the extreme. This implies that ideologies about women assume both force and specificity in particular economic and political contexts.

Social scientists have increasingly begun to examine the roles and statuses of

Arab women in the context of national politics and emerging state systems in their economic, political, and social dimensions.[13] It is at this juncture that the intertwining of gender and class becomes most apparent. The recent focus of inquiry has shifted from small-scale, local-level social organization to regional, national, and international processes of development and integration.

The involvement of Arab/Middle Eastern women in politics beyond the local level has usually been under the aegis of national politics. The struggles waged for independence from foreign domination in Algeria and Palestine, movements has been a questioning of national movements' and newly formed building process in Yemen furnish models for examining women's role in the political process. A common theme for both observers and women in these movements has been a questioning of national movements' and newly-formed states' commitment to gender equality. R. Sayigh succinctly stated one of the outstanding problematics in the study of women in national liberation movements when she pointed out '. . . the need to decide whether or not there is a problem of women independent of the collective national problem, and what is the correct relation between the two.'[14]

Challenging Fanon's vision of the revolutionary impact of armed struggle on Algerian women, J. Minces situates the dismal position of post-liberation Algerian women in the absence of a clear, ideological stance by the national movement on the nature of a post-liberation state and the role women play in it; in the nature of the participation of women (as auxiliaries or replacements for men), which inhibited the growth of a feminist consciousness, and the non-autonomous and appendage-like nature of women's organizations.[15] A protracted national crisis and a high level of violence compelled women to break traditional boundaries and engage in militancy; but once the war was over, women were reassigned to domesticity. F. M'rabet, in an exposé of the situation of women in post-revolutionary Algeria, contends that the petty-bourgeois leadership, with its stress on nationalism and tradition as the embodiment of cultural authenticity, manipulated traditional ideology, a prominent mobilizing force against colonial domination, in order to consolidate their class position.[16] Articulating the coincidence of gender and class oppression, M'rabet suggests that the state is unwilling to make the cost investments – education and subsidies for domestic labour and child care – necessary for women's integration into the public sector on an equal basis with men. Nor can the unemployment factor be ignored. To avoid social unrest as a consequence of high levels of unemployment, women were discouraged from seeking employment, and priority for jobs was accorded to men.[17] Cultivating the support of the Islamic clergy also played a significant role in the Algerian state's neglect of the issue of women.[18]

South Yemen provides an example of a quite different set of historical and political circumstances. The apparent success of South Yemeni women in avoiding demobilization in the wake of national liberation and state reformation attests to the necessity of scrutinizing state commitment to gender equality. One of the basic strategies of the Yemeni state in pursuit of social development has been to integrate women into the labour force to enlarge the human resource base, to integrate them into the political process to expand the support base of the regime, and to transform the family to accelerate the development process.[19] Unlike Algeria, Yemen suffered a labour shortage and women formed a largely untapped resource. Furthermore, the Yemeni state expressed its commitment to gender equality by curbing the power of the religious judiciary and introducing a Family Code that substantially revised a number of Islamic legal codes governing women's status in the family. A law was pressed into service to alter the family towards a nuclear structure and more egalitarian relations. New laws were to be instrumental in forming new personalities and identities based less in the family and more in women's role in production and politics.[20] The Yemeni example points to the need for examining both ideological promotions of gender equality as a moral and developmental issue, expressed in a reformed legal system, and women's actual access to economic opportunities, channels of power, and legal equality. In spite of being the most radical legal reform in the Arab world, a number of legal inequalities still prevail. (For example, men still retain more grounds for divorce than women, and the bride-price, although reduced, remains a legitimate transaction accompanying marriage.) The government of South Yemen perceives the need to refrain from openly renouncing Islam, and retained some of its legal strictures governing personal status matters.

With regard to Sudan, a country with one of the strongest Communist parties in the region, S. Hale locates the factors responsible for inhibiting the emergence of a strong autonomous women's movement or a party platform and practice that genuinely supports gender equality. She mentions the appendage-like relations that prevailed between the Party and the Women's Union, and concludes that they reproduced the hierarchical relations that prevail in capitalist society. The Party was less interested in transforming the position of women than in mobilizing women to recruit other women into the Party. Perhaps most significant, however, was the separation of the private from the political. Relations between men and women were determined to be 'private,' and thus not a 'political' issue meriting serious attention.[21] The pattern of internal segregation appears to be fairly common when women participate in national politics. What is apparent in the Sudanese case, and for the rest of the region, is that public and private domains are the sites of internal sexual segregation.[22] Women are not necessarily excluded from the public domain, but remain distant from the centres of power within it.

Iran serves as a useful example for examining the relationship of women to politics and state consolidation in the wake of the 1979 revolution. M. Hegland argues that the participation of Iranian village women in the anti-Shah, pro-Khomeini activities in their villages did not result in any substantial changes in their social position, since it was neither new nor did it fundamentally deviate from their previous local political participation. She also contends that during periods of strong state centralization, village political activities in general diminished in intensity, and this included those of women. With the weakening of the state, women reappeared in village politics. Contrasting urban women with village women, she notes that the village business, particularly trading, was conducted in a setting very close to or integrated into the home. In the cities, by contrast, the bazaar was clearly separated from the domestic sector. Village women were active in the family business and, as such, forged and maintained economic and political relations. Thus, village economic organization facilitated the role of women in local factional politics.[23]

Iranian feminist scholars are adamant that the emancipation of women is incompatible with an Islamic regime that mobilizes women for struggle but is quick to exclude them from the process of state consolidation, banishing them to veiled seclusion. Yeganeh writes that the Khomeini regime discovered the tremendous potential of women to mobilize and express their discontent, and reacted soon after victory to 'Islamize' their position by mandating veiling and proclaiming motherhood as the primary social duty of women.[24] The regime, now firmly in power, acted to demobilize women and reassign them to the domestic realm: 'Women did not participate in the Revolution as "women", but as members of different political and social forces. Yet after the Revolution they found themselves treated specially as women.'[25] A. Tabari notes that there is no contradiction between the traditional roles of women and their political activism when it is within an Islamic framework. Thus, the regime continues to maintain the presence of women in the political domain in such a manner as not to conflict with domesticity and remain within the ideological parameters of Islam.[26] For instance, the regime encouraged the formation of Muslim women's organizations devoted to mobilizing and sustaining support for the regime among traditional sectors of society. Having witnessed the potential for women's discontent to become a potent secular mobilizing force, as evidenced in the massive street march on International Women's Day in 1979, where large numbers of women protested against the increasing Islamization of their status, the regime decided to organize and encourage state-sponsored associations for Muslim women with a view to pre-empting such secular potential. Again, we encounter the pattern of women appearing in the militant political process when the state is reforming, and then being demobilized by force, if necessary.

No review of women and politics would be complete without at least a passing reference to the phenomenon of veiled activist women in Egypt, a subject of recent scrutiny by a number of scholars.[27] Some have contended that readoption of the veil is not a sign of seclusion and restriction, as it was in the past, but is rather an empowering phenomenon that facilitates women's movement in public, easing their presence in sexually mixed educational and work settings.[28] Others have argued that the veil casts women as sex objects, stressing their essentially sexual nature.[29] Whether the veil empowers or makes sex objects of women, veiled activists are visible on the streets and university campuses of cities such as Cairo. They are part of a larger Islamic resurgence in an area that seeks to establish an Islamic state and society where carefully delineated spheres of social life would be assigned on the basis of gender.

By and large, these cases indicate that the participation of women in national struggles can be extensive without involving substantial changes in the sexual division of labour, or the access of women to power in post-liberation states.

Women's increased integration into the national political process (and the labour force) has not been accompanied by a transformation in the control over women vested in the family and upheld in the legal system of most Middle Eastern states.[30] By examining one specific case study, the Palestinians, during the actual process of organizing for national liberation, a phase that in this case could be termed 'incipient state formation,' we can examine in depth some of the points brought out in this selective review of women's political activism in the region.

Palestinian women

The Palestinian national movement, crystallized around the PLO, represents approximately four and one-half million people, nearly half of whom are dispersed in various countries in the region and abroad. It faces a large. well-equipped military power that enjoys strong international support. Since its inception, the PLO has faced continuous military and political crises; with its evacuation from Beirut in the wake of the 1982 Israeli invasion of Lebanon, the PLO lost its last autonomous base of operations.[31]

The protracted nature of the Palestinian quest for self-determination has placed the exile community and those under Israeli occupation in a state of constant insecurity and crisis. Yet, following the PLO's 1969 assumption of control of the refugee camps in Lebanon, the PLO became a kind of embryonic government for the refugees, providing a wide range of quasi-governmental municipal and social services and economic enterprises far beyond those of a strictly military nature for which it is more commonly known. One source of the uniqueness of incipient Palestinian state formation stems from the fact that it was unfolding from adjacent countries.

Exile, national struggle, and incipient state formation had an uneven impact on women. At the same time, statelessness and the national movement have formed the axis around which women have organized, and both inform a certain continuity of position and consciousness. Women in the camps, for the most part poor and uneducated, are here the main focus.

Although essential changes had been set in motion during the first two decades of exile, the major impetus for initiating and sustaining a transformation in the roles of women occurred under the aegis of the Palestinian Resistance Movement. The Resistance furthered the structural transformations set in motion by exile and the destruction of a system of agricultural production, establishing the national and institutional framework for change and shaping its contours. Economic enterprises to employ women opened. and the national context of employment lent legitimacy to their new roles. During the 1950s, for example, it was not uncommon for young camp women to work as maids for wealthy urban families. By the early 1970s, the Resistance was providing women with opportunities for vocational training and employment, a move favourably received by the camp population as a step in the process of social development. Parents are often heard to justify a daughter's employment by commenting, 'She's working for the cause,' or, if she is enrolled in a vocational training programme, 'She'll be able to take care of her children.' Thus, changes in women's role were initiated by a national crisis, and then materialized, institutionalized, and legitimized by the Resistance, which lent them a patriotic, national context.

Women's political activism

With roots going back to the 1920s, when élite urban women organized demonstrations, strikes, and boycotts to protest against Zionist immigration and the British Mandate in Palestine, the Palestinian women's movement is one of the oldest in the Arab world.[32] During this period, women were organized around the Palestine Women's Union, which incorporated various women's associations, charities, and organizations.[33] The Union was the precursor of the current General Union of Palestinian Women (GUPW), a component part of the PLO. Until 1948, this movement remained largely isolated from the more spontaneous, diffuse, and militant actions of rural women in defence of their communities. Peasant women transported weapons and messages, hid fighters from the authorities, provided food for them and nursing care to the wounded, and as an omen of the future, a few women fought alongside the men.

The early women's movement posed no challenge to prevailing norms of domesticity, nor did the women themselves express any demands for change in their position. A now elderly woman, active in the 1936 and 1948 conflicts, recalls: 'We never thought we women had any problems. We were working in a revolution for the rights of men who had none. Our main concern was politics – the Palestine problem, though we did initiate and encourage education for girls.' Obviously, élite women's activism had not begun to challenge norms of female propriety, although it may have awakened the initial stirrings of feminist consciousness. The movement was nationalistic and patriotic. Women discerned no clear separation of their issues from those of a country under foreign rule and in danger of being expropriated by the increasingly militant Zionist movement. Indeed, at this early stage, women were vitally aware of the limitations on their movement of the absence of an independent state structure in which to pursue and consolidate reforms.[34]

With the emergence of the Palestinian national movement in the late 1960s, and the formation of a women's movement under the umbrella of the GUPW, a minority of women, largely middle class, once again assumed a visibly active role. Women are affiliated with Resistance organizations in a variety of ways: as friends, members, or full-time cadres. To be a friend (*sadiqa*), the most common category of affiliation for camp women, means that one identifies with and supports the policies of one of the various Resistance groups, works with them during crises, and can be counted on to attend their events in the camps. Kinship ties usually colour a woman's friendship with an organization; friends are often wives, sisters, and mothers of male members. A friend supports policies in political debates and discussions and identifies herself as a friend or supporter of a specific organization. The category of friend also connotes specific patterns of action. Friends attend Resistance events in the camp – such as lectures, films, seminars, funerals, demonstrations, and national holidays – and can be mobilized during crises to help the organization with nursing, preparing food, and undertaking civil defence and first aid tasks.

Members are either ordinary 'regular' members or full-time. When asked what they do in the Resistance, or of their relations to political organizations, women are quick to distinguish between those who are full-time, salaried members, and regular members. The latter are formally affiliated with an organization, are under the authority of a 'responsible' within it, and are expected to attend meetings and carry out certain assignments.[35] These women may also be students, housewives, or have other employment.

Full-time members, or cadres, work in the Resistance, either in its organizational or administrative sectors, for which they receive a salary. Fluehr-Lobban defines cadres as '. . . militants attached to a political party.' She deftly notes that militancy does not necessarily indicate involvement with armed struggle, but rather is a '. . . type of political involvement where women cadres are linked to political parties, even taking on leadership roles within that party.'[36] The term 'cadre' indicates the potential for higher political advancement in that as a woman continues to mature politically, becoming more proficient in the political theory of the organization and undertaking more responsible tasks, she will advance up the organizational ladder.

It is difficult to draw distinct boundaries between forms of affiliation. Women in the camps quite naturally draw a distinction between formal political affiliation and their own fluid form of community-based involvement, yet nearly every household in the camps is affiliated, in one way or another, with the Resistance. If a father or brother is a member of an organization, the whole family is often considered by itself and by others to be supporters or friends of that organization. Women are no exception to this type of kin-based, self-defined affiliation. Um 'Ali, mother of seven, was not active in the Resistance and rarely ever attended Resistance events in the camps, but if one were to ask her if she was affiliated, she would respond without hesitation: 'We belong to Fatah.' Her husband was a Fatah commando; his membership of that organization was his family's sole source of income, social services, and protection, and thus formed the overriding component of its political identity.

Women can be found in all sectors of the Resistance: military, political, and social. There is, however, a sexual division of labour within the Resistance; women tend to be most concentrated in the social field, and least in the military. In spite of several highly visible women who head social institutions, the vast majority remain distant from the centres of power and decision making. This division of labour is a replica of that of society at large and tends to reproduce the same types of hierarchical gender relations.

The PLO did not encourage the full integration of women into the military. Undoubtedly, many camp girls of high-school age were given military training courses on weekends or after school; the intent was less to engage them in full-time military work on an equal footing with men, and more to raise their political consciousness. The PLO sponsored political and military clubs for boys, the 'lions' (*ashbal*), and for girls the 'flowers' (*zahrat*). In these mass organizations, young girls and women were prepared to form a militia as a second line of defence in the event of attacks against the camps; however, these girls and the masses of trained women were not called upon to defend the camps, even during the siege and battle of Beirut in 1982.

On the one hand, PLO policy on women's military training was partly a result of a surplus of young men. On the other hand, concern with alienating what was perceived to be a conservative mass base served to circumscribe women's military mobilization. The division of labour in the Resistance relegates women to a back-up role in times of crises. During military attack, women may be mobilized for guard duty and to supervise relief efforts. Every organization has some full-time women in the military, but they are few in number.

Organizational work means building the organization, its mass base, and its institutions. The bulk of organizational work is carried out by full-time members, another feature which distinguishes them from regular members. What this often means is women cadres mobilize other women and cultivate mass support for the organization.

Women are also actively involved in administrative aspects of the Resistance. Social institutions are staffed primarily by women members and employees, yet they do not reach positions of power in these institutions or in the political echelons of the national movement as readily as men do. They are concentrated in social work which, due to the protracted and mass-based nature of the national struggle, has become a form of political work: women link the masses to the Resistance – they staff the bureaucracy and the social service sector, and mobilize others.

Increased autonomy
Women assumed more of a voice in managing their daily lives and choices during this period of political formation and Resistance autonomy. For example, during crises such as the civil war in Lebanon, some young women volunteered to fight, or joined organizations, and their duties mandated that they sleep away from home and work in close proximity to men. The pervasive crises in their communities left parents with little choice but grudgingly to accept both these departures from the consensus on women's behaviour and the lessening of direct control over their daughters.

In a society where arranged, endogamous marriages were the ideal, both education and the Resistance had a pronounced impact on marital arrangements. Women were acquiring the autonomy to refuse marriage to a man they did not like. They made use of the new public space available to them in education, work, and politics to form social relations outside the home and family. Prospective spouses were meeting and marrying as a consequence of working for the same national cause. Women cadres were expected to marry cadres from their organizations. The family-like atmosphere fostered among cadres expanded to encompass subtle forms of match-making and an endogamy based on political affiliation. Indeed, the family as an arena for marital arrangements was losing ground, as was corresponding family control over marriages.

Women may have enjoyed an amplified measure of individual autonomy, while collectively they were to face serious affronts. The national crises and the attacks to which the exile community was subjected assaulted domestic boundaries, leaving women with little choice but to have a strong stake in the political realm. As the Palestinian community in Lebanon became the target of military attacks, women increasingly became victims. During the 1975–76 Lebanese civil war, Palestinian women in the besieged East Beirut camp of Tal al-Za'tar were shot by snipers as they attempted to fetch water from exposed wells to carry back to their children, and many hundreds were massacred when the camp fell to its right-wing besiegers. The Sabra–Shatila massacres of 1982 targeted women and children.[37]

The slogan 'the political is personal,' the opposite of Western feminists' 'the personal is political,' takes on heightened significance when the stakes are physical survival. Vitally aware of the link between their daily lives and the regional and international political situation, Palestinian women are naturally hesitant to assign a separate quality to their struggle for equality. Instead, they view gender oppression as part of a larger totality of national and class oppression.[38]

A case study of a young Palestinian widow shows how a crisis situation and subsequent involvement in the resistance movement opened new avenues of participation and independence for women.

When I first met Randa, she and her five-year-old daughter were living in one room in the remains of a bombed-out school in Damour.[39] Several other families from Tal al-Za'tar had settled there, each setting up housekeeping in what had once been a classroom. Despite the absence of electricity, windows and running water, her sparsely furnished room was impeccably tidy. Water was hauled from a common tap outside the school building in large, colourful plastic containers. A common bathroom was shared among the inhabitants of the school, which included her widowed sister and her sister's two children.

Randa joined the Resistance when she was 25 years old, by then a widow and a mother of two children. She had lived most of her life in Tal al-Za'tar camp, which fell to the right-wing Christian Phalangists in August 1976, after nine months of siege and heavy bombardment. Her husband, along with hundreds of other men between the ages of 14 and 60, was lined up against a wall and shot the day the Phalangists entered the camp. The remaining residents fled to West Beirut.

Randa had never been politically active or had an interest in politics, nor had she worked outside the home after marriage. A strained financial situation led her to broach the subject of employment, but her husband forbade it. Unlike many women in Tal al-Za'tar, Randa did not participate in defending the camp during the siege. Seven months pregnant, just before the fall of the camp she went into premature labour and delivered a still-born child in the underground shelters. Her eldest child, six-year-old Mohammad, contracted polio during the siege and now lives in a children's home in Europe.

When Randa, her two children, and her widowed sister Jamila and her two children left Tal al-Za'tar, they initially lived with their parents in

Rashidiyeh camp in South Lebanon. Accustomed to living on their own, they were unable to tolerate reverting to a daily existence controlled by their parents and Randa's in-laws. The two sisters stayed only a few weeks with the family and then moved to Damour, a small coastal town approximately ten kilometres from Beirut. The PLO opened Damour as a refuge for the thousands of Tal al-Za'tar widows and their children, repairing war-damaged houses, setting up schools, kindergartens, and clinics, and opening small factories to provide women with employment and vocational training.

When Randa first arrived in Damour, she lived on a widow's monthly indemnity of 250 Lebanese lira (then approximately US$60.00) from the PLO's Office of Social Affairs. In need of more money and now concerned with contributing to her community's well-being in the aftermath of the calamity of massacre and dispersal, she began to work in the Social Affairs section of a political organization. Her first task was to visit families to determine who needed food, blankets, stoves, and medical care. At the same time, she started to embroider for the organization's workshop, and was subsequently elected to be its supervisor. She said she wanted to work for two reasons: 'I needed the money and wanted to do something to get out of the house and be productive. Our society almost imposes political activity on us. If I live here, I must be involved – there is no escaping it.' While she was in the workshop, members of the organization would drop in, asking her to read their newspapers and magazines and encouraging her to join as a full-time member, which she eventually did.

Although her in-laws strenuously opposed her new political activities and employment – 'What do women know about politics?' – she ignored their entreaties and persisted. Living away from them, financially independent, now committed politically and in custody of her children, she was able to ignore their opposition and that of her own parents.

Randa's assumption of her new duties led to a gradual transformation in her concept of self. As her activities increased, and she travelled frequently between Beirut and Damour attending political meetings, running an expanding economic enterprise, and hosting a constant stream of visitors to Damour, she was more than a mother and a widow. She was now a worker, an activist and a struggler. Her self-confidence was on the rise, as were her aspirations.

A widow and the sole support of her remaining daughter, Randa had also taken on responsibility for her unemployed, widowed, and illiterate sister and her two children. Recognizing that she had to support herself and a number of dependants, she quickly found community social work in Damour, which eventually led to her mobilization through the persistence of several women cadres who encouraged her to join. The material and emotional security of being politically affiliated in a situation where the national movement is the basis of the social infrastructure cannot be underestimated. Randa was alone with no male kin to support or protect her, and the Resistance provided a sense of belonging, identity, and protection, supplying the institutional framework for the expression of nationalist sentiment and commitment, and facilitated access to resources.

Damour was in no uncertain terms a community in crisis. The overwhelming majority of families were, like Randa's, female-headed households. Many women were traumatized by the loss of husbands and sons. With families fragmented and men largely absent, their economic future was bleak. The Resistance organized a set of community institutions and was the only sure source of economic security providing widows with indemnities and employment. In such a situation, where women had few alternative options, those who worked did so in Resistance enterprises.

Randa was mobilized as well as politicized by extreme crises: her husband had been executed, and her child born dead. Uprooted and traumatized by the siege of the camp and the expulsion and massacre of its inhabitants, she faced a domestic life essentially in ruins. In sum, she was completely alone to fend for herself and her daughter. Her political consciousness unfolded and matured after her move to Damour, reflected by her willingness to work for the community in the immediate days of chaos following resettlement in Damour.

Randa's case illustrates how crisis affects the mobilization potential of women and draws them into political organizations for a variety of motives and reasons: a desire to be an active and contributing member of the community, helping to defend it when under attack, and to survive financially. Unlike many women who are mobilized during crises only to return home once the level of violence diminishes, Randa's crisis mobilization was sustained and transformed into full-time militancy. Her traumatic experience of the fall of the camp and the female-headed structure that remained go far towards shedding light on why she was permanently mobilized.

Politicizing domesticity

A redistribution of domestic tasks has not accompanied the entry of women into the labour force or their political activism. The traditional domestic-based reproductive and productive roles of women have been charged with a new political meaning, and in some instances have been reinforced rather than weakened. The impact of this contradiction varies with class and age, however.

Political activism has only marginally affected women's identification with and management of the domestic realm. For most camp women, community-based political activism has been incorporated into the domestic routine. The domestic realm, the world of reproduction and production by women, has been infused with political responsibilities and meaning as it is mobilized for service to the national movement.

The majority of women in the camps afford priority to domestic responsibilities, but they do believe women can and should be politically active. These 'politicized housewives,' usually friends of an organization, satisfy traditional norms of fertility and domesticity, yet manage to engage in a range of informal political activities that link the Resistance to the camp community. Although not members of an organization, they carry on a complex set of parapolitical activities without damaging the social standing of their families in the community, or posing a threat to the moral consensus on what constitutes the proper place of women. Although not members of the Resistance, they see themselves as strugglers by virtue of their community-based political activism. For example, activities that fall into this category are attendance at demonstrations, strikes, and funerals; participation in Resistance events such as national celebrations and commemorations; and attendance at discussion sessions held in the homes of ordinary camp women, organized by the Resistance as a means of politicization and recruitment within the camps.

Politics have entered the domestic realm in full force, mobilizing domestic duties, and in the process politicizing their meaning and functions. For example, women's activities during military crises crystallize around the home and the provision of sustenance to the fighters: they bake the bread, prepare the food, and tend to the wounded. During air raids or shelling, children as well as old people must be quickly fetched and a decision made as to whether to stay put or to go to the underground shelters. Prolonged stays in often hot and overcrowded shelters mean that arrangements must be made to secure food, milk, and water for the children. Repressing their own anxieties, women stoically attend to their children's fears and needs, often risking death themselves to bring water from wells to the shelters. Wondering about the whereabouts and fate of the men of the family causes worry and frustration. The fear of destruction of homes and the loss of possessions is uppermost in the mind of every woman. The daily routine of cooking, cleaning, shopping, work, and school attendance is disrupted. Attacks bring the loss of loved ones, or providers or homes, and the prospect of becoming a widow or the mother of a martyr. Homes must be constructed anew, or old homes repaired. Women go to the shelters to encourage people to remain in the camps. Most importantly, these women feel that just to be a Palestinian woman raising a family in camps under continuous attack is a form of struggle. Using a political idiom, they often describe their existence and daily work as a form of struggle. The potential for widowhood or becoming the mother of a martyr is an ever-present fear. As the Palestinian lexicon was suffused with political terms, the discourse of women has been politicized. Women are now more than just wives and mothers: they are activists, martyrs, fighters, workers, and strugglers. Daily housework is described in a political idiom as a form of struggle (*nidal*). Yet this reflects more than just their adaptation of current linguistic usage. It expresses national sentiments of solidarity and support for the Resistance and underscores the communal burden of life in exile.

Reproduction has taken on political meaning as women describe their reproductive capabilities in political terms and consider reproduction a positive national action. Indeed, the discourse of women on reproduction – on the act of giving birth and raising children – has taken on militant overtones, expressed by their use of the military idiom to describe childbirth and care. For example, women jokingly refer to their *butin askari* (military womb), meaning that they are the producers of fighters. This is particularly so among older, uneducated women who are eager to feel they are making a contribution to the national cause and genuinely believe women have a role to play, but this role should not challenge the primacy of domesticity. To ensure more balance between domesticity and political activism, activist women see the reduction of the number of children they bear as a first step, accompanied by expanded day-care facilities. For now, few ask for a redistribution of domestic tasks between men and women, but instead seek a lessening of their content and burdens for women.

The role of women as childbearer, domestic manager, and wife has not been weakened, but has been expanded to include other activities – in this case, political. This process has not been an even one, however. Pinpointing the process of politicizing domesticity does not imply a denial of the remarkable advances and changes in the position of women. A number of Palestinian women are full-time activists, and increasing numbers of young girls and women are participating in the revolution. Nevertheless, the former remain a vanguard few.

Political activism corresponds closely with specific stages in the life cycle of women. From puberty to marriage are years when a woman is most likely to have strong political commitments – to want to be politically active and in the workforce. Once married, however, many women abandon or dilute their activism. Seasoned cadres remark bitterly, 'She has graduated,' of women who leave the struggle upon marriage. It should be added that it is not as though husbands suddenly demand that wives stay at home, or that housework suddenly becomes burdensome. This may be so, but it is just as evident that women voluntarily withdraw from work and politics upon marriage, considering domesticity their primary role. Political activism has become an accepted component of 'girlhood,' along with education and employment. Those women who continue political activism after marriage are very much in the minority, and they tend to be middle class, educated women whose husbands are also full-time activists.

Conflicting loyalties and demands have an uneven impact by class. Upper- and middle-class women can more easily become political activists and satisfy domestic demands by enlisting other women as 'shock absorbers'. The hiring of maids deflects the impact of extra domestic activities on gender relations within the family, cushioning husbands and children from a redistribution of domestic tasks. Poorer women who may have to work or want to engage in political activities often resort to relying for housework and child care on their eldest daughters, whose education can consequently suffer a serious setback, or draw on the exchange of labour that exists among women in extended kin groups. What is unfolding as women adopt new roles, in which case the burden of domesticity is shifted to other women (daughters, female relatives, and maids), depending on one's class affiliation, is that men are hardly undergoing equivalent pressures or expectations, a process that alleviates a fundamental source of pressure on unequal gender relations within the family.

Women and politics

Without losing sight of advances in the position of women under the sponsorship of a national liberation movement, critical questions should be posed in order to assess the consequences of women's activism for transforming gender relations.

With the Palestinian people scattered across a wide range of states, and a national movement in continuous flux and adaptation to constantly shifting objective realities, long-term social policies and their implementation are difficult on other than an immediate scale. Thus, the Resistance has yet to define the structure and ideology of the society it aspires to create in any liberated part of Palestine. Indeed, the national movement avoids expounding upon the nature, structure, and ideology of the state in the absence of a liberated territory; correspondingly, it hesitates to define the role of women in a future state. Shifting objective realities are not enough to account for this ambiguity.

Examining the military, political, and socio-cultural context in which the national movement operates, particularly its class basis, may shed light on why its objectives are not well defined. A woman leader explained that the then current (early 1982) 'advanced defensive stage' has largely shaped the contours of women's struggles, compelling them to assign political priorities. Insistent on the intimate link between their own struggle and the national situation, women put forth their own programmes, but are cautious about advocating and demanding changes in their personal lives – that is, the private realm of family relations and the personal status (Islamic) and customary laws that govern male–female relations and define the legal status of women – in order to avoid alienating large sectors of the population.

The political leadership of the PLO is also cautious about detailing the social and ideological parameters of a future state in order to retain the support of their own mass base, perceived as traditional and conservative. Organizations compete to recruit members, and appealing to traditional values can enhance mobilization campaigns in the camps and among the petty bourgeoisie.

The new Palestinian bourgeoisie, who emerged in the wake of 1948, had substantial capital but no secure territorial base. This emergent class readily lent financial and political support to the Fatah wing of the PLO.[40] Trying to amass capital, and subject to the vagaries of operating businesses in Arab countries with their often volatile shifts in the opportunities and rights granted to Palestinian exiles, the bourgeoisie was exceedingly aware of its need for a state if their financial ventures were to operate securely. The Fatah doctrine of a broad, united front representing a wide spectrum of Palestinian political opinion, although mainly appealing to nationalist sentiment, found a ready partner in this new class. Fatah did not clearly define the kind of economic system it envisioned in the proposed secular, democratic state, nor did it outline a programme of social reforms to accompany the process of struggle for national liberation. In this way it avoided jeopardizing an at times fragile national unity, and retained the support of the bourgeoisie who would hardly find their interests served by calls for radical social transformation that would upset the class and gender structures of society.

When the national question is the primary basis of political unity, there is a tendency to perceive national and social issues as separate realms of struggle, relegating the latter to a secondary position. This state of affairs is not peculiar to the Palestinian situation. In many national liberation movements, women are pressured to subordinate their own demands and needs in the interest of the broader struggle.[41]

Nevertheless, there are a number of views on women's struggles for equality within the Palestinian movement. Some consider that mobilizing women for the national struggle is setting the groundwork for liberation in the wake of national liberation. In this view, women are gradually setting the stage for their own liberation through an active role in militant politics that assaults traditional barriers and dilutes the force of convention. Another opinion contends that women must postpone their own particular struggle until the national question is solved. Like their early counterparts in the 1920s and 1930s, most women concede that, in the absence of a territorially based state with its own economy and legal system, it is difficult to institute reforms in the status of women.

The expression of a platform for women is seen as a potentially divisive issue that could lead to open confrontation with the normative consensus on the gender arrangements of Palestinian society. The leadership anticipates alienating its mass base. Such caution is expressed in the reluctance to intervene directly in the realm of domestic relations. Yet the Resistance does support women's rights to active political expression, as witnessed by its intervention in family quarrels when violence appears likely, in order to minimize individual family control over the means of force, and to protect women from abuse.

The General Union of Palestinian Women (GUPW), a PLO mass organization composed of women from all political factions, exerted efforts to raise the national consciousness of women and established institutions for their active participation in national life. The limited autonomy enjoyed by the Union in decision making and political stances has obstructed the emergence of a cohesive movement that could address issues specific to women, and speak for broad sectors of Palestinian women. It has also ensured political domination by some factions and cut short deviation from the dominant PLO policy.

Another facet of the relationship between the women's movement and the national movement is revealed in the tensions within the women's movement. The Union is a microcosm of the larger national movement, embodying its factions and potential lines of fissure. For instance, tension in the Union is often between women of varying political factions, each of whom vies to mobilize women for membership in its political organization rather than in the Union in general. The Union, controlled for the most part by Fatah women, the largest and dominant group within the PLO, would prefer to sponsor all projects for women rather than have its efforts duplicated by each organization in the PLO. Women from other organizations see this as a move by Fatah to monopolize all Palestinian social institutions, rather than as a step towards consolidating a women's movement. These factions, which disperse women across different groups, contribute to obstructing the emergence of a unified stance by women.

Palestinian women are in agreement that there is no contradiction between the sexes which could constitute the basis for struggle. Although women recognize the benefits that accrue to men through the subordination of women, they are vitally aware that equality with men in the current objective circumstances of the Palestinian people would only be equality in subordination and dispossession. Samia, a Fatah cadre, summed it up eloquently when she stated: 'How can we take our rights from men who have none?'

The absence of a formal commitment by the PLO to women's liberation, however, should be weighed against the complex of social institutions promoted by the Resistance, such as kindergartens and nurseries that allowed women to pursue activities outside the domestic realm, clinics that eased the burdens of health care in the family, and vocational training and salaried employment. The Resistance did attempt to give institutional expression to ideological promotions of gender equality. Randa's situation is a clear example of this. It was through the Resistance-initiated social infrastructure that she was able to build a new life for herself and her daughter, earn an income, and express her now evident national commitment. Liberal social tendencies and a generalized openness to change, fostered during the process of national struggle, led to critical examination and assessment of Palestinian culture and social values. The exile community evinced a readiness to explore new forms of cultural life and social relations. Socio-cultural change was given an institutional framework, ideological support, and legitimacy by the national movement.

Palestinians often say that new norms and values have been created in the process of women's experience in exile and participation in the Resistance. It is to these new norms that the PLO has been responsive, rather than a force of explicit creation. For example, most Palestinians now strongly support a woman's right to choose her own husband. The Resistance has taken no formal stand on the issue, but it will occasionally intercede to prevent a forced marriage, just as it will intercede to prevent violence over the question of honour. Was this a policy to protect women and ensure their newly formulated rights based on an ideological commitment to promote their liberation, or was it an attempt by the PLO to assert and maintain control over its mass base and to recognize household and family organization and relations? The question becomes: what was the intent of the Resistance towards women? Was it simply reacting to a generalized openness to liberal thinking? It is doubtful that any sophisticated attempt at social engineering was being made in order to weaken pre-existing structures.

Conclusion

We have seen that Middle Eastern women have scarcely been politically marginal. In local politics, their role is clearly based in the kinship matrix. They are politically present by virtue of membership in a kin group, village, tribe, or sect. Palestinian women act not solely as members of families, but as members of a dispossessed national community under constant assault. The social constraints on women are being questioned and weakened, but it is still debatable to what extent fundamental, long-term change has occurred.

Political developments, in this case a national crisis and a resistance movement, have had an uneven impact on women. The clearest variation seems to be by class. Women in the camps tended to incorporate political roles into domestic roles, whereas upper- and middle-class women have been able somewhat to escape the burdens of domesticity. They have done this by shifting its burdens to other women, or by reducing its content by lowering the number of children borne and maintaining an increased standard of living. This is one of the factors making for the unevenness in the position of Palestinian women. There are, however, continuities that serve to define a common ground between all Palestinian women: the national crisis or the state of being stateless, and, second, the nature of the social controls to which they are subjected – that is, control over their mobility, life choices, and sexuality. It is these two basic social elements, women's constrained autonomy, maintained by similiar cultural institutions across class and sectarian cleavages, and the national struggle, that have the potential to define a common ground for Palestinian women.

The protractedness of the Palestinian national struggle and its cyclical character – the struggle goes through periods of prolonged, extreme tension, as in the civil war in Lebanon, and periods of relative calm interspersed by occasional flare-up, as in the years between 1977 and 1982 – can have contradictory implications for the mobilization of women. Crises bring women out of their homes and into community and political activity in a support capacity; yet most return to their homes and domestic lives once the crises have subsided. For some, activism is cut short by onerous domestic duties; many see their role in the national movement as helpers in times of crisis. Some women willingly worked with the Resistance when the camps were under siege, but their mobilization was never carried to its logical conclusion of full-time militancy. Although crisis and the protractedness of the struggle can have positive consequences for the mobilization of women, they also tend to deflect attention from the stringent planning of mobilization campaigns. Crisis also deflects attention from explicitly women's or social issues, emphasizing political and military issues instead. The civil war in Lebanon was, however, to provide the real impetus for the development of Palestinian social institutions.

Although the Resistance did not express a firm commitment to transform gender relations and ideologies, or the division of labour, it is hardly likely that permanent changes can take place outside a party or state framework. Political activism can signal the beginning of the process of undermining domesticity as the primary social role and source of status for women. The national movement has been responsive to the new political roles of women. Liberal, paid maternity leave and flexible work schedules allow women to bear children and not be penalized, as are women in many other countries. Women are not forced by institutional imperatives to choose between motherhood and political activism. Indeed, the women's movement has not striven so much to grant women reproductive freedom and legal rights as much as it has achieved an embryonic reconciliation between the role of women in reproduction and production, and political activism. Yet, it is apparent that women's participation in national struggles can be extensive without involving fundamental changes in the division of labour, definitions of the role or position of women, or ultimately the access of women to power in post-liberation states. Reducing the domestic content and identities does not necessarily indicate a greater measure of autonomy. When control of women in the family and hierarchical gender relations remain largely intact, political activism and economic participation may simply mean the double burden and a continuation of control in new forms.

Notes

1. This essay is based on two years (1980–82) of research in Lebanon for the author's PhD dissertation in anthropology. Writing was funded by the D. T. Sabbagh Foundation.

2. For literature on women and Middle East politics, see L. Ahmed, 'Feminism and Feminist Movements in the Middle East, a Preliminary Exploration: Turkey, Egypt, Algeria, People's Democratic Republic of Yemen,' in A. Al-Hibri (ed.), *Women and Islam* (Elmsford, NY, Pergamon Press, 1982); C. Fluehr-Lobban, 'The Political Mobilization of Women in the Arab World,' in J. Smith (ed.). *Women in Contemporary Muslim Societies* (London), Associated University Press, 1980); S. Hale, 'The Wing of the Patriarch: The Emancipation of Women and Revolutionary Parties – a Sudan Chapter,' *MERIP Reports*, no. 138 (1986); M. Hatem, 'The Enduring Alliance of Nationalism and Patriarchy in Muslim Personal Status Laws: The Case of Modern Egypt,' *Feminist Issues*, vol. 6, no. 1 (1986); M. Hegland, '"Traditional" Iranian Women: How they Cope,' *Middle East Journal*, vol. 36, no. 4 (1982); M. Hegland, 'The Political Roles of Aliabad Women in Community Politics and in the Iranian Revolution,' *MERIP Reports*, no. 138 (1986); A. Marsot, 'The Revolutionary Gentlewoman in Egypt.' in L. Beck and N. Keddie (eds.), *Women in the Muslim World* (Cambridge. Mass.. Harvard University Press, 1978); T. Philipp, 'Feminism and Nationalist Politics in Egypt,' in L. Beck and N. Keddie (eds.), *Women in the Muslim World*; J. Peteet. 'Women and the Palestinian Movement: No Going Back?' *MERIP Reports*, no. 138 (1986); R. Sayigh, 'Encounters With Palestinian Women Under Occupation,' *Journal of Palestine Studies*, vol. 10, no. 4 (1981); and J. Tucker. 'Women and Politics in Nineteenth Century Egypt,' *MERIP Reports*, no. 138 (1986).

3. See M. Rosaldo, 'Women, Culture and Society: A Theoretical Overview,' in M. Rosaldo and L. Lamphere (eds.), *Women, Culture and Society* (Palo Alto, Calif., Stanford University Press, 1974) for an elucidation of a theoretical construct dividing social life into public and private spheres, a construct that became a focus of intense critical examination.

4. L. Sweet. 'The Women of Ain ad-Dayr.' *Anthropological Quarterly*, vol. 40, no. 3 (1967), p. 179.

5. S. Joseph, 'Working Class Women's Networks in a Sectarian State: A Political Paradox,' *American Ethnologist*, vol. 10, no. 1 (1983) examines the role of women in maintaining the integrity of Lebanese sects.

6. Where a primary aspect of a state's integration into the world capitalist market revolves around exporting labour, as in North Yemen, the impact on women's labour varies. With male migration some women may find themselves freed from domestic and agricultural labour, with increased leisure time; for others, however, male absence does not alleviate the productive roles of women. See C. Myntti. 'Yemeni Workers Abroad: The Impact on Women.' *MERIP Reports*, no. 124 (June 1984).

7. L. Sweet. 'The Women of Ain ad-Dayr,' *Anthropological Quarterly*, p. 174.

8. L. Beck, 'Women Among the Qashqa'i Nomadic Pastoralists in Iran,' in L. Beck and N. Keddie (eds.). *Women in the Muslim World* (Cambridge. Mass.. Harvard University Press. 1978), pp. 353–4.

9. *Ibid.*, p. 367.

10. *Ibid.*. p. 369.

11. B. Aswad. 'Key and Peripheral Roles of Noble Women in a Middle Eastern Plains Village.' *Anthropological Quarterly*. vol. 40, no. 1 (1967), pp. 148–9.

12. B. Aswad, 'Key and Peripheral Roles of Noble Women . . .'; L. Sweet, 'The Women of Ain ad-Dayr'; L. Sweet. 'In Reality: Some Middle Eastern Women.' in C. Matthiasson (ed.). *Many Sisters: Women in Cross-Cultural Perspective* (New York. The Free Press. 1974).

13. See *MERIP Reports*. no. 138 (1986). an issue largely devoted to women and politics in the Middle East; M. Hatem, 'The Enduring Alliance of Nationalism and Patriarchy in Muslim Personal Status Laws.'

14. R. Sayigh, 'Encounters with Palestinian Women under Occupation,' p. 3.

15. J. Minces. 'Women in Algeria.' in L. Beck and N. Keddie (eds.). *Women in the Muslim World*.

16. F. M'rabet. 'Excerpts From Les Algériennes,' in E. Fernea and B. Bezirgan (eds.), *Middle Eastern Women Speak* (Austin, University of Texas Press, 1977).

17. Migration to France absorbed a substantial quantity of Algerian surplus labour. See M. Bennoune. 'Maghribin Workers in France,' *MERIP Reports*, no. 34 (January 1975).

18. See M. Lazreg. 'You Don't Have to Work, Sisters! This is Socialism.' Paper presented at the Annual Meeting of the Middle East Studies Association. New Orleans. 1985.

19. See M. Molyneux. 'Legal Reform and Socialist Revolution in Democratic Yemen: Women and the Family,' *International Journal of the Sociology of Law*. vol. 13 (1985), p. 154.

20. *Ibid.*

21 S. Hale. 'The Wing of the Patriarch.'

22. Suad Joseph. personal communication.

23. M. Hegland. 'The Political Roles of Aliabad Women' (1986).

24. N. Yeganeh. 'Women's Struggles in the Islamic Republic of Iran.' in A. Tabari and N. Yeganeh (eds.). *In the Shadow of Islam: The Women's Movement in Iran* (London. Zed Press. 1982).

25. *Ibid.*, p. 35.

26. A. Tabari. 'Islam and the Struggle for Emancipation of Iranian Women,' in A. Tabari and N. Yeganeh (eds.). *In the Shadow of Islam*.

27. See F. El-Guindi. 'Veiled Activism. Egyptian Women in the Contemporary Islamic Movement.' *Peuples Méditerranéens*, nos. 22–23 (Special Issue: Femmes de la Méditerranée) Jan.–Feb. pp. 79–89; M. Hatem. 'The Enduring Alliance of Nationalism and Patriarchy.' pp. 33–35; J. Williams. 'Veiling in Egypt as a Political and Social Phenomenon.' in J. Esponsit (ed.). *Islam and Development* (New York. Syracuse University Press, 1980).

28. F. El-Guindi. 'Veiled Activism.'

29. M. Hatem. 'The Enduring Alliance of Nationalism and Patriarchy.'

30. See M. Hatem. 'The Enduring Alliance of Nationalism and Patriarchy.' for a detailed examination of this argument.

31. A substantial body of material has appeared in the wake of the 1982 Israeli invasion of Lebanon. See M. Jansen. *The Battle of Beirut: Why Israel Invaded Lebanon* (London. Zed Books. 1982); R. Khalidi. *Under Siege: PLO Decisionmaking During the 1982 War* (New York. Columbia University Press. 1986); S. Nassib and C. Tisdall. *Beirut. Frontline Story* (Trenton. NJ. Africa World Press. 1983); *Journal of Palestine Studies*, vol. 11. no. 4, vol. 12. no. 1 (Summer/Fall. 1982); and *Race and Class*, vol. 24. no. 4 (Spring 1983).

32. See L. Ahmed. 'Feminism and Feminist Movements in the Middle East.' in A. Al-Hibri (ed.). *Women and Islam*. for a review of women's movements in the region.

33. M. Mogannam. *The Arab Woman and the Palestine Problem* (London. Herbert Joseph. 1937) provides a first-hand account of the early Palestinian women's movement. the only such work in English.

34. M. Mogannam clearly recognized the need for an independent state when she states in

regard to women's rights '. . . such measures of reforms can only be introduced by National Governments, or by persons deriving their authority from the people.' *Ibid.*, p. 53.

35. The term 'responsible' (Arabic: *masoul*) refers to one superior in rank and responsibilities in a political organization, and implies a relation of hierarchy. In striving for more egalitarian relationships among members, the Resistance adopted this term, which is less hierarchical than formal military terms of rank.

36. C. Fluehr-Lobban, 'The Political Mobilization of Women in the Arab World,' in J. Smith (ed.), *Women in Contemporary Muslim Societies*, p. 242.

37. A. Kapeliouk, *Sabra and Chatila: Inquiry Into a Massacre* (Belmont, Mass., American Association of American–Arab University Graduates, 1983) provides a detailed and comprehensive account of the massacre of Palestinians in the Sabra-Shatila refugee camps in the wake of the Israeli entry into West Beirut in September 1982.

38. See M. Hatem, 'The Enduring Alliance of Nationalism and Patriarchy,' for a critique of the 'survival' approach to the study of Middle Eastern women.

39. Damour, a small coastal town on the road between Beirut and Sidon, was attacked by the Joint Forces (an alliance of Lebanese progressive parties and Palestinian organizations) during the civil war in January 1976. Its inhabitants fled, and the town was settled in the Autumn of 1976 by Palestinian refugees from the Tal al-Za'tar camp in East Beirut.

40. P. Smith, *Palestine and the Palestinians 1876–1983* (New York, St. Martin's Press, 1984) documents the history of this class in the wake of the 1948 Palestinian diaspora and provides an analysis of its early support for the Fatah wing of the PLO.

41. For a rather different situation, see S. Urdang, *Fighting Two Colonialisms: Women in Guinea-Bissau* (New York, Monthly Review Press, 1979) where she illustrates how women in Guinea-Bissau were able to incorporate their interests into the revolution. In the course of the struggle against the Portuguese and for social transformation, fundamental transformations in women's social positions ensued.

9. Palestine and the Palestinians

Pamela Ann Smith

In 1947, the Arab population of Palestine numbered 1,303,585, 70 percent of whom lived in the rural areas.¹ Thirty-four years later, the Palestinian population totalled almost 4.5 million, of which 2.6 million, or just under 60 percent, were living outside the territory of mandatory Palestine, that is, outside Israel and the occupied territories of the West Bank, Gaza Strip, and al-Himmah. Today, the largest Palestinian community is in Jordan, where Palestinians constitute more than half the population. Other sizeable communities are found in Lebanon, Syria, Kuwait, and Saudi Arabia, with smaller concentrations in the other Gulf states, and in Egypt, Libya, Iraq, and Cyprus (see Table 9.1).

More than 100,000 Palestinians reside in the United States. Many of them are Christians originally from the West Bank towns of Ramallah, Beit Jala, and Bethlehem. Some Palestinians who worked for the Palestine government during the Mandate period emigrated to Britain, where they were joined by others, including several thousand students, in the 1960s and 1970s. The Palestinian communities in Brazil, Argentina, Chile, and other parts of Latin America were originally established by immigrants fleeing conscription under the Turks during World War I; their numbers increased after 1948, and today the communities in Latin America, which are among the wealthiest in the diaspora, count four generations.

The impoverishment of the peasantry

Although some of the well-to-do Palestinians who enjoyed family or business connections in other parts of the Arab world had begun to leave Palestine shortly after the United Nations General Assembly called for the partition of the country in November 1947, the vast majority of the refugees left after fighting broke out between the Haganah – the underground Jewish army – and Palestinian irregulars, and later, after May 14, 1948, during battles between the Haganah, the Arab Legion (Transjordan), and the armies of Egypt, Syria, and Iraq. Many initially sought safety in Lebanon, Syria, or other parts of Palestine, particularly during the heavy fighting in the Galilee in the Spring of 1948 and after the massacre of 254 villagers in Deir Yasin in April of that year.

Table 9.1
The Palestinian population, 1981

Country	Palestinian Population		Percent of Total
Arab Oil States:		594,295	13.4
Kuwait	299,710		
Saudi Arabia	136,779		
Oman	50,706		
United Arab Emirates	36,504[a]		
Qatar	24,233[a]		
Libya	23,759		
Iraq	20,604		
Bahrain	2,000		
Other Arab States:		1,774,671	39.9
Jordan (East Bank)	1,148,334		
Lebanon	358,207		
Syria	222,525		
Egypt	45,605[a]		
Europe and the Americas:		124,856	2.8
United States	104,856		
West Germany	15,000[b]		
Latin America	5,000[b]		
Other:[c]		120,116	2.7
Total outside Palestine:		2,613,938	58.8
Palestine:			
West Bank	833,000		
Israel	550,800		
Gaza Strip	451,000[a]		
Total in Palestine:		1,834,800	41.2
Total Palestinian Population:		4,449,138[d]	100.0

Source: *Palestinian Statistical Abstract, 1980* (Damascus, PLO Central Bureau of Statistics, 1981).
[a] Eric Rouleau, in his *Les Palestiniens: D'Une Guerre à l'Autre* (Paris, La Decouverte/Le Monde, 1984), notes that the figures for 1981 do not count the Palestinian population of al-'Arish, returned to Egypt in April 1982; that the PLO representative in Abu Dhabi puts the figure for the Emirates at closer to 70,000; and that the PLO office in Doha estimates the number in Qatar has risen to 30,000 or more.
[b] Figures for 1970, taken from Nabeel Shaath, 'High-Level Palestinian Manpower,' *Journal of Palestine Studies*, vol. 1, no. 2 (Winter 1972), p. 81. The total for West Germany and Latin America has been deducted from the PLO's figure for 1981 of 140,116 for 'other' countries.
[c] Includes Eastern Europe as well as Canada, Australia, Africa and other parts of Asia.
[d] There is an unexplained discrepancy between the total Palestinian population listed here (as taken from the *Palestinian Statistical Abstract, 1980*) and the actual total.

Others fled to the West Bank and Transjordan after the entry of the Arab Legion, seeking refuge in territories held by the Jordanian forces. Still others, including many from Jaffa and the southern coastal districts, sought the protection of the Egyptian army and fled to the Gaza Strip, or to Egypt itself.

By January 1949, when a programme of food rations had been organized, the number of refugees registered for relief was estimated at almost one million.[2] Makeshift camps were gradually set up to house those who originally had sought shelter in army barracks, convents, schools, orchards, barns, and caves. By the end of 1949, an estimated 430,000 Palestinians were housed in these camps; another 250,000 had managed to find accommodation with friends or relatives, or through charitable institutions, but were still registered for free food rations.[3] Over the years, the natural increase in the refugee population also led to an increase in the numbers registered for relief; by March 1966, the figure had reached 1.3 million. Of these, the majority lived in Jordan (including the West Bank), with 164,000 in Lebanon, and 139,000 in Syria.[4]

The overwhelming majority of those in the camps and registered for relief were either peasants who had owned their own homes and land in Palestine, or tenant farmers and sharecroppers who had tilled plots in or near their native villages. Unlike those who had experienced urban life, received an education, or had business contacts abroad, the peasantry was uniquely deprived because its source of livelihood, the land, was lost. While a few were able to flee with livestock, household goods, and some agricultural tools, the lack of suitable agricultural land in the neighbouring countries in which they took refuge, combined with the relatively high rates of unemployment which already existed in the agricultural sector in the host countries, meant that most of the peasant refugees were unable to escape the poverty and loss of skills that confinement in the camps over years, and even decades, entailed.

Furthermore, the fact that the purchase of agricultural land by Palestinians was forbidden, except on the West Bank and in Jordan, meant that even those who did manage to accumulate some wealth in exile often were unable to re-create their former way of life. Reduced to a landless proletariat, the peasants were forced to take up what work they could find, primarily as seasonal labourers in agriculture, in the building trades, or in the few industries which existed around the urban centres in Jordan, Lebanon, and Syria. Several thousand were employed by the United Nations Relief and Works Agency for Palestine Refugees in the Near East (UNRWA), established in 1950, as construction workers, or in the production of essential goods – shoes, clothing, textiles, soap, and bricks – needed in the camps.

The rapid development of Saudi Arabia and the Gulf states in the 1950s provided another avenue of employment. By the end of 1953, 3,000 Palestinian refugees were employed by the Arabian American Oil Company (ARAMCO) in Saudi Arabia, where their previous experience with modern tools and equipment in Palestine and their familiarity with the English language made them particularly valuable as foremen. Palestinian workers were also imported to build port, rail, and residential facilities in Saudi Arabia and the Gulf states, and to work as seamstresses, tutors, and personal maids in private homes. A few who had worked in the oil refineries in Palestine, in the railways, or in the Palestine police found jobs in the public sector industries of Kuwait and Qatar, as well as in Saudi Arabia.[5]

Palestinian discontent with the working conditions in the oil industry and in the Gulf states, however, soon led to a series of strikes and demonstrations in Kuwait, Bahrain, Qatar, and Saudi Arabia. In 1956, when the unrest escalated into protest against the combined Israeli, French, and British invasion of the Suez Canal, the local regimes clamped down sharply lest the discontent spread to their own populations. Hundreds of Palestinian workers were deported, and others were banned from jobs in sensitive sectors.[6] By 1958, only those Palestinians with professional qualifications, such as engineers, urban planners, doctors, and educators, were allowed to work in the Gulf states in large numbers.

The growth of the bourgeoisie

In contrast to the peasantry, those Palestinians whose assets consisted of movable property or transferable skills were often able to make a new life in exile that, with time and effort, even surpassed the standard of living they had enjoyed in Palestine. In contrast to the picture often portrayed by Zionists, on the eve of the establishment of the state of Israel, Palestine was one of the most modern regions in the Middle East. As a result of the wartime prosperity which had resulted from the awarding of huge government contracts from the British, the beginning of oil exporting from Haifa, a significant rise in agricultural exports to Europe, and the development of corporate forms of business, many Palestinian merchants amassed considerable wealth in the form of stocks and shares, bank deposits, cash, and financial investments abroad.

Some 44.7 million Palestinian pounds (US$179 million at 1945 exchange rates) in capital, or about 16 percent of the total capital owned in the country, was held by the non-Jewish population in the form of assets that could be transferred abroad.[7] Balances held in sterling accounts in London were easily accessible to those forced into sudden exile, and the release of blocked accounts held in the Palestinian branches of Barclays Bank and the Ottoman Bank following international negotiations in the early 1950s provided additional sums for rebuilding lives in the diaspora. Some £10 million was estimated to have been transferred to Jordan in the form of bank deposits and cash during the same period.[8] (The magnitude of such a sum can be gauged by the fact that this figure equalled the total amount of money in circulation in the Hashemite Kingdom at the time.)

These sums enabled many Palestinians to invest in new businesses, or to re-establish their companies in neighbouring Arab countries. Yusif Baydas, a foreign exchange dealer in mandatory Palestine, invested funds obtained by colleagues from Barclays, along with other earnings he had made after the devaluation of the Palestine pound, to start a new money exchange business in Beirut which, in 1951, became the Intra Bank. By early 1966, Intra was the largest financial institution in Lebanon. Its holdings included the Hilton and Phoenicia Hotels in Beirut; shares in Middle East Airlines, the port of Beirut, as well as a shipyard in France; mining companies registered in England; and real estate along the Champs Elysées in Paris, Fifth Avenue in Manhattan, and Park Lane in London. Intra also owned banks, brokerage houses, and trading companies in Geneva, Rome, New York, Frankfurt, São Paulo, Dubai, Liberia, Sierra Leone, and Nigeria.[9]

The Arab Bank, originally founded in 1930 by a Palestinian peasant from the village of Beit Hanina, 'Abd al-Hamid Shuman, managed in 1948 to transfer some of its funds, records, and staff to Amman, where its reputation for paying claims immediately helped it to expand throughout the Arab world. By the mid-1960s, in addition to more than a dozen branches in the Arab countries, its holdings included affiliates in Switzerland, West Germany, and Nigeria. The bank's auditor, Fu'ad Saba, moved the offices of his firm, Saba and Company, to Beirut and Amman. In 1955, the Arab Bank began working for international oil companies in the Gulf, and was thereby able to take on many more American clients who were expanding their operations in the Middle East. The Arabia Insurance Company, whose founders included Sulayman Tannus (also a member of the Arab Bank's Board of Directors), moved to Beirut, and from there set up additional branches in Jordan, Kuwait, Bahrain, Qatar, Dubai, Abu Dhabi, Sudan, Libya, Tunisia, Morocco, and Britain.[10]

Emile Bustani, a Lebanese entrepreneur who had studied engineering in Britain before emigrating to Palestine during World War II, gained useful contacts working on government projects for the British during the war. After 1948, his firm, the Contracting and Trading Company (CAT), obtained huge contracts in the oil fields in the Gulf states (many of which were still British protectorates), Aden, Syria, and Lebanon.[11] The Consolidated Contractors Company (CCC), founded in 1963 by three Palestinians – Hassib Sabbagh, Muhammad Kamal 'Abd al-Rahman, and Sa'id Tawfiq Khuri – also specialized in projects in the Gulf, as well as in Libya and Nigeria. By the early 1970s, it was doing business worth an estimated US$60 million a year, and its founders were considered to rank among the wealthiest men in the Palestinian diaspora.[12]

The decline of the ruling families

Palestine's indigenous ruling class – which by 1948 consisted of the notables who had access to high positions in the Islamic courts, schools, and administration, as well as the main landowning families – suffered a mixed fate after the establishment of the state of Israel. The Mufti of Jerusalem, al-Hajj Amin al-Husayni, who had led the resistance to the partition of the country, was exiled to Egypt, and later took up residence in Lebanon, where he died in the early 1970s. His opponents, those families like the Nashashibis who allied themselves with King 'Abdallah and who accepted the annexation of the West Bank by Jordan in 1950, found themselves faced with a dilemma: either to accept Hashemite hegemony and the opportunities it offered for prosperity and for securing influential positions in the Jordanian government, or to continue insisting on the independence of Palestine and the resumption of the armed struggle against the Israeli occupation of their homeland.[13] The first promised security and the maintenance of their class position, but at the cost of losing any claims to represent their own people; the second threatened them with the loss of their lands, estates, and government positions but, in the eyes of the majority of refugees, would have buttressed their claim to speak for the Palestinians as a whole.

While discontent simmered on both the East and West Banks of the newly enlarged Kingdom of Jordan, the ruling families concentrated their efforts on trying to obtain reforms in what was then basically a tribal system. But their demands for constitutional rule, a modern civil service, and economic and social development programmes – particularly on the West Bank – met with strong opposition from the new king, Hussein, who had inherited the throne after his grandfather's assassination in 1951 and the subsequent illness of his father.

In 1956, when a nationalist coalition government led by Sulayman Nabulsi obtained a majority in the Chamber of Deputies and in the cabinet, the pro-Hashemite loyalists within the Palestinian ruling class were again divided. Those from the previous cabinets feared that the economic and social reforms demanded by Nabulsi – whose coalition included support from the Ba'th Party and the Communists – went too far, particularly in their recognition of trade union rights and the promotion of indigenous industrial capital at the expense of the import/export trade, in which some of the most prominent Palestinian families were involved. They were also concerned that Nabulsi's determination to end British control over the Arab Legion, and its influence in Jordan, would leave them vulnerable to the demands of the more radical Palestinian intellectuals sympathetic to the Ba'th, the Communists, and Egyptian President Nasser.

Others, however, particularly the youngest members of these families, who had been trained in the West and who sympathized with the pan-Arab parties, supported Nabulsi's attempts to open the kingdom's administration to Palestinians, and to the principle of promotion based on merit rather than on tribal or clan affiliation. Some, like Qadri Tuqan, a member of a prominent West Bank family that had built up strong business connections on the East Bank, had already stood as Communist candidates. Others, such as Tahsin 'Abd al-Hadi, Anwar Nusaybah, and Hikmat al-Masri, had resisted attempts by the court and the cabinet both to nullify the elections and to disband the Chamber of Deputies, and thereby helped to pave the way for Nabulsi's victory.[14]

The king's subsequent dismissal of parliament and declaration of martial law in April 1957 solved the issue. Political parties were banned, and the leaders of the opposition, including Nabulsi and other Palestinian deputies who supported him, were arrested. The landing of British paratroopers in Amman and in other parts of Jordan in July 1957, after a reported coup attempt, effectively put an end to the attempts at reform.

Those Palestinians who had played an active role in the opposition found themselves either deported, or forced into exile if they were not already detained. While some subsequently made their peace with the monarchy in the 1960s, loyalists within the ruling families continued throughout the period to reject demands from their own constituents for social and economic change, and for a resumption of the nationalist struggle against both the Israeli occupation of their homeland and Jordanian annexation of the West Bank.

In return, they were rewarded with important positions in the Jordanian government. Various members of the Nashashibi, Tuqan, Dajani, 'Abd al-Hadi, Jayyusi, and Nusaybah families were appointed to seats in the Upper Chamber and/or cabinet, while others held high ministerial posts throughout the period of Jordanian rule in the West Bank. Others were given key posts in the armed forces, served as ambassadors in Jordanian embassies abroad, or were encouraged to stand for the Chamber of Deputies. This, together with Jordan's policy of providing salaries for the mayors, judges, municipal officials, and civil servants in the West Bank, enabled these clans to continue in power at a time when Palestinians elsewhere in the diaspora were turning to other leaders in their efforts to obtain their national rights.

Nationalism and class, 1967 to 1982

The outbreak of the 1967 War and the Arab defeat led to a new exodus of Palestinians from the West Bank and Gaza. Some were refugees from the 1948 War who had been living in camps in the newly occupied territories or in the Golan Heights, and who were forced to leave for the second time in their lives. Thousands of others left later as the military occupation and the expansion of Jewish settlements deprived them of their homes and livelihoods, and left them vulnerable to economic stagnation and political oppression. As a result, by 1972 the number of Palestinians registered for relief had risen to 1.5 million, or about half the total Palestinian population at the time. More than 40 percent of these, 640,000, were housed in refugee camps of one kind or another.[15]

Three years later, the outbreak of civil war in Lebanon added still more to the relief lists. By 1979, after the 1976 Phalangist onslaught against the refugee camp of Tal al-Za'tar and the shantytown of Qarantina and the brief 1978 Israeli occupation of southern Lebanon, the number had increased to 1.8 million. After the Israeli invasion in June 1982, the subsequent massacres and fighting in the camps of Sabra and Shatila, and the destruction of others both in Beirut and in the South, the figure is believed to have risen to more than two million.[16]

The creation of a new working class

The dispersal of the peasantry and the sudden separation of a whole class of people from their livelihoods created a new landless proletariat, or sub-proletariat, within Palestinian society. Many of those on relief were elderly, those whose skills had deteriorated during long years of unemployment, or women and children whose providers had been killed, had enrolled in the various guerrilla movements, or had left the camps in search of work elsewhere.

These figures do, however, disguise another trend among the displaced peasantry, particulary since 1967: the achievement of self-sufficiency by large numbers of refugees who, as a result, left the camps, and in many cases withdrew from the relief rolls. Despite the absolute increase in the numbers of those needing assistance, the relative share of the population registered for relief, as a proportion of the total population, actually declined prior to the Israeli invasion of Lebanon in 1982. While complete data is still lacking, a crude estimate indicates that this share had fallen from about 76.7 percent of the total population in 1949, to only about 41 percent in 1979 (see Table 9.2).

Table 9.2
Palestinians registered for relief as a percentage of the total Palestinian population, 1949 to 1979

Year	Number Registered for Relief	Total Population	Percentage
1949a	1,000,000	1,304,000	76.7
1979	1,804,000	4,390,000	41.1

a As no population figure for 1949 is available, the 1947 figure given by Janet Abu Lughod was used.

Sources: Janet Abu Lughod, 'Demographic Transformations in Palestine,' in Ibrahim Abu Lughod (ed.) *The Transformation of Palestine* (Evanston, Ill., Northwestern University Press 1977), p. 155; *Palestinian Statistical Abstract, 1980* (Damascus, PLO Central Bureau of Statistics 1981); UNRWA annual reports (New York, UN, selected years).

The available evidence suggests that refugees achieved self-sufficiency either by finding work in agriculture, the building trades, and industry, or by emigrating to areas such as Saudi Arabia and the Gulf states, where work, both skilled and unskilled, was available. Some refugees also managed to set up small shops and businesses of their own in the shantytowns and urban quarters of the larger cities such as Beirut and Amman. Women often supplemented family income by taking in sewing and laundry, in addition to working in the fields of local landlords. Children found work as street vendors, messenger boys, and as agricultural labourers.

Unlike the period before 1967, when the neighbouring countries found the refugees an economic burden, the emigration of large numbers of Lebanese, Syrians, and Jordanians to the Gulf led to the employment of Palestinians in the local economies of these countries to replace those who had left; similarly, the rapid increase in disposable income made possible by the remittances sent back from the Gulf states after the growth of oil exports led to a rising demand for labour in the neighbouring Arab countries, particularly in the urban areas.

Only a few examples can be given here, but the change was perhaps most remarkable in Jordan. Government development plans, which emphasized both agriculture and industry, led to an increase in the numbers of Palestinians employed seasonally to harvest crops and install new irrigation works and greenhouses; others found jobs in food processing factories, in warehouses, metal fabrication workshops, textile plants, and garages, as well as in construction and public utilities. In Lebanon, Palestinian refugees found work in the port of Beirut, as well as in industry, construction, and agriculture. Unlike the situation in Jordan, however, most of these jobs were temporary. (For example, of the 4,845 Palestinians from the camps employed in Lebanese industry, construction, and utilities in 1971, only 390 had permanent jobs.[17]) In Syria, government policies tended to preclude the employment of Palestinians in agriculture, but some managed to obtain employment in service industries, construction, and the building trades. Others who had obtained vocational training in government schools were employed in local manufacturing.

By far the largest change came with the increased emigration of large numbers of Palestinians to Saudi Arabia, Libya, and the Gulf states after the rapid increase in oil exports in the mid-1960s and the commencement of huge new industrial and infrastructural development projects following the fourfold rise in oil prices in 1973 and 1974. Unlike the situation in the late 1950s and early 1960s, the pressing need for labour led to a relaxation of immigration restrictions, although most Palestinian workers were still prevented from bringing their families with them or from settling permanently in these countries. Preference was given to those with vocational training (including those refugees from the younger generation who had obtained an education in UNRWA schools or abroad) or previous work experience. Remittances sent by these workers to their families in the camps often enabled the family to leave the camp, to build a new home or business, or to provide higher education for a sister or brother. A few of the camp residents employed in the Gulf later established businesses of their own, and they themselves became successful entrepreneurs.

The bourgeoisie: challenge and retreat

While the rapid development of the Gulf in the late 1960s and 1970s also led to an increase in contracts obtained by Palestinian corporations and additional business for Palestinian banks and entrepreneurs, their ability fully to tap these new opportunities was severely eroded by the growth of local bourgeoisies in Saudi Arabia and the Gulf states, beginning in the late 1950s. In Saudi Arabia, an agreement signed by the government and ARAMCO in 1957 stipulated that not less than 70 percent of those employed in the oil industry should be Saudis. While the lack of suitable applicants hindered progress at first, by 1964 the percentage of Saudis employed in supervisory and management posts in the industry had risen to 52 percent.[18] This was accompanied by government pressure on ARAMCO to award related contracts to Saudi entrepreneurs, a policy that was also encouraged by US aid funds to the kingdom. ARAMCO's special department on Arab industrial development began to farm out construction and maintenance work to Saudi contractors, and to provide them with the capital, tools, equipment, and raw materials needed to complete the job.

At the same time, ARAMCO began moving into other areas, such as the construction of roads, schools, housing, and power and water facilities, which were also given, where possible, to Saudi contractors. Many of these Saudis later became extremely wealthy entrepreneurs in their own right, running holding companies covering the import of vital industrial and consumer goods, banking, insurance, shipping, petrochemicals, and local manufacturing. By the late 1960s, Palestinian entrepreneurs, who lacked the easy access to ARAMCO's capital subsidies and technical expertise, as well as to government permits, import licences, and development funds, found competition difficult.[19]

In Kuwait, legislation encouraging the employment of nationals was followed in 1965 by the promulgation of a new Industrial Law, which gave the government control over all sectors of the economy, including construction, manufacturing, and banking. All industrial firms were subject to nationalization which stipulated that Kuwaiti shareholders own 51 percent or more of the total shares. Non-Kuwaiti firms were banned from setting up financial and banking institutions.[20] Such measures meant that Palestinian companies had to share their profits with their new majority shareholders, and became dependent on the shareholders for vital import/export licences, working and building permits, and contracts.

Elsewhere, the advent of new regimes which shunned private enterprise, banned capital exports, or discouraged the establishment of companies by non-nationals further limited the opportunities available to Palestinian entrepreneurs. The fall of the monarchy in Iraq in 1958, and its replacement by a republican regime led by Major General 'Abd al-Karim Qasim, led to sweeping changes in the economy that deprived foreigners of the right to repatriate profits or to engage in banking and foreign exchange transactions. In 1964, when the Ba'thists came to power, all industrial sectors came under government control, and publicly-owned companies were established to run the major industrial and commercial sectors, thereby eliminating much of the work previously awarded on contract to private firms, both Iraqi and Palestinian.

The overthrow of King Idris in Libya and the installation of a republic headed by Mu'ammar Qadhafi in September 1969 led to the arrest of many Palestinians who had served as advisers to the king, or as civil servants in the government control. and publicly owned companies were established to run industries were nationalized a year later, and most Palestinian firms were forced to leave or submit to a Libyan takeover of their assets. In Syria, the restrictions on private enterprise introduced in the late 1950s and 1960s left some scope for Palestinian activity in retail trade, construction, and transport, but the continuing decline of the Syrian economy due to the war of attrition with Israel in the early and mid-1960s, the devastation caused by the 1967 war, and the lack of development funds adversely affected the private sector in general.

By the late 1960s, Palestinians who had successfully managed to rebuild their businesses abroad or to establish new ones modelled on the corporate lines common in the West found themselves at a distinct disadvantage. Unable to translate their new economic power into the kind of political influence that would enable them to secure their position in society and in the economy, they came to the conclusion that only by creating a state of their own in Palestine would they be able to compete successfully with the other growing bourgeoisies in the Arab world. Their commitment to Palestinian nationalism was further reinforced by the fate suffered by some of their compatriots in the preceding decade.

Two cases were particularly relevant. The first was the relative decline of CAT following the sudden death of Emile Bustani in a plane crash in 1963. While foul play has never been proved, many Palestinians regarded the crash, and the subsequent limitations suffered by his company, to be linked both to Bustani's intention, announced shortly before his death, to run for the presidency of Lebanon and to his determined campaign for Arab economic integration in a way that would have encouraged the use of oil revenues for the benefit of all Arabs, irrespective of nationality.[21] Bustani's success, they felt, had become too great to be tolerated by his erstwhile rivals.

Even more dramatic was what happened to Intra Bank and to Yusif Baydas. Following a series of sudden withdrawals by members of the ruling families in Kuwait and Saudi Arabia, the Central Bank of Lebanon refused to provide a loan to Intra, even though its assets outweighed its liabilities. The bank's subsequent collapse in October 1966 not only left thousands of depositors deprived of their funds, but also removed a source of finance, managerial expertise, and employment for many other talented Palestinians who had been encouraged by Baydas or by Intra. The bank's prized assets were turned over to its creditors in the US, Kuwait, Qatar, and Saudi Arabia, while Baydas himself was left bankrupt and later died of a heart attack in Switzerland.[22] For the scores of Palestinian companies he had helped to establish, his death and the collapse of Intra were blows from which many never recovered.

The ruling families under Israeli occupation

The Israeli occupation of the West Bank and Gaza Strip in June 1967 removed a major source of support for those elements within the traditional ruling families who had remained loyal to the Hashemites and who had accepted the Jordanian annexation of the West Bank. Although Jordan continued to pay salaries to municipal officials and civil servants, the imposition of Israeli rule dealt a devastating blow to the trade patterns which both the West Bank and Gaza had established in the aftermath of the 1948 war. The traditional landowners were among those worst affected. The important orange crop in

Gaza, for example, could no longer be easily exported to Arab markets via Jordan, while the Israeli policy of confiscating land and water resources, both for new Jewish settlements and for the cultivation of cash crops for export, reduced the larger landholdings and added to the difficulty of making commercial agriculture viable in the West Bank and Gaza Strip.

Those individuals within the ruling families who had set up new industries and trading companies on the East Bank continued to thrive, both because of the demand created by the huge influx of new refugees and because of rising demand in Saudi Arabia and the Gulf states. Their kin in the occupied territories, however, suffered from the new military regulations imposed by the Israelis and from the competition they suddenly faced from Israeli exports to the territories. While at first the ability to export to Israel provided some impetus for the establishment of new agricultural, urban construction, and property development industries, the imposition of sales taxes, the loss of skilled labour, and the lack of basic infrastructure made it difficult for many segments of the traditional families to adapt to the new conditions.[23]

A major blow came in 1974 following the civil war in Jordan, when the endorsement of the PLO by the Arab summit conference in Rabat led the monarchy to reduce its support for its clients within the Palestinian aristocracy. Policies were established to 'Jordanize' the kingdom and to remove Palestinians from influential posts in the cabinet and in the civilian administration. Development funds, salaries, and agricultural and industrial subsidies were no longer readily available to the loyalist families on the West Bank. Those who protested found the kingdom's divide-and-rule tactics tended to favour their rivals.

By the mid-1970s, even those elements of the landed aristocracy in the West Bank that had supported the Hashemites against the nationalist demands of Palestinians living in the other Arab states had begun to declare openly their support for the PLO and for the creation of a separate Palestinian state in the West Bank and Gaza Strip. While they, like the bourgeoisie, had come to believe that their interests could only be protected in a state of their own, their decision to support the PLO also reflected the growing radicalism within the occupied territories that had begun to undermine their own positions, a trend that was confirmed in the 1976 municipal elections when both Communist Party and pro-PLO candidates succeeded in gaining control of several important posts in the West Bank.[24]

The Palestinian diaspora, 1982 to 1985

The years 1982 to 1985 were dismal for all Palestinians, whatever their position in Palestinian society. Developments in Lebanon were particularly painful: the Israeli invasion in June 1982 and the subsequent massacre in the camps of Sabra and Shatila were followed by extensive fighting in the South and the 'war of the camps,' which first broke out in May 1985. Having already been subjected to the internecine conflict of a decade of civil war, Palestinians living in the camps and in the cities of Beirut, Sidon, Tyre, and elsewhere found their lives and livelihoods even more threatened than before. Families were divided, as many of the young men were evacuated from Lebanon when the PLO's fighters were dispersed to other parts of the Arab world.

By the middle of 1984, UNRWA's assistance had helped 15,000 families to rebuild their shattered homes, but funds were insufficient to rebuild many training centres, hospitals, clinics, water distribution facilities, workshops, and schools that had been damaged or destroyed. Many refugees living outside the camps received no assistance at all after the Phalangist-dominated government refused to give permission to rebuild homes located outside the existing camps.[25] By the end of June 1985, another 683 Palestinians had been killed, 2,000 wounded, and 30,000 rendered homeless by attacks on Sabra, Shatila, and Burj al-Barajneh camps in Beirut. Another 1,500 Palestinians were missing, and the lack of medical resources meant that many of the wounded were left untreated.[26]

Elsewhere in the diaspora, the fragmentation of the PLO and the determination of countries like Egypt and Jordan to negotiate with Israel meant that the Palestinians living in these countries were kept under an even tighter rein than usual. In Syria, the hostility of the government towards Yasir Arafat and Fatah provided another element of friction in what was already a tense situation, particularly after the eruption of fighting in north Lebanon at the end of 1983 between those forces loyal to Arafat and those supported by Syria.

Unfortunately, the conflicts in Lebanon also coincided with economic retrenchment in Saudi Arabia and the Gulf states. As a result of the drop in oil revenues, government spending plans were cut back sharply and contracts were cancelled or delayed. Contractors, particularly local Arab and Palestinian firms, were often the last to be paid. While some of the larger Palestinian companies could bide their time by cutting staff and costs, or by obtaining work outside the Gulf states, the recession drastically reduced the opportunities available to both those within the camps who had sought to emigrate to the Gulf, and to those professional, educated Palestinians already living in these states. Pressure in Kuwait, Qatar, the United Arab Emirates, and Saudi Arabia to reduce the amount of work given to non-nationals grew as a result, and by mid-1985, many Palestinians were being barred from entry. Relatives were often forbidden to visit their kin living in these states, and those Palestinians on the verge of retirement faced the prospect of losing their right to stay once their work permits expired.

With families divided and sons, daughters, and grandchildren often separated permanently as they went to Beirut, London, and the US for schooling, medical care, or jobs, the wealthier middle and upper middle class Palestinians in the Gulf found their lives more constrained than before. Compared to their compatriots in Lebanon, the West Bank, or Gaza, they were more fortunate, but, like the displaced peasantry, they could take little comfort in the various peace plans being negotiated in the West. Unless, and until, they are also given the right to return to their homeland, they face endless years of statelessness – with all the insecurity this implies – however comfortable their economic positions relative to other Palestinians in the diaspora.

In contrast, the Palestinians living in the West Bank could at least look forward to some hope of progress in talks between Jordan and the PLO aimed at achieving an Israeli withdrawal and the creation of an autonomous state. Yet even here it was far from clear how much land would be given back – assuming that the talks met with success – given Israel's continued intransigence on the issue of recognizing the PLO. In the meantime, the repression continued, and with it an upsurge in militancy among Palestinians in the occupied territories that reflected both their growing impatience and their determination to roll back the occupation following Israel's partial withdrawal from Lebanon.

For the old ruling class, the talks could not come soon enough. They held out the hope of reducing the threat they faced from the rapid radicalization that in the 1980s had led to an upsurge in Islamic fundamentalism and in support for the Communist Party in the West Bank and Gaza. With the decline of the Israeli economy, the rise in unemployment in the occupied territories, and the escalating inflation, such radicalization seemed likely to spread, rapidly barring progress on the proposed talks between Jordan, the PLO, Israel, and the US.

For all segments of the Palestinian population, both in the diaspora and among those still living in their homeland, the importance of the nationalist struggle assumed a new dimension in the 1980s, however split their leadership appeared to be to the outside world. The ringing endorsement that Arafat received at the Palestine National Council meeting in Amman in November 1984 underlined this, irrespective of the support various Palestinians felt for one or another of the contending factions within the PLO. In private, Palestinians from all social backgrounds expressed criticism of this or that leader, of the way the PLO was organized, or simply of the divisions themselves; Arafat nevertheless continued to symbolize the determination to achieve their national goals despite the divisions, the various policies of the Arab states, or Arafat's own inability to translate the world's growing sympathy for their cause into the kind of action needed on the part of the US and Israeli governments to make possible genuine progress on a peaceful settlement.

By the mid-1980s, despite the differences expressed by Palestinians on strategic or tactical goals – the wisdom of accepting a smaller state in the West Bank and Gaza, an alliance with Jordan, or the continuation of the armed struggle – Palestinian nationalism had become a national cause that transcended divisions of class, place of exile or origin, religion, and gender. In this the PLO, whatever its other failings, had succeeded.

Notes

1. Janet Abu Lughod, 'The Demographic Transformation in Palestine,' in Ibrahim Abu Lughud (ed.), *The Transformation of Palestine* (Evanston, Ill., Northwestern University Press, 1977), p. 155.

2. This estimate was made by William St. Aubin, the delegate of the League of Red Cross Societies. See his article, 'Peace and Refugees in the Middle East,' *The Middle East Journal*, vol. 3, no. 3 (July 1949), p. 251.

3. S. G. Thicknesse. *Arab Refugees: A Survey of Re-Settlement Possibilities* (London, Royal Institute of International Affairs, 1949), p. 102. See also the *Annual Report of the Secretary-General of the United Nations, July 1, 1948 to June 30, 1949* (New York, United Nations, 1949) and the final report of the Economic Survey Mission sent to the area by the UN in 1949 (UN A/AC 25/6, Part 1).

4. United Nations Relief and Works Agency (UNRWA). *Registration Statistical Bulletin*. UN Document A/6018, No. 1/66 (First Quarter, 1966), p. 27.

5. See David Sperling, 'The Arabian American Oil Company Goes to Lebanon,' (Cambridge, Mass., Center for Middle Eastern Studies, Harvard University, 1965); Thomas Stauffer, 'The Industrial Workers,' in S. N. Fischer (ed.) *Social Forces in the Middle East* (New York, Greenwood Press, 1968); and David H. Finnie, *Desert Enterprise: The Middle East in Its Local Environment* (Cambridge, Mass., Harvard University Press, 1958); and Smith, pp. 172–3.

6. Sperling, 'The Arabian American Oil Company Goes to Lebanon,' p. 2; Finnie, *Desert Enterprise*, p. 102; Fawaz Turki, *The Disinherited: Journal of a Palestinian Exile* (New York, Monthly Review Press, 1972), p. 89; and *Al-Jazirah al-Jadidah* (The New Peninsula, Journal of the People's Democratic Republic of Saudi Arabia, n.p., 1972) (trans. by the Arab Support Committee, Berkeley, Calif.) pp. 4–5.

7. Of the total capital owned in Palestine in 1945 amounting to 281 million Palestinian pounds, £P 132.6 million was owned by the non-Jewish population. Of this, about £P 74.8 million was invested in land and another £P 13.1 million in agricultural buildings, tools, and livestock. The remainder, £P 44.7 million, was invested in industry, stocks, and commodities, or invested abroad. About £P 1.3 million had been used to purchase automobiles and other forms of motorized transport. See *A Survey of Palestine*, 2 vols. (Jerusalem, Government of Palestine, 1946) vol. 2, p. 569.

8. UN Department of Economic Affairs, *Review of Economic Conditions in the Middle East, 1951–1952*, Document E/2353/Add. 1, ST/CA/19/Add. 1 (New York, UN, March 1953), p. 114.

9. For details of Intra's holdings, see *New York Times*, October 1966 to January 1967.

10. J. C. Hurewitz, *The Struggle for Palestine* (New York, Greenwood Press, 1968), pp. 189–90; *Palestine Personalia* (Tel Aviv, 1947).

11. For a history of the company, see William W. Miller, 'The CAT Company,' (master's thesis, American University of Beirut, 1955).

12. *Annuaire des sociétés libanaises par action* (Beirut, Middle East Commercial Information Centre, 1970). See also *Who's Who in the Lebanon, 1974* (Beirut, Publitec Publications, Gedeon House, 1974) and the article on Hassib Sabbagh by Colin Smith, 'A Palestinian's Dream of Home,' *Observer*, 9 February 1975.

13. Under the terms of the armistice agreement between Israel and Transjordan signed in April 1949, King 'Abdallah had agreed to prevent all 'land, sea or air military or para-military forces . . . including non-regular forces' from committing any warlike or hostile act against 'the military or para-military forces' of Israel. [The text appears in Ann Dearden, *Jordan* (London, R. Hale, 1958), pp. 201–8.] Thereafter, infiltrators were likely to be shot or imprisoned. In December, Palestinians on the West Bank and in Jordan were declared Jordanian citizens and subject to Jordanian laws.

14. For details of the election and of the previous debates within parliament and the cabinet, see Aqil H. Abidi, *Jordan: A Political Study, 1948 to 1957* (London, Asia Publishing House, 1965). Dearden and Marius Hass, *Husseins Königreich: Jordaniens Stellung im Nahen Osten* (Munich, Tuduv Verlagsgesellschaft, 1975).

15. Edward Hagopian and A. B. Zahlan. 'Palestine's Arab Population: The Demography of the Palestinians,' *Journal of Palestine Studies*. vol. 3. no. 4 (Summer 1974).

16. Annual reports of the director-general of the United Nations Relief and Works Agency (UNRWA). *Palestinian Statistical Abstract, 1980* (Damascus, PLO Central Bureau of Statistics. 1981). p. 361.

17. Basim Sirhan. 'Palestinian Refugee Camp Life in Lebanon.' *Journal of Palestine Studies*. vol. 4. no. 2 (Winter 1975). p. 101.

18. Kemal Sayegh. *Oil and Arab Regional Development* (New York. Greenwood Press, 1978). pp. 85, 87.

19. For details of ARAMCO's operations. see Finnie. *Desert Enterprise*; and Stephen Longrigg. *Oil in the Middle East* (London, Royal Institute of International Affairs. 1968).

20. See M. W. Khoja and P. G. Sadler. *The Economy of Kuwait: Development and Role in International Finance* (London. Macmillan. 1979). p. 125; and Naseer H. Aruri and Samih Farsoun. 'Palestinian Communities and Arab Host Countries,' in Khalil Nakhleh and Elia Zureik (eds.). *The Sociology of the Palestinians* (London: Croom Helm, 1980). p. 136.

21. Bustani's own views on employing Palestinians and on regional economic integration are available in his book *Marché Arabesque* (London. R. Hale. 1961).

22. Details of the collapse are available in *New York Times*. 16. 19. 20. and 30 October 1966 and 17 November 1966. See also *The Banker*. vol. 122. no. 551 (January 1972); and Michael Field. *A Hundred Million Dollars a Day* (London, Sidgwick and Jackson. 1975). pp. 138–42.

23. Interviews with Rashid Shawa. Bassam Shaka'a. Muhammad Milham. and Muhammad Z. Nashashibi in London. May 1980 to June 1981. See also Jamil Hilal. *al-Diffah al-Gharbiyyah: al-Tarkib al-Iqtisadiyyah w-al-Ijtima'iyyah, 1948–1974* (The Economic and Social Structure of the West Bank. 1948–1974) (Beirut. 1974); Emile Sahliyeh. 'West Bank Industrial and Agricultural Development: The Basic Problems,' *Journal of Palestine Studies*. vol. 9. no. 2 (Winter 1982); Hisham Awartani. 'West Bank Agriculture: A New Outlook.' *Al-Najah University Research Bulletin*, no. 1 (Nablus. 1981); 'Atallah Mansour. 'West Bank Aid.' *Events* (London). 17 October 1977; and Sarah Graham-Brown. 'The West Bank and Gaza: The Structural Impact of Israeli Colonization.' *MERIP Reports*. no. 74 (January 1979).

24. On the growth of the Communist Party on the West Bank and in Gaza during the middle and late 1970s, see Salim Tamari. 'The Palestinian Demand for Independence Cannot be Postponed Indefinitely.' *MERIP Reports* (October–December 1981).

25. *Report of the Commissioner-General of UNRWA to the UN General Assembly July 1, 1983 to June 30, 1984* (New York. UN. 1984).

26. Medical Aid for Palestinians (MAP). 'Beirut Camps Appeal' (London). August 1985.

10. The Armenian National Question

Paul Saba

The twenty-fourth of April 1990 will mark the 75th anniversary of the beginning of the first campaign of genocide in the 20th century: the systematic and premeditated extermination of 1.5 million Armenians by the Turkish government. For many decades this atrocity was largely forgotten by world opinion, the memory of it kept alive only by the worldwide Armenian diaspora and a few sympathetic historians and political activists. The magnitude of the tragedy is arresting even for a world which has seen so many other mass murders. Two-thirds of the Armenians living in the Ottoman Empire were killed between 1915 and 1923 on orders from the highest levels of government.[1] Although Turkey was one of the defeated powers in World War I, the victorious allies took no steps to punish the perpetrators of this crime.

If the world as a whole chose neither to remember nor to respond, in some quarters the fact of the massacres and, more importantly, the fact that those responsible went unpunished were not forgotten. International indifference to the Armenian genocide in no small part paved the way for the Holocaust which later engulfed six million Jews, as the following story suggests. In 1939, one week before launching the German army into Poland and thereby inaugurating World War II, Adolph Hitler met with his military commanders to present them with his plans for the forthcoming invasion. Exhorting them to exterminate mercilessly the Jews, Poles and Slavs in their path, he brushed aside the objection of one general who suggested that the Nazis might some day be held accountable for these crimes. 'Who after all,' he reminded them, 'speaks today of the annihilation of the Armenians? The world believes in success only.'[2]

In contemporary Turkey the government continues to profit from its 'success' of 1915–23, sparing no effort to ensure that few remember Armenia or the Armenian genocide. The official Turkish position is that the massacres never occurred.[3] The small Armenian community which survives in Turkey today is closely monitored, while history books have been rewritten to remove any mention of their national past. Turkey is also extremely sensitive to any foreign references to the genocide. When the Turkish government learned in 1982 that Israel was set to host an International Conference on the Holocaust and Genocide at which the Armenian massacres were to be discussed, its immediate threats against Turkish and other Jews caused the Israelis to sever all official ties to the conference.⁴ Absurd as it may seem, even British tourists in Turkey who happen to photograph old buildings where (unknown to them) massacres of Armenians occurred have been arrested, while a deputy manager of Lufthansa airlines was put on trial for possession of an old globe on which 'Armenia' was marked.⁵ What the Turkish government insists remain hidden, the Armenian diaspora has kept alive. When traditional leaders and quiet diplomacy failed, an Armenian revolutionary movement opted for direct action. Since 1975 a whole series of armed attacks have been directed against Turkish diplomats and other officials in Europe and North America.⁶ With the formation, in 1983, of the Armenian Democratic Front which broke with the narrow militarism of pre-existing Armenian revolutionary groups, the movement has shown its growing political maturity.⁷

In recent years a great number of works have appeared on the Holocaust and the inadequacy (to use the most charitable word) of Western responses to the plight of European Jewry under Nazism.⁸ The Armenian massacres, too, provide an illuminating perspective on genocide in the 20th century and the world's failure to act against it. At the same time the Armenian question, both in its past and present configurations, illustrates the ineluctable problem of national oppression and national resistance within the world capitalist system. For it was not the 'barbaric nature' of the Turks which was responsible for this genocide, as has been alleged by certain historians,⁹ but rather the social and national contradictions which Turkey experienced as a result of the process of its integration into the world capitalist order, and the effects of those contradictions on its internal disintegration.

The Ottoman Empire

An adequate understanding of the Armenian massacres of 1915 is impossible without an accurate picture of the character of the Ottoman Empire at the end of the 19th century. Created in 1300, the Ottoman state rose to become the most powerful empire in the world in the 16th century under Suleiman the Magnificent, when it stretched from the gates of Vienna in the west to Persia in the east, from the Ukraine in the north to the Mahgreb and Arabia in the south.¹⁰ Theoretically, the Ottoman social formation has perhaps best been described as a combined articulation of a dominant Asiatic mode of production¹¹ with forms of petty commodity production and merchant capital.¹² The economic basis of Ottoman power was the wealth of its vast territories, including strategically important Mediterranean coastlines, the Levant, North Africa, the Balkans, and the agricultural and commercial bounty which these provided.¹³ The strength of the Osmanli state lay in its absolute ownership and control of all wealth within the Empire,¹⁴ particularly its collection of agricultural surplus, tax revenues, and control over internal trade,¹⁵ its military prowess, a fervent if rigid theology, and a vast government bureaucracy.

A whole series of factors at the end of the 16th century, however, combined to halt Ottoman territorial expansionism and eventually to force the Empire back upon itself. The strength of Persia in the east blocked the growth of the house of Islam in that direction. The rise of absolutist states in Europe in the late 16th and early 17th centuries and the impact of their conquests in the New World and the Far East gave Europe an increasing economic, technological, military and, eventually, commercial advantage. Internally, the primary factors fostering this decline were the beginnings of an endemic revenue collection crisis, caused chiefly by rising military expenses, a population increase in Anatolia, price inflation and a growing loss of political control over merchant capital and trade. The Ottoman state and the Islamic religious hierarchy were generally hostile to industry and entrepreneurial innovation, urban centres were neglected, and agricultural production was never accompanied by improvements in rural technology. Commercial activity, despised by the Turks, largely devolved onto minority peoples within the Empire: Greeks, Armenians, Jews. State despotism, technological parasitism and theological obscurantism were all powerful obstacles to Ottoman progress.[16]

It is, therefore, particularly remarkable, given the political contraction of the Empire beginning in the 16th and 17th centuries, and these various economic impediments, that the Ottoman commercial economy remained dynamic and vigorous at least until the beginning of the 19th century. Only thereafter did it begin a precipitous decline under the impact of its own internal contradictions and its peripheralization in relation to European capitalism.[17] As Turkey was inexorably drawn into the world imperialist system, it experienced all the dislocations, transformations and catastrophic social contradictions which flow from the subordination of states to the logic and hierarchy of the capitalist mode of production on a world scale.[18] As capitalism spreads in this manner it must, of necessity, smash or restructure the ancient social formations surrounding it, and these tend to fall apart, as Tom Nairn has pointed out, along fault lines contained inside them – fault lines which are almost always ones of nationality and/or religion.[19] The Ottoman Empire, being a polyglot admixture of nations, peoples and religions, was particularly vulnerable in this regard. The encroachments of Western imperialism produced not only the collapse of a once great empire, but also the terrible human tragedies which accompanied its death throes, the Armenian genocide being one of the most horrific.

The Ottoman crisis of the 19th century

At the close of the 19th century the Ottoman Empire, although considerably shrunken in size from its days of grandeur, was nonetheless still a far-flung political entity, encompassing a seemingly endless diversity of geographical formations, nationalities, languages, religions, and forms of economic and social life, precariously linked together by a powerful despotic state, military force and the crushing weight of historical tradition.[20] Geographically, the Empire varied from the Hellespont, separating Europe from Asia, across the elevated plateaux of Anatolia and Asia Minor surrounded by a whole series of mountain ranges, toward the Tigris and Euphrates river valleys to the marshes of Mesopotamia, the Levantine coast and the deserts of the Arabian peninsula. Its population included Turks, Macedonians, Tartars, Circassians, Armenians, Kurds, Arabs, Greeks and Albanians, each with their own distinct history, ethnic culture, and social dynamic.[21] Although Muslims predominated (the Sultan, in addition to his temporal powers, was Caliph of the Muslim faith), the Druze, Jews, and Catholic, Protestant and the various Eastern Orthodox churches also were established, and even enjoyed a degree of legal recognition.[22]

The Ottomans were no less diverse economically.[23] Although major commercial cities and seaports were closely linked to the world market with their inhabitants conversant in the latest forms of finance and trade, various forms of pre- and semi-capitalist land tenure and social organization prevailed in the countryside, in fact, if not in law. Here the majority of the population dwelled and was subject to the exactions of both the central government and local oligarchies. Even more remotely, in the east, Kurdish and Circassian bands maintained a marauding nomadic existence while in the high Cilician mountains Armenian villagers continued to live lives which were indistinguishable from those of their medieval ancestors.

The Ottoman economy at the end of the 19th century was based overwhelmingly on commercial agriculture and, to a lesser extent, on handicraft production; industrialization was as yet unknown. There were no capitalist enterprises in the Ottoman Empire prior to the 19th century, apart from Egypt which, after 1882, was occupied by the British.[24] Nineteenth-century indigenous attempts at economic modernization were stifled by a series of commercial treaties imposed upon the Empire by the European powers resulting in a flood of cheap imported Western goods and the consequent collapse of local artisanal production. The speed with which this transformation was accomplished is quite remarkable. In 1825, Turkey had supplied almost all of Britain's cotton fabric imports, yet by 1855 the Ottomans were importing over 121 million metres of cotton fabrics from England.[25] The few industrial enterprises which did manage to develop were dominated by foreign capital or capital belonging to non-Turkish minority groups. As late as 1913 there were a mere 269 industrial enterprises in Turkey, of which only 242 were actually functioning. Their capital was supplied as follows: 10 percent by foreigners, 50 percent by Greeks, 20 percent by Armenians, 5 percent by Jews and only 15 percent by Muslim Turks.[26]

A direct result of this overall economic underdevelopment was the deplorable state of Ottoman finances. As noted earlier, the Empire had been suffering endemic revenue crises since the late 16th century. In the 19th century these crises were intensified by a number of new factors. A chronic trade deficit caused by the importation of large quantities of foreign products was exacerbated by numerous loans obtained in Western Europe, not for economic development, but for military and imperial extravagances. Between 1854 and 1875 one billion dollars was borrowed from Western banks, yet all efforts to raise sufficient internal revenues to reduce the constantly growing debt were unsuccessful.²⁷ The Ottoman government was rushing towards bankruptcy and in 1875 declared that it would no longer be able to honour its obligations. The resulting financial crisis provided a new opportunity for the Great Powers to tighten their grip on Turkey; in 1881 the Sultan turned complete control of the economy over to a specially created European-dominated organization – the Ottoman Public Debt Administration – which proceeded to an economic reorganization of the Empire for the further benefit of Western imperialism.²⁸

The effects of this financial disaster were felt throughout the Ottoman territories. The treasury had been depleted to pay off the foreign debt, and government expenses could not be met. Bureaucrats who went unpaid resorted to increased corruption, while everywhere harsher and more onerous methods of taxation were imposed, primarily upon the peasant masses and minority nationalities. The population reacted to these new indignities with anger and dissension, while national-minded Turks grew increasingly resentful of Europeans, and those minority peoples within the Empire whom they considered pro-European.²⁹ No one could yet foresee the extent to which Turkish reaction, unable effectively to resist the encroachments of the European powers, would turn its wrath against much more vulnerable internal targets, including the oppressed Armenian nationality.

The Ottoman Empire and the Great Powers
The seizure by Europeans of the Ottoman economy in 1881 was the culmination of a long process of imperialist penetration which had begun in the 18th century. Each one of the Great Powers – Austria, Russia, Britain, France and, later, Germany – was contending for international supremacy, and the Ottoman Empire figured in the strategy of all.³⁰ Each sought to influence, control or dominate the Turkish economy and state, if not to dismember the Empire and annex its territories. Austria desired to expand its own empire into south-eastern Europe. Russia, too, coveted the Balkans, inhabited by its fellow Slavs, as well as Turkish access to the Mediterranean and the Persian Gulf. Again and again the Czars were to champion the demands of the Armenians for freedom from Ottoman rule as a pretext to increase their access to these waterways. At the same time, England and France were engaged in fierce commercial rivalries, for which the Turkish import market and government loans were the chief prizes. Britain, whose mercantile policies were destroying the Ottoman economy, was dominated in its decision making by a concern to block Russian expansion, and it supported the maintenance of the Ottoman Empire as a bulwark against the Czar. Nonetheless, Britain, too, claimed to champion minority rights in Turkey, including those of the Armenians.³¹

Thus, the fortunes of the Ottomans, caught in the middle of these rivalries, shifted with the shifting balance of world power and politics. When, in 1853, Czar Nicholas I of Russia, whose military might represented a constant threat to the decaying Ottoman state, labelled Turkey 'the sick man of Europe,' the phrase was so apt that it stuck.³² If the great powers were intent on gaining maximum advantage from the decline of this invalid, none was yet ready to take such action as would decisively change the status quo and thereby risk a major clash between them. They were all fearful that, as the condition of the patient deteriorated, the intensified rivalry of the surviving heirs to divide his possessions might result in an international military confrontation.[33] This fear proved to be well founded. Time after time, a crisis in the Empire brought the Powers into conflict, as with the Crimean War, only to have them pull back just short of international conflagration. The pattern was constantly repeated until this precarious equilibrium was shattered forever in World War I.

Dramatic signs that this framework of Great Power relations would not last forever appeared in the 1820s with the emergence of a destabilizing factor which upset the calculations of both the imperialists and the Turkish ruling class. Pressure had begun to build along the fault lines of nationality and religion within the empire, and it was not long before a whole series of social earthquakes began to shake the foundations of this centuries-old system. Oppressed peoples within the Ottoman Empire, chafing under a brutal and corrupt administration, and increasingly influenced by nationalism, pan-Slavism and other foreign ideologies, rose in revolt. The initial centre of this rebellion was Greece, but it soon spread to the rest of the Balkans and then Asia Minor.[34] In 1875, Bosnia and Herzegovina revolted. Bulgaria followed in 1876, in part over the harsh new taxing policy which resulted from the government's declaration of bankruptcy, in part due to Muslim attempts to suppress its Christian faith. They were soon joined by Montenegro and Serbia. When Russia, aided by Rumania, entered the fray in 1877 by invading Turkey, ostensibly on behalf of its brother Slavs, the tide turned decisively against the Ottomans. The so-called Russo-Turkish War was over in less than a year.[35]

The Armenian question first became an issue in international diplomacy as a result of this war.[36] In the peace treaties which followed, the Ottomans were forced to grant independence to Rumania, Montenegro and Serbia; autonomy to Bulgaria; and to submit to an Austria protectorate over Bosnia and Herzegovina.[37] Russia had occupied parts of Turkish Armenia during the fighting, and Britain was insisting on their return to the Turks. A strong Armenian delegation travelled to the peace conferences at San Stefano and Berlin to attempt to convince the Great Powers to redress Armenian grievances. Their efforts were brutally rebuffed: in exchange for Turkish surrender of Cyprus to England, Britain defended the Ottoman demand for the return of Armenian territory seized by Russia. Under British pressure the Russians agreed to the abandonment of a certain amount of Armenian territory, accepting in exchange empty Ottoman promises of reform. Nonethelesss, Russia managed to retain additional parts of ancient Armenia to those she had seized from Persia in 1827 and from Turkey in 1828–29.[38]

After much negotiation, the Treaty of Berlin contained, among its many articles, a weak and unenforcible statement relating to the Armenian situation. In it the Ottoman government promised that it would carry out improvements and reforms in the Armenian provinces, subject to Great Power supervision, and that it would guarantee the security of Armenians living there.[39] Having previously expected to be granted the same independence won by the Balkan peoples through force of arms, Armenians saw their hopes cruelly dashed at the peace conferences. They put little stock in the empty promises of the Ottoman government, and were dismayed by the callous indifference of the Great Powers to Armenian aspirations. All too soon they would learn to their sorrow just how little the promises of the Ottoman government meant, and how unconcerned the Great Powers were in enforcing a treaty when only Armenian lives and liberties were at stake.

Armenia before the Ottoman conquest

Geographically, the Armenian homeland of classical and Byzantine times (known historically as Greater Armenia) encompasses some 120,000 square miles of high volcanic tablelands, broken by rugged mountains and wild rivers located in eastern Anatolia, south of the Caucasus Mountains.[40] The Caspian Sea lies to the north-east of Greater Armenia, the Black Sea to the north-west. The bulk of this territory is virtually uninhabitable, consisting of windswept mountains, many over 10,000 feet, including Mount Ararat, which rises to 17,000 feet.[41] The mountains of this compact geographical unit might appear to make Armenia a natural fortress. The fact that they run west to east, however, exposes Armenia on two sides, and historically it has been subject to a whole series of invasions precisely from those directions, with devastating effect. Rich in mineral deposits, Armenia contains a number of fertile regions, including the Araxes river valley. The climate of Armenia is harsh: frigid winters of up to eight months alternating with short, hot, dry summers. Although the rivers are numerous, few are navigable; the headwaters of the Tigris and Euphrates are to be found in Armenia.[42]

Lesser Armenia, which came to be populated in a later period, is 250 miles of Mediterranean coast in Cilicia, in south-west Anatolia, ranging from the Taurus mountains down to the sea, north of the Gulf of Iskanderun (Alexandretta). The area has several ports and was a strategic centre of international trade from ancient times. Armenians, who began to move into this region in the 11th century, were active in commercial affairs in coastal towns as well as establishing cities and villages in the mountains and plains. From here they also spread to trading centres throughout the Middle East, Europe, and Asia.[43]

In spite of its inhospitable climate and terrain, Greater Armenia has been continuously inhabited since the Old Stone Age, with a settled, civilized population since before the 14th century BC. In the 9th century BC, its first unitary state, the Kingdom of Urartu, was established.[44] Overrun by Assyria and then by the Persians, Armenia came under Greek influence when Alexander the Great conquered Persia in 331 BC. With the weakening of the Greek Empire after Alexander's death, Armenia revolted and won its independence, developing a flourishing empire of its own, aided by its strategic location on the main trade route between Europe and India and China. Coveted by its powerful neighbours to the west (Rome) and east (Persia), Armenia was also racked by internal conflicts. In 66 BC, King

Tigran's forces were defeated by a Roman army and, for the time being, Armenian independence came to an end.[45]

Situated as it was on the eastern boundary of the Roman Empire with Persia, any shift in the balance of power between the two could not but affect Armenia. Rome's fall and the rise of its weaker Byzantine successor provided the Persians with their opportunity, and, in 387 AD, after much fighting, a partition of Armenia between the two empires was forced. Interestingly enough, this period of disunity saw a number of developments which helped to foster and strengthen Armenian ethnic cohesion and self-consciousness. In 301 AD, Armenia was the first nation to convert to Christianity. While this event secured Armenia's links to the west rather than to its Zoroastrian, or later Muslim, neighbours, the Armenian Orthodox Church developed its own independent doctrine and liturgy, and rejected the supremacy of both the Papacy and the Greek Orthodox Patriarchate.[46] Given what Fernand Braudel has written about the relationship between mountain geography and religion, the independent development of Armenian orthodoxy should not be surprising.[47] In 404 AD, the Armenian alphabet was invented, thereby providing a basis for the translation into Armenia's own independent Indo-European language of works from the west, the preservation of its rich oral cultural tradition, as well as the composition of original writings, and the creation of an educated intelligentsia.[48]

These developments were interrupted in the seventh century by the rising tide of Islam which overwhelmed Persia and pushed back the Byzantine borders. In 650, Armenia became part of the Arab caliphate and it was not until the ninth century that it managed to regain its independence, a state of affairs which lasted only 160 years. In 1045, it was annexed by the Byzantines once more only to be overrun shortly thereafter by the Seljuk Turks.[49] Much of the Armenian nobility was wiped out in this period.[50] One of the byproducts of this defeat was a mass migration out of Great Armenia to the west. This was not only the beginning of the Armenian diaspora, it was also the origin of an independent Armenian principality (Lesser Armenia) in Cilicia on the shores of the Mediterranean.[51] This new state lived a precarious existence, attempting to ally with its neighbours for security, and to profit from international trade. Co-operating with the Crusaders on their way to the Holy Land, Lesser Armenia sought to win the support of Europe, but could not withstand the Muslim offensives which swept through Asia Minor in the 14th century, ultimately falling to the Mameluke Sultans of Egypt in 1375, who were, in turn, forced into submission by the Ottoman Turks.[52]

While Lesser Armenia was losing the battle to maintain its independence, the history of Greater Armenia was one of 'almost uninterrupted woe and disaster.'[53] Its seigneurial social formation suffered acutely from a series of invasions by eastern nomadic pastoralist peoples.[54] First there were the Mongol hordes (1236), then those of Tamerlane (1386–88), then various warring Turcoman tribes. Finally, in 1514, half of the Armenian plateau fell to the Ottoman Empire, with the remainder being conquered by Suleiman the Magnificent 20 years later.[55] A new era in Armenian history had begun.

Armenians under Ottoman rule

The Armenia which the Ottomans incorporated into their Empire was in a deplorable state. The various invasions had depopulated much of the country, destroyed organized social life, and ruined the economy. The remaining inhabitants were reduced to abject poverty, or else flight to alpine strongholds.[56] Although it was hoped that Ottoman rule would bring much-needed stability, this was not immediately the case. Armenia continued to exist as a distant outpost on the volatile Persian border, and sporadic warfare continued until a 1639 peace conference at which the eastern part of Armenia was ceded to Persia.[57] The Ottoman solution to the problem of maintaining a strong military presence on this border was forcibly to transfer into Armenia alien populations, primarily Kurds, but also some Turks and Turcoman tribesmen. The Kurds, still essentially nomadic, were promised perpetual immunity from taxation if they would act as a militia to guard the Persian frontier. This they did – as well as seize Armenian land and harass its people. By the 19th century Armenians were a minority in their own country, being outnumbered by the combined population of Kurds and Turks.[58]

The foundation upon which the Ottoman Empire and its minorities policies were constructed was the combination of two traditions, the Muslim religion and Osmanli dynastic history. Each of these helped to shape Ottoman policy vis-à-vis the conquered peoples under its control.[59] In regard to religion, the Ottoman Sultans recognized the right of non-Muslim peoples to practise their faith subject to governmental supervision. The Sultan, for example, created the position of Armenian Patriarchate in Constantinople with authority over all adherents of Armenian Orthodoxy within the Empire, and a jurisdiction which overrode the established hierarchy of the Armenian church itself.[60]

At the political level, the Armenian people, as with other non-Turkish peoples, initially were allowed to maintain a certain degree of their autonomy in accordance with the 'millet' system.[61] Each community (millet) within the Empire was entitled to a large measure of internal self-government, without direct Turkish interference, provided that the community paid its taxes and created no disturbances. Matters of marriage, inheritance, education, the settlement of disputes between members of the same community, and similar day-to-day affairs were all the responsibility of the millet. In this regard the millet system was similar to the limited autonomy granted to sections of medieval Jewry in Europe, of which the charter given to Polish Jews by Sigismund Augustus in 1551 is the most developed example.[62] What the Armenians gained by the millet system in their internal affairs, they lost in terms of their relations with the Muslim majority. Ottoman practice provided that Muslim law was inapplicable to non-Muslims so that whenever there was a conflict involving members of both communities, the Muslim could petition to have his case heard in a Muslim religious court where non-Muslim testimony was either forbidden, or later, consistently disregarded.[63]

Other policies were equally detrimental, subjecting Armenians to numerous discriminatory practices. Because they were Christians they were not allowed

to bear arms, a situation which prevented them from taking effective action
against marauders and predatory neighbours. Armenians were required to pay
special taxes, which more often than not meant suffering extortion at the hands
of greedy or corrupt officials. Although they were not required to serve in the
military, until the mid-eighteenth century they were victims of the *devshirme*, or
boy-collection, in which Christian children were snatched from their parents,
raised as Muslims and sent into the slavery of the Ottoman civil service.[64] A
final disability to which they were subject related to the Kurdish militia within
their midst; the Armenians were required to provide free winter quarters to the
Kurds and their flocks. Inasmuch as this burden had to be endured for periods
of four to six months each year it further impoverished the already poor
peasant masses, who frequently found themselves in debt to the local Turkish
or Kurdish beys.[65] Limited self-government in their own community could not
lessen the stigma of second-class status everywhere else, and the Armenian
population suffered under the oppressive weight of imperial power and local
depredations.

The Armenian national awakening

At the end of the 19th century, according to various estimates, there were
between three and a half and four million Armenians dispersed among three
empires (Ottoman, Russian and Persian) and a world wide diaspora. Two-
thirds of these lived under Ottoman rule.[66] Common religion, a common
language and a history of oppression linked them together as did a certain
common social structure: the absence of an historical nobility, a large peasant
base and a more numerous middle class than existed in other Eastern
societies.[67] Armenians can be said to have constituted a nation of a special type.
Unlike many other nations, they had a large and wealthy diaspora population;
unlike the Jews, another diaspora nation, they continued to inhabit their
ancient homeland in significant numbers. Like the Kurds, their homeland was
both occupied and divided among several states.[68] The majority of Armenians
were peasants, but three other classes should also be noted here. First, there
was the Armenian comprador bourgeoisie, consisting of bankers, financiers,
the clerical hierarchy and high government officials. Located primarily in
Constantinople and Tabriz, they maintained close ties to the Turkish and
Persian states but had little or no contact with the broad masses of Armenians
in their ancient homeland. Second, there was a large middle class of small
traders, artisans and merchants in cities and towns throughout all three
empires whose commercial dealings brought them into frequent and
sympathetic contact with foreigners. Finally, there were the Armenian
mountaineers, spirited, independent warriors who inhabited the remote alpine
fastnesses of Greater Armenia and Cilicia, and who, unlike their brethren, kept
and manufactured their own arms.[69]

Since the 14th century, Armenian merchants had traversed the known world,
trading in Europe and even China. By the 16th century, extensive networks of

Armenian merchants stretched from the Philippines and Far East to India, Iran, and Europe. Travelling as far north as Moscovy and Sweden, they traded in much of Europe and Asia, as well as points south, including Portuguese Africa.[70] In the wake of these commercial ventures, established Armenian communities emerged throughout Europe, Asia and North America. The influence of the Armenian middle class and the presence of a large number of intellectuals in the diaspora communities in Europe and North America, with strong ties to Armenia itself, distinguished Armenia from other Eastern states, linked it to the West, and powerfully contributed to making Armenia the first Eastern nation to take the path of revolution.[71]

The sources of the Armenian national awakening were several. Relatively more liberal conditions in Russian-occupied Armenia fostered the development of radical and populist ideas which gradually filtered across the Turkish border. Because of its proximity, and because Russia had historically championed the rights of Turkish Armenia, many Armenians looked to Russia for leadership and even hoped for Russian military intervention to liberate them from the Turkish yoke. The presence in Armenia of foreign Catholic and Protestant missionaries meant that many of the Armenian youth were being exposed to contemporary European intellectual currents. European ideas were also reaching Armenia through the return of sons of the Armenian bourgeoisie in Constantinople who had been sent to Europe to be educated. Finally, Armenian intellectuals in the West were influenced by the development of 19th century nationalism to anticipate the eventual independence of their own homeland.[72]

The first stirrings of unrest in Armenia itself in the 19th century were largely spontaneous demonstrations of popular dissatisfaction, rather than conscious national revolts. Like other rural mountainous areas, Armenia had a long history of social banditry and primitive rebels of the type discussed by Eric Hobsbawm.[73] A certain degree of unrest could always be attributed to these traditions, while other occurrences appear to have represented a response to the generalized grievances of several groups, not just the Armenians. The uprising in the town of Van in 1862, for example, seems to have united the Armenian city dwellers with the Kurdish peasants of the outlying areas against their common Turkish oppressors.[74] The more important rebellion in the Cilician mountain stronghold of Zeitun in the same year, however, already shows evidence of a significant role played by revolutionary Armenian intellectuals.[75]

In examining the Armenian revolutionary movement in relation to indigenous political developments in other Eastern and Middle Eastern countries in the same period, one is struck by three things: its precocity, its pronounced military character, and the influence of socialism within it.[76] In 1885, the first Armenian political party, the Armenakans, was formed. Its platform called for self-defence against Ottoman violence and demanded that the Great Powers, particularly Russia, rescue Armenia from Turkish misrule. Given its basic bourgeois democratic character, and its lack of an international perspective on the nature of Armenian oppression, the party's practical activity eventually degenerated into anti-Kurdish violence, which worked to divide these two minority peoples.[77] The first Armenian revolutionary party, the Hunchaks, was formed in Geneva in 1887 by a group of Marxist students. Influenced by Russian populism as well as by the Russian Social Democrat G. V. Plekhanov, the Hunchak programme called for both national liberation and socialism, and advocated a multinational strategy of co-operation with revolutionaries throughout the Ottoman and Russian empires. By the 1890s, the Hunchaks were established in a number of cities in the Empire, in Europe, America and the Russian Caucasus.[78]

During this same period, a number of different Armenian revolutionary groups were formed in the Russian Empire; in 1890, they came together to form the Dashnaktsutiun, or Armenian Revolutionary Federation (ARF).[79] The Hunchaks joined the new Federation, but the two organizations soon separated. The ARF, while describing itself as socialist, was primarily a nationalist organization, calling for a people's war and foreign intervention to rescue Armenia from the Turks. As the revolutionary movements grew in size and influence, they surpassed the more moderate nationalist groups and even began to challenge the hegemony of the traditional, Armenian clerical leadership and the conservative Armenian bourgeoisie. The year 1890 saw a number of incidents which testify to the rising tide of the Armenian revolutionary spirit. In June, revolutionaries fired on Turkish troops called to disperse a peaceful demonstration in a cathedral churchyard in Erzerum. In July, similar fighting broke out in Constantinople between soldiers and Armenian demonstrators. In September, a group of Armenian partisans attempted to cross the Russian border and raid Turkish territory.[80] In the midst of these events, other developments on the international level and within the Ottoman Empire itself were pushing the Armenian situation into a new and dangerous phase.

Pan-Islamism and the 1894–95 massacres
In 1876, immediately prior to the outbreak of the Russo-Turkish war, a new Sultan, Abdul Hamid II, had assumed the throne, and proclaimed a new constitution.[81] Celebrated by Turkish liberals, the document had called for an elected parliament based on proportional representation for all nationalities, freedom of religion, education and the press, as well as equality of taxation. It soon had become apparent, however, that Abdul Hamid had no intention of implementing a constitutional programme. Using the war as an excuse, he prorogued parliament in 1878 and shelved the constitution, continuing to rule by imperial decree.[82]

The Ottoman ruling class, with the Sultan at its head, resented the humiliating consequences of their wartime defeat, viewing them as only the latest examples of European interference, with all the destructive effects on traditional social and political relations which such interference implied. Nor did it escape their attention that certain minority peoples, acting as intermediaries in the process of Turkish integration into the world economy,[83] were profiting from the development of capitalism within the Empire in a manner in which the Turks were not. The response of the Ottomans to these developments was profoundly ambivalent; at once they sought to resist European encroachment and to take over 'its vital forces for their own use.'[84] What the Empire needed was its own form of imperial cohesion, one which would unite the traditional classes and peoples in the face of a common challenge posed by the West and its native 'agents.'

Abdul Hamid, reactionary and obsessive, played a central role in formulating the Ottoman response. He launched a series of initiatives, relying equally on his religious and secular authority. On the ideological front he looked to Islamic tradition as an organizing principle. The result was the implementation of a vigorous Pan-Islamic policy in an effort to weld together the Turks and potentially dissident Muslim minorities within the Empire. Militarily, he established a new fighting force, the Hamidiye, named after himself. These were cavalry regiments of Kurdish tribesmen organized on the model of the Russian Cossacks and sent to the provinces, including Armenia, ostensibly to act as a frontier corps, but in reality to restrain a rebellious population.[85] Like their 17th century predecessors, the Hamidiye were given free rein in the outlying areas, which they used more to plunder the Armenians and other local inhabitants than to patrol the border. Pan-Islamism and the Hamidiye were effective tactics; they strengthened Kurdish loyalty to the regime, hampered the revolutionary movement and drove a new wedge between the Kurdish and harassed Armenian peoples.

Another Hamidian initiative should also be noted here. The Armenians were already suffering the effects of the Ottoman land policy which had been developing in response to the penetration of capitalist relations within the Empire. In the course of the 19th century, this policy was codified in a number of legal reforms which gave *de jure* recognition to various pre-existing forms of private property. These precedents were now seized upon by the Ottoman regime in the course of its struggle against the rebellious Christian minorities in order forcibly to dispossess them of their traditional holdings to the benefit of wealthy local Turkish and Kurdish landlords whose loyalty was assured. Armenians, already a minority in their own country, were increasingly being driven off land which had been worked by their ancestors for centuries.[86]

While the Turkish government was intensifying its oppression of the Armenians, the Russian government, to whom the latter had previously looked for protection, was also undergoing a change of attitude with regard to the Armenian question. Once the issue of Turkish mistreatment of this Christian people had been a handy excuse for Russian interference in Ottoman affairs. Now support for Armenian independence from the Ottomans was seen as a liability which might easily strengthen the already powerful multinational revolutionary movement in the Russian Caucasus which was demanding the right of self-determination for Russia's own oppressed peoples. As the focus of Russia's geopolitical interests shifted elsewhere in the 1890s, a certain Russian–Turkish rapprochement emerged, constituting an anti-revolutionary united front directed against all rebellious peoples, including the Armenians.[87] These changes, together with the lethargy and indifference of the Western powers, created a climate which would enable the Turkish government to respond mercilessly and with impunity to any further manifestations of Armenian nationalism. Given increasing oppression, a rising tide of Armenian struggle, and an international climate which favoured the Ottomans, a bloody confrontation was inevitable.

The detonating spark of this confrontation was struck by the very economic crisis which imperialist penetration and Hamidian exploitation had helped to create. In 1895, Turkish government authorities entered the mountainous district of Sasun in Greater Armenia to double the already heavy rent which Armenian villagers had been paying to local Kurdish chieftains.[88] The villagers refused to submit and drove off the government agents. Seizing upon this incident, Turkish troops and Kurdish tribesmen were sent into the area to hunt down and punish the Armenian rebels. Before long, three thousand were dead, women had been raped and mutilated, and children had been dashed against the rocks.[89] The eventual European outcry against this massacre forced Abdul Hamid to issue a series of paper reforms, while behind the scenes he was cold-bloodedly instigating a wave of additional massacres of Armenians throughout eastern Turkey. Organized with great precision beforehand, the killings were carried out by military units under the direction of government officials. For these massacres Abdul Hamid earned the nickname, the 'Red Sultan.'

Space does not here permit a full account of the carnage or the terrible atrocities committed, but thousands were massacred in major Armenian cities and towns. Some 1,000 Armenians were killed in Trebizond; in Arabkir, 2,800. In Urfa 8,000 were massacred, 3,000 burned alive in a cathedral in which they had sought refuge. In August 1896, mass murder spread to Constantinople where for two days bands of Turks, many directed by police agents, roamed the streets, unopposed, killing and looting. When the rampage subsided, between 5,000 and 6,000 Armenians were dead. Estimates of the total casualties from the massacres which were committed between 1894 and 1896 include 100,000 killed, 50,000 dead of starvation, 40,000 forcibly converted to Islam, and 100,000 driven into exile.[90] The extent of the Great Powers response to these events was the issuance of notes to the Sultan urging him to adopt additional reforms and to seek out and punish the perpetrators, when they knew full well that his own government was responsible. Fearing once again that a significant weakening of the Ottoman Empire would upset the European balance of power, they abjured more decisive action.[91] In the context of big power politics, the Armenians were expendable. As one historian who has studied British Armenian policy makes clear:

... Britain's interest in Armenian territory far outweighed her concern about the Armenian people. The result was that no security whatever was asked for, or given, for reforms. No effective pressure was put on Turkey for their implementation. Consequently, while the stipulations and the constant reminders about reform aroused, on the one hand, the hopes of the Armenians, they laid them open, on the other, to the hostility and reprisals of the Turks, and helped to cause successive massacres.[92]

The Young Turk revolution

These massacres not only depopulated the Armenian countryside, they also gave further impetus to the systematic robbery by Turks and Kurds of the remaining inhabitants. In despair, many Armenians fled to the mountains where revolutionary activity increased and guerrilla warfare posed a serious threat to Ottoman authority. With extensive popular support, revolutionaries managed to keep whole provinces in turmoil, driving out government tax collectors, and killing Kurdish and Turkish landlords and usurers.[93]

During this same period the Hamidian regime was facing a danger of a different sort, the growing power of the nascent Turkish bourgeoisie. In the Istanbul military academies, as well as among small groups of Turkish exiles in Europe, the seeds of Ottoman dissidence were beginning to take root. In 1902, in Paris, the first congress of Ottoman liberals (popularly known as the Young Turks) was held, bringing together Turkish, Armenian, Kurdish, Arab, Greek, Albanian, Circassian and Jewish delegates to debate alternatives to Osmanli tyranny.[94] Immediately, two divergent approaches to the future Turkish state made themselves known. One, represented by Abdul Hamid's nephew, Sabah al-Din, called for a Turkey consisting of a decentralized federation of equal nationalities. The other, represented by the Committee of Union and Progress (CUP), stood for a centralist policy of Ottomanization, or more extremely, Pan-Turkism. Initially, however, the liberal movement spoke as if it was genuinely committed to an end to the brutalities of Abdul Hamid, and minority liberals and revolutionaries, including the Armenians, threw their support behind the Turkish dissidents. For the first time, many Armenians abandoned their traditional orientation towards reliance on foreign powers to free their homeland in favour of a policy of internally generated transformation of Ottoman rule.[95]

If liberal intellectuals set the ideological tone for the Young Turk movement, it was only military power which could bring down six hundred years of Osmanli rule. In Macedonia, Turkey's last significant territorial bastion in Europe, Christians and Muslims alike seethed with discontent over the indifference, incompetence and brutality of Ottoman administration. In 1908, patriotic army officers in Salonika, who had previously enrolled in secret societies affiliated with the Committee of Union and Progress, organized an armed revolt within the Third Army Corps and threatened to march on Constantinople to enforce the constitution which Adbul Hamid had discarded in 1878.[96] The Sultan, recognizing his precarious military position, immediately capitulated to their demands, restoring the constitution and ordering elections for a new Chamber of Deputies. Popular acclaim was general, culminating in an unprecedented fraternization between the various Ottoman nationalities. Recognizing that he could not crush his opposition by force, Abdul Hamid waited for an opportunity to restore his former despotism.

Thus was inaugurated a period of dual power. The Sultan and the traditional ruling class could no longer rule in the old way, but continued to exercise broad power through the unreformed state apparatuses, including sections of the army, the secret police, and the clerical hierarchy. The Young Turks, mostly military officers with limited civilian support from a small and weak national bourgeoisie, were neither strong enough nor sufficiently experienced to seize the reins of power themselves.[97] A constitutional government existed on paper, and an elected Chamber of Deputies met and debated, but the Sultan continued to maintain control through his own selection of government ministers. When, in 1909, the Congress of Young Turks finally sought to deprive him of this prerogative, the counter-revolution decided to strike. Supported by the First Army Corps, the bureaucracy, and reactionary clerical interests, the Sultan seized command in Constantinople, and attempted to reverse the gains of the previous year. The Committee of Union and Progress reacted swiftly, dispatching troops to the capital. Within twelve days the counter-revolution was suppressed, Abdul Hamid deposed and parliament restored. A new sultan was proclaimed, one who would pose no threat to the Young Turks, now firmly in command. New articles were written into the constitution, reducing the sultan to a largely ceremonial role and establishing the supremacy of the Chamber of Deputies. But real power now rested with the CUP.[98]

The revolution betrayed

Just as the counter-revolutionary movement in the Russian revolutions of 1905 and 1917 was characterized by pogroms organized against the Jews, so the Ottoman counter-revolution went hand in hand with pogroms against the Armenians. The attempted coup in Constantinople was accompanied throughout Cilicia by massacres of Armenian villagers in which some thirty thousand were killed.[99] Most disturbing of all, however, was the fact that massacres continued even after the Young Turks were restored to power. It was subsequently claimed that these later atrocities had been planned by officials of the Committee of Union and Progress, and while the government publicly disavowed those who were responsible, it failed actively to punish them.[100] Armenians, alarmed by the Cilician massacres, nonetheless continued to give qualified support to the Young Turk revolution, if only as a defence against the restoration of Hamidian despotism.

Historians can debate whether or not a genuine bourgeois democratic regime could possibly have developed in Turkey in the years that followed the Young Turk revolution. In fact, a combination of external and internal factors worked to block any such outcome. From the revolution's beginning, oppressed nations within the Empire seized the occasion to declare their independence, while foreign powers sought to take advantage of Turkish internal disorder for their own gain. In 1908, Bulgaria announced its independence; soon after Crete revolted to unite with Greece. Austro-Hungary annexed Bosnia-Herzegovina and in 1911–12, Italy invaded and conquered Libya. Finally, in 1913, a united Balkan alliance drove the Turks out of Macedonia. Within the remnants of the Empire other oppressed nationalities, including the Armenians and the Arab peoples, were demanding greater autonomy or self-determination.[101]

The effects of the Ottoman Empire's disintegration along national and religious lines on the Young Turk leadership and the weak bourgeoisie which it represented was profound. Dissension within the movement increased, liberalism waned, and the proponents of federation and the equality of nationalities were isolated. The regime, unable to create new institutions, merely exploited traditional mechanisms of rule for its own purposes.[102] Turkey jolted towards military dictatorship, and Turkification became the dominant ideology in leading CUP and government circles. Pan-Turkism, as theorized by the CUP, was an extreme expression of the contradictory and ambivalent response of Turkish nationalists to Western penetration and its destructive impact on the unity of the Ottoman Empire. On the one hand, Pan-Turkism was an extremely virulent form of nationalism, a very Western ideology. On the other hand, it was a nationalism which was consciously and deliberately anti-Western, xenophobic, and predicated on the glorification of the Turk's distant pagan past. Racialism, chauvinism, militarism, and a disregard for much of traditional Islam were all features of Pan-Turkism. Taken together, this combination of ideological elements foreshadowed a similar ideology which was to emerge in Germany in the 1920s: Nazism.[103]

Pan-Turkish theorists conceptualized Turks as a master race, and envisioned the forcible creation of a great empire ('Turan') of all 'Turo-Aryan' peoples throughout Asia. Russia, the Slavic peoples and Armenians were all seen as obstacles to this goal. The Turks were to be united in a new purified state in which there would be no place for 'alien' peoples. The CUP's efforts at popular mobilization of the Turkish masses on the basis of nationalist appeals, racial intolerance and Nazi-like cults of the Turk's pagan past created a climate of growing intolerance for all minority peoples within the Empire.[104]

In its practical application in Armenia, Pan-Turkism meant the acceleration of the theft of Armenian land by Turks and Kurds begun under Abdul Hamid, an end to equality before the law, and other disabilities. By 1913, conditions for Turkish Armenians were scarcely better than they had been under the 'Red Sultan.' As Europe moved closer to war, the Young Turk government which had previously forged an alliance with Kaiser Wilhelm's Germany saw in the conflict a basis for realizing its irredentist dream at Russia's expense: 'the Pan-Turkish aspirations cannot come to their full development . . . until the Moscovite monster is crushed . . .'[105] On October 30, 1914, the Ottoman Empire entered World War I on the side of the Central Powers.

The destruction of Turkish Armenia
One of the principal battlefronts in the Asian theatre of the war was the Caucasus, Russia having strategic bases in its Armenian provinces. The Ottoman Third Army was sent into Armenia in the hopes of mounting an anti-Russian offensive which would begin their reconquest of ancient Turan. Within two weeks of the campaign, however, 80 percent of the troops had been killed either by Russian forces or by the terrible Caucasian winter.[106] Defeated in battle, the Young Turks determined to strike at an easier target. In early February 1915, the Central Council of the Committee of Union and Progress decided upon the systematic extermination of all Armenians within the Ottoman Empire.[107] Armenian sympathy for Russia and their illegal possession of arms provided the pretexts, while the absence of Allied observers

in the area as a result of the war provided the opportunity for Turkish reaction to strike its blow virtually unobserved.

Planned, supervised and directed at every level by the Committee of Union and Progress with a fierce blend of racial fanaticism and 20th century rationalism, unrestrained by remorse or conscience, the same pattern of extermination was employed throughout the Armenian provinces.[108] It was a pattern which, in many respects, foreshadowed the Holocaust visited upon European Jewry by the Nazis. First, Armenian government officials and employees were dismissed, then Armenian soldiers were removed from combat positions and assigned to labour battalions where they were worked to death. In the towns and villages, all Armenian able-bodied adult males were ordered to present themselves at a certain place and time for resettlement. Once assembled, they were either jailed for several days, or immediately marched out of town. In either case, as soon as they had been transported to a remote location, they were massacred by their military escorts. Several days later, old men, women and children were similarly assembled and forced to march 'endlessly, along pre-arranged routes, until they died from thirst, hunger, exposure or exhaustion.'[109] They were sent into deserts, marshes or other inhospitable locales, subject along the way to rape, assault, plunder and murder at the hands of their military escorts or the local population. The Armenians in Constantinople and other large cities were rounded up, sent to the interior and murdered.

Concentration camps were set up in remote areas for the few who survived the forced marches. In some cases, enormous pits were dug into which Armenians by the hundreds were thrown to die in agony. Government orders were clear: 'The Armenians must be exterminated. If any Muslim protect a Christian, first his house shall be burnt; then the Christian killed before his eyes, then his [the Muslim's] family and himself.'[110] Wherever there was resistance, the brutality increased. In Moush, thousands of women and children were driven into pre-prepared wooden sheds where they were burned to death. In accordance with the government's racial policy no one could be spared. Armenian orphans were ordered to be taken out and killed, even those who had been adopted by Turkish parents. Imperial Germany, Turkey's principal ally during the war, knew of the massacres and chose to do nothing.[111]

In two places, however, popular resistance and the presence of foreign troops prevented massacres. The capture of the city of Van by Russian troops in May 1915 relieved a small body of Armenian fighters who had refused to surrender their community to the Turks. In the mountains of Musa Dagh, villagers heroically held off a large Turkish force long enough for French ships to arrive and rescue over 4,000 persons.[112] Other than these two isolated examples, the year 1915 was one of disaster for the Armenians. Before the war it has been estimated that there were between 1,500,000 and 2,000,000 Armenians in the Ottoman Empire. By 1916, some 250,000 had managed to flee to Russia and escape the carnage. Another 1,000,000 were killed, half of them women and children. Of the approximately 600,000 survivors, about 200,000 were forcibly converted to Islam. The remaining 400,000, mostly in refugee and concentration camps, suffered a wretched existence. Some 50,000 to 100,000 of these were killed during the Turkish invasion of the Caucasus in May–September 1918. while approximately another 250.000 were murdered in 1919–23 during post-war attempts by survivors to return to their homes.[113]

After the genocide

The military defeat of the Ottoman Empire in World War I spelled the destruction of the Committee of Union and Progress. The leaders of the Young Turk government fled the country. Allied troops entered Istanbul; Cilicia was occupied by the French, and Smyrna (Izmir) by the Greeks. Meanwhile, Armenia declared its independence and even the Turkish government was forced to recognize the new state in 1918.[114] The victors, already fighting over the spoils of war, initially endorsed Armenian independence with the same lukewarm enthusiasm which they had displayed towards Armenia on so many previous occasions. Meanwhile, the Bolshevik victory in Russia changed forever the international community and, quite unexpectedly, gave Turkey a new lease on life. The Bolsheviks, beset by civil war and sixteen invading armies, were no longer military masters of the Caucasus. The victorious allies, facing unrest, civil disorders and Bolshevik agitation within their own countries, were more concerned with the Communist danger than with a resurgent Turkey. Mustapha Kemal ('Ataturk'), heading a military provisional government in Ankara, seized upon the weakness of the Soviet government and the indifference and division of allied forces to begin a military offensive for the recapture of the lost Ottoman territories.[115]

In 1920, Kemalist forces took the offensive in Cilicia. In March of the following year France signed a treaty evacuating the region and restoring it to Turkish rule. Military force was also applied towards independent Armenia from 1920 through 1923 against an array of Armenian government forces, local revolutionaries and the Soviet Red Army. The allies made it known that they would do little to help maintain Armenian independence. It was at this time that a portion of the former Russian Armenia declared itself a Soviet state. Comprising one-tenth of historic Armenia, it is today the Soviet Republic of Armenia. The rest was recaptured by Kemalist forces and forcibly incorporated into the new Turkey. On July 24, 1923, the Treaty of Lausanne. which made no mention of Armenia, was signed by the allies and the soon to be proclaimed Turkish Republic.[116]

Although those who bore chief responsibility for planning and perpetrating the Armenian massacres fled to Germany, no attempt was made to have them extradited to Turkey to stand trial for their crimes. In 1919, a few lesser CUP leaders were arrested, tried and convicted, but only one of any significance was executed. In 1921, a military court of appeals annulled a number of sentences and set the murderers free.[117] The Western powers stood by and did nothing; there would be no Nuremberg Trial for the Turkish war criminals. The true character of Western concern for Armenian grievances was demonstrated during the Turkish recapture of Smyrna in September 1922. While a fleet of British, French, Italian and American warships was anchored in the harbour, the Turks sacked and burned the city, looting, raping and massacring its Greek and Armenian inhabitants. No attempt was made by the victorious allies to intervene to stop the carnage or to rescue the many victims. The United States finally landed sailors for one purpose only: to protect a Standard Oil Company plant.[118] This small incident is one more example of the fact that the repeated assurances of support which the Western powers had provided the minority peoples in the Ottoman Empire were mere propaganda; their primary concern was and would always remain the same: working together profitably with the Turks.

By the mid-1920s Turkish Armenia ceased to exist. But Armenian revolutionary nationalism, although it had previously emerged in a specific conjuncture, thereafter took on a life of its own, both in Soviet Armenia and throughout the diaspora. The Young Turks sought to eliminate the Armenian question as an internal political problem, but only succeeded in internationalizing it. The Armenians never accepted the Lausanne Treaty; they publicized continuing Turkish atrocities in the 1920s and, after World War II, pressed the United Nations to reopen the issue of Turkish occupied Armenia.[119] The impact of all this activity on world opinion, however, was negligible. The revival of Armenian revolutionary violence against representatives of the Turkish government throughout the world in 1975 has not only proved that the Armenian question is very much alive, it has also brought the issue to world attention. The collective memory of the Armenian people, in spite of the massacres, or perhaps because of them, has never faded. Instead, it remains a powerful material force which time and distance cannot erase.[120] In this regard it is not unlike two other national liberation movements in the Middle East: those of the Kurdish and Palestinian peoples.

Armenia, Kurdistan, Palestine

Like the Armenians, the Kurds and the Palestinians have a long record of struggle for national self-determination. They, too, have suffered a lonely and fragmented history of oppression and exile. They, too, have been compelled to take up armed struggle as a means of redressing fundamental grievances and calling world attention to their plight. Finally, the repression of their national aspirations and the resulting diverse forms of their resistance and rebellion are key factors in the continuing volatile situation in the Middle East.

These common features, however, should not obscure the very real differences which exist among the various movements. As noted earlier, the Armenian people were the first Eastern nation to take the revolutionary road, in large part due to their specific economic history, class composition and the influence of diaspora communities in Europe and America. Also, Armenia enjoyed a certain era of independence, first before the Ottoman conquest, and later, briefly, after World War I, unlike either the Kurds or the Palestinians who have never achieved national statehood. For the Kurds and Palestinians the absence of an historical legacy of national independence, a relatively underdeveloped economy and the lack of established modern classes all impeded the process of nation building, stunted the development of a patriotic intelligentsia, and contributed to the late development of national consciousness and organized forms of national liberation struggle. The Kurdish and Palestinian national liberation movements only appeared on the world stage in this century, in the epoch of imperialism when the options open to such movements in the so-called 'third world' were already extremely limited.[121]

All of these differences notwithstanding, certain contemporary features and problems of all three of these movements deserve mention here as they relate to issues of current politics and strategy. These include the problem of building and maintaining unity within the national liberation struggle itself, the question of armed struggle, and the difficult problem of forging an effective alliance policy. Obviously, in an historical article such as this one, we can only touch on these issues and their inter-relationship in the most cursory fashion.

National liberation: two roads

A critical examination of the way in which these three movements have responded to the above enumerated issues provides us with some extremely valuable evidence which may be read as a verification of certain recent theoretical advances in Marxism.[122] There has always been a current in Marxism which argued that because modern nations and the ideology of nationalism arose with the rise of capitalism, that ideology had an inherent bourgeois class essence. While revolutionaries in oppressed nations, in the epoch of imperialism, might find it necessary to champion the national liberation struggle and revolutionary nationalism in wars for independence, once independence was finally achieved nationalism would have to be abandoned for genuinely socialist class ideologies.

Other currents in Marxism, following the path inaugurated by the great Italian theorist Antonio Gramsci, recognize that every ideology does not have a pre-given and immutable class essence. Instead, disparate ideologies and the ideological elements which compose them only take on a specific class character through class and social struggles within societies and revolutions. It is in these processes of social transformation that ideologies and ideological elements develop and are transformed, processes in which ideologies and ideological elements are articulated and rearticulated by becoming part of the programmes and discourses of fundamental classes, and thereby taking on some of the characteristics of those classes. Thus, nationalism, according to this view, is not inherently bourgeois. It is simply that historically the bourgeoisie has articulated nationalism to its dominant class discourse so as to constitute the many varieties of bourgeois nationalism. Transformed and rearticulated to a revolutionary socialist discourse, many of the ideological elements of nationalism can equally serve the cause of socialism. The failure of certain Marxists to grasp the changeable nature of ideologies in general, and the ideology of nationalism in particular, has been central to their underestimation of the significance of the experience of national liberation struggles, particularly since World War II. As Regis Debray noted a number of years ago, 'there will never be socialism without revolutionary nationalism,' and 'the near silence of European Marxists on "the question of nationalism" will one day be seen as the most costly and ruinous of all historical omissions.'[123]

Given the above described Marxist orientation, a cluster of important lessons can be drawn from the experience of modern national liberation movements, the implications of which are both immediately relevant and far-reaching. First, the national liberation struggle and its ideology, nationalism, have no pre-given or inherent social or political content. Both are rather sites of class and popular struggle, arenas of constantly shifting contention between different class forces and political subjects. The hegemony within the national liberation struggle of certain classes and popular forces, their political practices and the results of their efforts to transform nationalism by articulating it to their own ideologies are what give a definite political and social content to any national liberation movement and its nationalist ideology.[124]

The current crises and transformations within the Kurdish, Palestinian and Armenian movements are a direct result of such struggles for hegemony between different social forces and different political/ideological orientations. While the parties and issues vary from one movement to another, the stakes are everywhere the same. On one side are forces which more or less imperfectly recognize and insist upon an understanding of national liberation within a framework which is independent, political and socialist, democratically determined and conscious of the need for respectful mutual relations with allies on the basis of common political and strategic interests. On the other side are forces for which a combination of the following elements are key: the nation and the national liberation struggle themselves are their own politics and end; military strategy and tactics and the military style are pre-eminent without regard for the targets, either among the movement's enemies or in terms of the settlement of differences within the movement itself; a willingness to enter into relationships of subordination to erstwhile allies for short-term gains without regard for the movement's long-term interests.

Revolutionary militants within and without these three movements cannot maintain a position of neutrality in such struggles, any less than they should urge upon the combatants a false unity for its own sake. Genuine solidarity and common struggle require something other than mutual blind endorsement: they necessitate principled criticism and concrete political support. And they also require that we ourselves be willing to be judged and held accountable to these same standards.

A new unity in Kurdistan

Historically the Kurdish national liberation struggle has always been the most underdeveloped and divided of the three movements under discussion here, in no small part due to the fact that the Kurds have been dispersed among five different states (Turkey, Iran, Iraq, Syria and the USSR).[125] Traditionally, the chief areas of Kurdish struggle have been Iraq and Iran, both of which have witnessed tremendous popular uprisings and protracted wars for Kurdish autonomy or independence.

The principal Kurdish organization in Iraq for many years, the Kurdish Democratic Party (KDP), was founded in 1945. As chief organizer and leader of the Kurdish movement in that country, it directed a multitude of activities culminating in a major war of liberation which lasted from 1961 until 1974. In 1975, policy errors including excessive reliance on Iranian aid led to the collapse of the revolutionary war amid bitter recriminations.[126]

In Iran, the dominant Kurdish group, the Iranian KDP (KDPI) had a relatively broad political base, despite its underground status during the reign of the Shah, in addition to a detailed programme of 'autonomy for Iranian Kurdistan within the framework of a democratic Iran.' In the 1960s, however, its activities were circumscribed by Iranian support for the Kurdish struggle in Iraq and consequent Iraqi Kurdish hostility to any activity in Iran which might jeopardize that aid.[127] This situation only began to change in the late 1970s when Kurdish revolutionaries played a significant role in the popular uprisings which brought an end to the Pahlavi regime.

The Iran–Iraq Gulf war dramatically altered the conditions facing the Kurdish movements in both these countries, as well as the organizational balance of forces within them. Before the war, the Iranian Kurds had faced a determined military offensive on the part of Iran's army and Revolutionary Guards while Iraqi Kurds were attempting to profit from a precarious and limited autonomy agreement with the Baghdad regime. But the legacy of years of indifference to transnational Kurdish unity, the vestiges of political underdevelopment, and the lack of a socialist orientation in the context of a Middle East increasingly shaken by national and class contradictions and inter-imperialist rivalries could no longer be ignored. The traditional Kurdish nationalist organizations proved themselves slow to respond to the new situation. As a result, they have begun to be superseded by newer organizations, operating upon more advanced political premises.[128]

The Gulf war found Iraq unable to fight on two fronts simultaneously; it was obliged to offer further concessions and a ceasefire to the Kurdish population. This situation considerably improved opportunities for pro-Kurdish activities, and the more favourable climate witnessed the rapid growth of the leftist Patriotic Union of Kurdistan (PUK) whose political sophistication and longstanding ties to other Kurdish groups in Iran and Turkey represent a departure from past traditions.[129]

In Iran, the stronger government forces stepped up their offensive in Kurdistan, inflicting devastating losses upon KDPI guerrillas. Most tragic of all, it has been reported that Iranian-supported KDP troops fought alongside the Iranian army in these campaigns against their fellow Kurds. In spite of these adverse conditions, the socialist Komaleh group has greatly increased its strength among the Kurdish masses in relation to the KDPI. Like the PUK, it favours Kurdish unity across state boundaries and has worked with Iraqi- and Turkish-based Kurdish groupings. As one observer has remarked, for the first time a Kurdish movement may be emerging which transcends narrow tribalism and no longer confines itself to the boundaries imposed on it at the turn of the century.[130]

Split in the Palestinian movement

If the Gulf war has dramatically altered the balance of forces in the Kurdish movement, pushing it towards a new unity, the 1982 Israeli invasion of Lebanon has produced crises and resulting splits in the Palestinian and Armenian revolutionary movements, both of which had previously been based there. The origins of this development must be located in the manner in which the weaknesses of the Lebanese state allowed these movements to organize themselves virtually unfettered, up to and including the freedom to create military formations within its borders. The result was that significant sections of the Lebanese-based contingents of the PLO and the Armenian Secret Army for the Liberation of Armenia (ASALA) began to develop an autonomous existence – the PLO fighters in isolation from the majority of the Palestinian people in the occupied territories and the Armenians from the strong diaspora-based popular movements which had arisen in support of the ASALA.[131] And, because of their ability to develop a military presence in Lebanon and to use it as a base from which to conduct armed actions, the tendency towards militarism within these organizations was further encouraged. Then came the Israeli invasion. Once the PLO and ASALA lost their bases in Lebanon, many sought refuge in Syria where these tendencies towards autonomy and militarism became even more pronounced. Meanwhile, the majority of the militants in both national liberation movements outside of Lebanon and Syria were moving in the opposite direction, towards a political rather than a narrowly military strategy, and against the indiscriminate use of violence and terror. With neither side willing to make fundamental concessions, splits were inevitable.[132]

Within the PLO, the split began with a revolt in Fatah and culminated in the 17th Palestine National Council in November 1984. The 17th PNC formally divided the PLO between the vast majority of the Palestinian movement, led by Yassir Arafat, which is publicly committed to an all-sided political solution determined democratically by the Palestinians themselves, and the Fatah minority and other pro-Syrian forces of the 'National Bloc,' who would effectively subordinate the Palestinian struggle to Syrian national interests and a narrowly military strategy. (The short-lived 'Democratic Alliance' attempted unsuccessfully to straddle the fence between these two positions.)[133]

The same demarcation between the PLO majority and the National Bloc manifests itself in sharply differing lines on the issue of alliance policy. For the Palestinian movement, the principal community which must be strategically engaged in order to achieve some measure of national self-determination is Israeli Jewry (as the most far-sighted PLO leaders have always recognized). The 17th PNC reaffirmed this fact by calling for a dialogue with all Jewish and Israeli forces ready to accept the creation of a Palestinian national state and the return of Palestinian exiles. The Syrian-backed National Bloc, on the contrary, not only rejected dialogue with progressive Israelis but actually engineered the assassination of PLO leaders who have advocated and taken part in discussions of this kind. Indeed, its member organizations have never hesitated to use force in an attempt to resolve political differences within the movement.[134]

The fundamental differences which divided the two Palestinian camps were formally overcome at the 19th PNC in Algiers in 1988 with the victory of the Arafat line. This was primarily a result of the intifada in the occupied territories and new diplomatic openings for the PLO in the West which dramatically demonstrated the soundness of the strategy proposed by the Fateh majority and its allies.

Split in the Armenian revolutionary movement

Just as the Israeli invasion of Lebanon helped to spark a split in the PLO, it also precipitated a crisis in the Armenian revolutionary movement. Lebanon had been the base of a number of Armenian guerrilla groups, notably the most prominent of these, the ASALA. With the Israeli invasion and occupation, many Armenian activists, particularly the military wing of the ASALA, shifted their operations to Syria, where they developed a close working relationship with the pro-Syrian minority in the PLO. The resulting increase in ASALA armed actions against civilians, which critics have called 'blind terrorism,' also provoked sharp controversy within the ASALA and its diaspora supporters, ultimately leading to a split in 1983.[135]

The two sides in this division share many similarities with the warring factions in the PLO. The more left-wing, political elements advocate a long-term political strategy based on an explicit political programme and the establishment of ties with Turkish, Kurdish and other revolutionary groups in Turkey and within exile communities. They reject acts of individual terror aimed at civilians and the use of military force to settle differences within the movement itself. These elements have now formed the ASALA-Revolutionary Movement (ASALA-RM) and their diaspora supporters the Democratic Front. They appear to enjoy the support of the majority of revolutionary-minded Armenians, including those previously associated with the ASALA. The nationalist–military wing, on the other hand, continues to call itself the true ASALA and tends to preoccupy itself with military actions which have included bombings in airports, Turkish travel agencies, and in the Istanbul bazaar. Its leaders have not hesitated to use terror and murder against opponents within the ASALA.[136] As with the PLO these differences are matters of fundamental political principle, the compromise of which would only seriously weaken the long-term viability of the movement itself.

The principal beneficiaries of this struggle within the Armenian revolutionary movement have been, of course, the Turkish government and its chief friend, the government of the United States. The Reagan administration, for example, did more than simply support the Turkish military. At least twice it has gone on record in opposition to the demand that Turkey recognize and acknowledge responsibility for the Armenian genocide, at one point even denying that the genocide ever occurred.[137] The failure to punish the Turkish war criminals of 1915 paved the way for the Holocaust of 1939–45. The struggle for recognition and retribution for the Armenians is a struggle against the war criminals of today and tomorrow.

Notes

1. Gerard Chaliand and Yves Ternon, *The Armenians: From Genocide to Resistance* (London, Zed Press 1983), p. 36.

2. Quoted in Dickran H. Boyajian, *Armenia* (Westwood, NJ, 1972) p. 311.

3. E. K. Sarkisian and R. G. Sahakian, *Vital Issues in Modern Armenian History* (trans. and ed. by Elisha B. Chrakian) (Watertown, Mass, 1965).

4. *Jewish Currents* (April 1983).

5. *MERIP Reports*, no. 121 (February 1984).

6. Chaliand and Ternon, *The Armenians*, pp. 4 –10.

7. See *Sardarabad*, vol. 1, no. 1 (February 1984).

8. The most recent influential work on this theme published in the United States is David S. Wyman, *The Abandonment of the Jews: America and the Holocaust, 1941–1945* (New York, 1984).

9. See, for example, James Nazer, *The First Genocide of the 20th Century* (New York, 1968) and Charles A. Vertanes, *Armenia Reborn* (New York, 1947).

10. Lord Kinross, *The Ottoman Centuries* (New York, 1977), part III.

11. The Asiatic mode of production can be defined as:

> a situation in which the agricultural producer is a free peasant and his surplus is appropriated in the form of taxes by the state. Only state officials belong to the class of surplus appropriators. Thus the unit of reproduction is defined by the extent of state authority.

Huri Islamoglu and Caglar Keyder, 'Agenda for Ottoman History,' *Review*, vol. I, no. 1 (Summer 1977) p. 37, note 18. On the Asiatic mode in general, see Anne M. Bailey and Josep Llorbera (eds.) *The Asiatic Mode of Production* (London, 1981). For serious critiques of the concept, see Barry Hindess and Paul Q. Hirst, *Pre-Capitalist Modes of Production* (London, 1975), ch. 4, and Perry Anderson, *Lineages of the Absolutist State* (London, 1979), pp. 462–549. The problem with critiques of this concept is that they have not been able to come up with a better theoretical concept with which to replace it.

12. Islamoglu and Keyder, in *Review*, p. 37.

13. Fernand Braudel, *The Perspective of the World*, trans. Sian Reynolds (New York, 1984) pp. 466–71.

14. The virtual absence of private property in land was the fundamental characteristic of Asiatic despotism according to Marx. See Anderson, *Lineages*, p. 365, n. 7.

15. Anderson, *Lineages*, pp. 366–67; Islamoglu and Keyder, in *Review*, pp. 37–8, 40.

16. Anderson. *Lineages*. chapter 7. passim.

17. Braudel. *Perspective*. pp. 467–84.

18. Charles Bettelheim. 'Theoretical Comments.' in Arghiri Emmanuel. *Unequal Exchange: A Study of the Imperialism of Trade* (New York. 1972) pp. 289–99.

19. Tom Nairn. 'The Modern Janus.' *New Left Review* no. 94 (November–December 1975) pp. 3–29.

20. Anderson. *Lineages*. chapter 7. passim.

21. Chaliand and Ternon. *The Armenians*. pp. 20–25.

22. Sydney Nettleton Fisher. *The Middle East* (New York. 1968) pp. 300–303.

23. Islamoglu and Keyder. *Review* passim.

24. Maxime Rodinson. *Islam and Capitalism*. trans. Brian Pearce (New York. 1973) p. 122.

25. Berch Berberoglu. *Turkey in Crisis* (London. 1982). p. 3.

26. Rodinson. *Islam*. p. 124.

27. Fisher. *The Middle East*. p. 320.

28. Berberoglu. *Turkey in Crisis*. p. 4.

29. Christopher J. Walker. *Armenia: The Survival of a Nation* (London. 1980). p. 89.

30. Kinross. *The Ottoman Centuries*. chapter 33.

31. Walker. *Armenia*. pp. 90–91; Akaby Nassibian. *Britain and the Armenian Question. 1915–1923* (New York. 1984). pp. 267–68.

32. Kinross. *The Ottoman Centuries*. p. 483.

33. Nassibian. *Britain and the Armenian Question*. p. 13.

34. Walker. p. 64.

35. Fisher. pp. 310–11.

36. Walker. p. 94.

37. Fisher. p. 312

38. Walker. pp. 114–15.

39. Nassibian. p. 8.

40. Sirarpie Der Nersessian. *The Armenians* (New York. 1970). p. 11.

41. David M. Lang and Christopher J. Walker. *The Armenians* (London. n.d.). p. 6.

42. Der Nersessian. *The Armenians*. p. 12.

43. Louise Nalbandian. *The Armenian Revolutionary Movement* (Berkeley. 1963). pp. 3. 15.

44. Walker. p. 20.

45. Walker. pp. 20–23.

46. Der Nersessian. chapter V.

47. Braudel claims that mountainous regions remain on the fringe of civilizations and therefore new religions can make 'massive. though unstable. conquests in these regions.' Braudel. *The Mediterranean and the Mediterranean World in the Age of Philip II*. trans. Sian Reynolds (New York. 1972). vol. 1. pp. 34–8.

48. Nalbandian. *Armenian Revolutionary Movement*. p. 11.

49. David M. Lang. *The Armenians* (London. 1981). pp. 51–6.

50. Walker. p. 31.

51. Walker. p. 32.

52. Nalbandian. pp. 15–17.

53. Walker. p. 31.

54. Anderson. *Passages From Antiquity to Feudalism* (London. 1974) pp. 218–19. 274.

55. Walker. pp. 31. 85.

56. Walker. p. 85.

57. Nalbandian. p. 17–18.

58. Lang and Walker. *The Armenians*. p. 8.

59. Anderson. *Lineages*. pp. 363–7.

60. Walker. p. 86.

61. Walker. pp. 86–7.

62. S. M. Dubnow. *History of the Jews in Russia and Poland*. trans. I. Friedlaender (Philadelphia. 1916) I. pp. 105–6.

63. Walker. p. 87

64. Anderson. *Lineages*. pp. 366–7.

65. Walker, p. 89.

66. Anahide Ter Minassian, *La Question Armenienne* (Paris, 1983).

67. Ter Minassian, *La Question Armenienne*, p. 120.

68. Gerard Chaliand (ed.), *People Without a Country: The Kurds and Kurdistan* (London, 1980), p. 11.

69. Walker, pp. 94, 95.

70. Braudel, *The Wheels of Commerce*, trans. Sian Reynolds (New York, 1982), pp. 154–7. See also Mesroub J. Seth, *Armenians in India from the Earliest Times to the Present Day* (Calcutta, 1937) and Sirapi De Neisessian, *The Armenians* (New York, 1970).

71. Ter Minassian, pp. 121–2.

72. For an excellent discussion of the rise of the Armenian revolutionary movement, see Ter Minassian, pp. 113–35.

73. *Primitive Rebels* (New York, 1959); *Bandits* (New York, 1969).

74. Nalbandian, p. 78.

75. Nalbandian, p. 71.

76. Ter Minassian, pp. 121–2.

77. Walker, pp. 126, 129.

78. Nalbandian, chapter 5.

79. Nalbandian, chapter 7.

80. Walker, pp. 131–3.

81. Fisher, p. 326. See also Roderick Davison, *Reform in the Ottoman Empire 1856–1876* (Princeton, N.J., 1963).

82. Kinross, p. 530.

83. Caglar Keyder, 'The Political Economy of Turkish Democracy,' *New Left Review* no. 115 (May–June 1979) p. 7.

84. Nairn, in *New Left Review*, no. 94, p. 12.

85. Walker, pp. 133–4.

86. Anderson, *Lineages*, p. 389; Walker, pp. 177–8.

87. Lang, *The Armenians*, p. 113.

88. Walker, pp. 136–41.

89. Walker, p. 141.

90. Ter Minassian, p. 30. See also Yves Ternon, *Armenia: History of a Genocide*, trans. Rouben C. Cholakian (Delmar, N.Y., 1981).

91. Kinross, pp. 562–3.

92. Nassibian, pp. 267–8.

93. Walker, pp. 177–8.

94. Walker, p. 179.

95. Walker, p. 179.

96. Kinross, pp. 573–4.

97. Kinross, p. 575.

98. Fisher, p. 342.

99. Chaliand and Ternon, p. 31.

100. Walker, p. 187.

101. Nassibian, p. 26.

102. Anderson, *Lineages*, p. 390, note 47.

103. Walker, p. 191.

104. Walker, pp. 189–92.

105. Nassibian, p. 29.

106. Walker, p. 199.

107. Lang, pp. 23–4.

108. Walker, pp. 202–3.

109. Walker, p. 203.

110. Walker, p. 207.

111. On Germany's knowledge of and role in the massacres see Johannes Lepsius, *Deutschland und Armenien, 1914–1918* (Potsdam, 1919).

112. Lang, pp. 26–7.

113. Walker. p. 230.
114. Fisher. pp. 381. 383.
115. Berberoglu. pp. 9–10: Nassibian. p. 229.
116. Chaliand and Ternon. p. 114.
117. Chaliand and Ternon. pp. 87–93; Walker. p. 344.
118. Walker. pp. 345–6.
119. Vertanes. *Armenia Reborn*.
120. Donald E. Miller and Lorna Touryan Miller. 'Armenian Survivors: A Typological Analysis of Victim Response.' *Oral History Review*. vol. 10 (1982) pp. 47–72.
121. Chaliand. *People Without*. p. 15: William B. Quandt. Fuad Jabber. Ann Mosely Lesch. *The Politics of Palestinian Nationalism* (Berkeley. 1973). pp. 15–42.
122. Ernesto Laclau. *Politics and Ideology in Marxist Theory* (London. 1977); Laclau and Chantal Mouffe. *Hegemony and Socialist Strategy* (London. 1985).
123. 'A Letter from Regis Debray.' *Atlas*. (May 1969).
124. Laclau. *Politics and Ideology*. pp. 100–119.
125. Chaliand. *People Without*. pp. 11–17.
126. Chaliand. *People Without*. pp. 180–92.
127. Chaliand. *People Without*. pp. 124–5.
128. *The Middle East* (May 1984) p. 48.
129. Ibid.
130. Ibid.
131. *Israel & Palestine* no. 110 (December 1984) p. 16.
132. Ibid.. pp. 8–9. 16; *The Middle East* (October 1983) pp. 27–8.
133. *Israel & Palestine* no. 110. pp. 8–9. 16: no. 113 (April/May 1985) p. 21.
134. The tragic fighting in Lebanon after the revolt in Fatah and the assassination of Fahd Kawasmeh are only two examples.
135. *The Middle East* (September 1983) pp. 8–20: October 1983. p. 28; June 1984. pp. 29–30.
136. *The Middle East* (June 1984) pp. 29–30: *Sardarabad*.
137. Christopher Hitchens. 'Minority Report.' *Nation* (April 13. 1985).

Index